LEVEL II PRACTICE EXAMS – VOLUME 1

SCHWESER 2018 LEVEL II CFA® PRACTICE EXAMS VOLUME 1

©2017 Kaplan, Inc. All rights reserved.

Published in 2017 by Kaplan, Inc.

Printed in the United States of America.

ISBN: 978-1-4754-5970-8

HOW TO USE THE LEVEL II PRACTICE EXAMS

Thank you for purchasing the Schweser Practice Exams. We hope that you find this volume effective and user-friendly. The following suggestions are designed to help you get the most out of these practice exams and prepare for the actual Level II Exam.

Be ready for a new format. The format of the Level II exam is different from Level I. The exam consists of item sets, which are vignettes or short cases followed by six multiple-choice questions (CFA Institute calls these "mini-cases"). There will be 20 item sets (120 questions) on the exam: 10 item sets (60 questions) in the morning and 10 more item sets (60 more questions) in the afternoon. Each question is worth 3 points (and is allocated 3 minutes), and there are 360 total points available. Each question will have three possible choices (A, B, or C).

Any topic can be tested in the morning and/or the afternoon, so you might have an economics item set in the morning and another one in the afternoon. Don't spend a lot of time contemplating which topics might appear in which session.

Save the practice exams for last. Save the practice exams for the last month before the exam. A good strategy would be to take one exam in each of the three weeks leading up to the test. Do your best to mimic actual exam conditions for at least one of the practice exams (e.g., time yourself, have someone turn the heat down and up so that you go from freezing to boiling, hire a construction crew to do some blasting outside your window).

Remember, no matter how challenging we make our practice exams, the actual exam will be different. Also, mainly due to the stress of the exam day, your perception will be that the actual exam was much more difficult than *any* practice exam you have ever seen.

After you have completed an exam, use your results as a diagnostic tool to help you identify areas in which you are weak. One good way to accomplish this is to use your online access to Performance Tracker. This is a tool that will provide you with exam diagnostics to target your study and review effort, and allow you to compare your scores on practice exams to those of other candidates.

Make sure you understand the mistake(s) you made on every question you got wrong (or guessed on). Make a flashcard that illustrates that particular concept, carry it around with you, and quiz yourself until you are confident you have mastered the concept. This "feedback" loop (practice exam, diagnosis of results, identification of concepts yet to be mastered, study of those concepts, and then another practice exam) is a very effective study strategy in the last month before exam day.

Topic Area	Guideline Topic Area Weight
Ethical and Professional Standards	10 to 15%
Quantitative Methods	5 to 10%
Economics	5 to 10%
Financial Reporting and Analysis	15 to 20%
Corporate Finance	5 to 15%
Equity	15 to 25%
Fixed Income	10 to 20%
Derivatives	5 to 15%
Alternative Investments	5 to 10%
Portfolio Management	5 to 10%
TOTAL	100%

Expect the unexpected. Be prepared for difficult questions on unexpected topics. Only one thing is certain about the exam: you will be surprised by some of the questions.

Guess if you are stumped. It should take you approximately 18 minutes to read the vignette and answer the six questions that make up each item set. Don't fall behind: successful candidates know when to cut their losses by guessing and moving on. If you're stuck, try to eliminate one of the incorrect answers, and then pick one of the remaining choices. If you successfully eliminate one choice you know is wrong, you have a 50/50 chance of selecting the correct answer. There is no penalty for guessing.

Be ready for more than just number-crunching. Your reading comprehension ability is an important component of success on the Level II exam. The vignettes will be long and full of information. Your job is to find the important pieces of information and answer the questions correctly.

There are two approaches to these item sets. You can read the vignette first and then tackle the questions, or you can read the first question and then go back to the vignette to find the data needed to answer it. We recommend the second approach because it saves time and helps you to focus on the details you need. When taking the practice exams, experiment with both techniques and do what works best for you!

My thanks to the Schweser team. I would like to thank all of my colleagues at Schweser for their commitment to quality. Kaplan Schweser would not be the company it is, nor could it provide the products you see, without the help of these content and editing professionals.

You may expect me to end this introduction with a "good luck on the exam." However, you need not be lucky to pass Level II. With your hard work and our assistance, luck will have nothing to do with it. Instead, I'll simply say, "See you next year at Level III."

Best Regards,

Bijesh Tolia

Dr. Bijesh Tolia, CFA, CA
VP of CFA Education and Level II Professor

Kaplan Schweser

Exam 1
Morning Session

Question	Topic	Minutes (Points)
1 to 6	Ethical and Professional Standards	18
7 to 12	Quantitative Methods	18
13 to 18	Economics	18
19 to 30	Financial Reporting and Analysis	36
31 to 36	Equity Valuation	18
37 to 42	Fixed Income	18
43 to 48	Derivatives	18
49 to 54	Alternative Investments	18
55 to 60	Portfolio Management	18

Test Answers

1. (A) (B) (C)
2. (A) (B) (C)
3. (A) (B) (C)
4. (A) (B) (C)
5. (A) (B) (C)
6. (A) (B) (C)
7. (A) (B) (C)
8. (A) (B) (C)
9. (A) (B) (C)
10. (A) (B) (C)

11. (A) (B) (C)
12. (A) (B) (C)
13. (A) (B) (C)
14. (A) (B) (C)
15. (A) (B) (C)
16. (A) (B) (C)
17. (A) (B) (C)
18. (A) (B) (C)
19. (A) (B) (C)
20. (A) (B) (C)

21. (A) (B) (C)
22. (A) (B) (C)
23. (A) (B) (C)
24. (A) (B) (C)
25. (A) (B) (C)
26. (A) (B) (C)
27. (A) (B) (C)
28. (A) (B) (C)
29. (A) (B) (C)
30. (A) (B) (C)

31. (A) (B) (C)
32. (A) (B) (C)
33. (A) (B) (C)
34. (A) (B) (C)
35. (A) (B) (C)
36. (A) (B) (C)
37. (A) (B) (C)
38. (A) (B) (C)
39. (A) (B) (C)
40. (A) (B) (C)

41. (A) (B) (C)
42. (A) (B) (C)
43. (A) (B) (C)
44. (A) (B) (C)
45. (A) (B) (C)
46. (A) (B) (C)
47. (A) (B) (C)
48. (A) (B) (C)
49. (A) (B) (C)
50. (A) (B) (C)

51. (A) (B) (C)
52. (A) (B) (C)
53. (A) (B) (C)
54. (A) (B) (C)
55. (A) (B) (C)
56. (A) (B) (C)
57. (A) (B) (C)
58. (A) (B) (C)
59. (A) (B) (C)
60. (A) (B) (C)

Exam 1
Morning Session

Use the following information to answer Questions 1 through 6.

For the past 15 years, Susan Luna, CFA, Kyle Lawson, CFA, and Matt Miller, CFA, have worked together as equity analysts and then equity portfolio managers in the investment management division (BIMCO) of Broadway Life Insurance Company. For the past five years, the three associates have worked together managing the BIMCO Aggressive Growth Fund (BAGF). During their management tenure, the BAGF had excellent performance and was well recognized in the financial press.

Just over one year ago, Broadway Life was acquired by a larger company, Gobble Insurance, and as part of the consolidation process, BIMCO was closed. The closure allowed Luna, Lawson, and Miller to start their own investment management firm, Trio Investment Management LLC (TIM). TIM focuses on the small capitalization growth equities area. This is the same investment focus as the BAGF, but TIM will have individually managed accounts. Several cases have arisen calling for interpretation as to consistency with CFA Institute Standards of Professional Conduct.

Case 1

TIM markets its investment management services by contracting with small, local bank trust departments. One of the newest bank trust clients for TIM is Shadow Mountain Bank and Trust. Judy Sampson, CFA, the trust officer for Shadow Mountain, has scheduled a meeting with a potential client. When Lawson arrives for the client meeting, he finds that all the TIM marketing material, including biographies of TIM portfolio managers, has been relabeled by Sampson as the Shadow Mountain Wealth Management Team. Sampson has also added the performance of BAGF into the current TIM Equity Composite Index portfolio and relabeled the resultant combined graph, the Shadow Mountain Equity Composite Index. Sampson states that making such changes would probably please clients and improve the chances of acquiring additional trust management accounts for Shadow Mountain and TIM. Lawson goes along and makes the presentation to the potential client using the Shadow Mountain marketing material and the relabeled BAGF/TIM equity performance record.

Case 2

Susan Luna of TIM is meeting with Sol Wurtzel, an institutional salesman for Turn Byer, a large national brokerage firm. Luna complains that TIM's technology costs are too high, especially their outside software services costs. TIM currently subscribes to two investment-related software services. The first software vendor is StockCal Software Services (StockCal), which provides valuation and stock-charting capabilities that TIM uses in its equity research and selection process. The other vendor is Add-Invest Software (Add-Invest), a software program providing account management and performance evaluation reporting, which TIM uses in developing monthly reports for all clients. In response to Luna, Wurtzel suggests that Turn Byer has an excellent soft dollar trading desk and would be willing to offer to cover TIM's StockCal and Add-Invest expenses through soft dollar commissions. Luna then reviews TIM's projected commission dollars for the year and decides there are more than enough soft dollars to pay the StockCal, AGF, and Add-Invest Software bills combined. Luna believes she can be assured of excellent trade execution from Turn Byer and improved profitability for TIM because of the increased use of soft dollars. Luna then directs that the StockCal and Add-Invest software services be paid for with soft dollar or client brokerage dollars.

Case 3

Sol Wurtzel, the equity salesman for Turn Byer, has referred several clients to TIM over the past year. In fact, Wurtzel referrals currently account for almost 20% of the assets managed by TIM. The principals of TIM decide to reward Wurtzel, either by doubling the commissions paid on trades executed through Turn Byer on Wurtzel's referral accounts, or by paying Wurtzel a cash referral fee for each additional TIM account opened by a Wurtzel referral. The principals agree that any cash referral fee would need to be disclosed to clients in advance.

Case 4

Luna notes that her clients have become increasingly aware of the directed client brokerage/soft dollar commissions issue. At a recent meeting with one of her large pension clients, Service Workers Union Local No. 1418, the subject of directed commissions came up. Upon learning of the commission dollars available to their account, the Union trustees directed Luna to use their client brokerage of approximately $25,000 to donate to a think tank called the Hoover Study Center of Unions at Samford University. Service Workers trustees believe the Hoover study will increase the public awareness of the benefits unions offer to their members and increase union membership. Luna concurs with the trustee's judgment on increasing union enrollment as a great goal, and follows the client's instructions and makes the $25,000 contribution to the Hoover Study Center. Another client, Rosa Lutz, has asked Luna to credit the soft dollar client brokerage proceeds from her personal retirement accounts to Roswell Academy, to update their computer lab. Luna agrees that a new computer lab for Roswell Academy is greatly needed, and she allocates $10,000 of Lutz's commission dollars to Roswell Academy.

1. Did Sampson and/or Lawson violate the CFA Institute Standards of Professional Conduct with respect to presenting the TIM biographies to the client?
    A. Yes, both Sampson and Lawson violated the Standards.
    B. Yes, Sampson violated the Standards, while Lawson did not.
    C. Neither Sampson nor Lawson violated the Standards, because such outsourcing is permitted.

2. Sampson's use of the relabeled BAGF investment performance record violates CFA Institute Standards:
    A. only if Sampson fails to include written disclosures as to the true source and nature of the performance record.
    B. only if Sampson does not have written permission from Gobble Insurance to use the performance data.
    C. unless Sampson includes written disclosures as to the true source and nature of the performance record and has written permission from Gobble Insurance to use the performance data.

3. Did Luna violate the CFA Institute Standards of Professional Conduct by using soft dollar commissions to pay TIM's software subscription costs to StockCal and/or Add-Invest?
    A. Both StockCal and Add-Invest software services may be paid for with soft dollars.
    B. Neither StockCal nor Add-Invest software may be paid for with soft dollars.
    C. It is acceptable to use soft dollars to pay for the StockCal software but not the Add-Invest software.

4. Would either compensation arrangement to reward Wurtzel for client referrals violate the CFA Institute Standards of Professional Conduct?
    A. Both compensation arrangements would be violations, regardless of any disclosures to clients.
    B. The increased commissions plan would be a violation, while the cash referral fees would not be a violation.
    C. Both compensation arrangements are allowed, as long as they are fully disclosed, in advance, to all clients and prospective clients.

5.   Is the use of client brokerage to make the $25,000 educational contribution to the Hoover Study Center of Unions a violation of the CFA Institute Standards of Professional Conduct?

   A. Yes, because TIM must ensure that client brokerage fees are directed to the benefit of the client.

   B. Yes, because client brokerage must only be used to pay for goods and services directly related to the investment decision-making process.

   C. No, because the client brokerage has been spent at the specific direction of the client.

6.   Is the use of client brokerage to make the $10,000 contribution to the Roswell Academy a violation of the CFA Institute Standards of Professional Conduct?

   A. Yes, because client brokerage must only be used to pay for goods and services directly related to the investment decision-making process.

   B. Yes, because client brokerage of tax-deferred accounts cannot be used to make charitable contributions.

   C. No, because the client brokerage has been spent at the specific direction of the client.

Use the following information to answer Questions 7 through 12.

William Shears, CFA, has been assigned the task of predicting sales for the specialty retail industry. Shears finds that sales have been increasing at a fairly constant rate over time and decides to estimate the linear trend in sales for the industry using quarterly data over the past 15 years, starting with Quarter 1 of 2004 and ending with Quarter 4 of 2018. On January 1, 2019, Shears estimates the following model:

$$sales_t = b_0 + b_1 t + e_t \qquad (1)$$

where:
sales = quarterly sales (measured in \$ millions) for the specialty retail industry
b_0 = intercept term
b_1 = slope
t = time variable (quarter number)
e = random error

Exhibit 1 provides the results of the linear trend regression.

Exhibit 1: Linear Trend Regression

	Coefficient	Standard Error
Intercept	10.0	3.50
Trend	16.0	6.55

Shears also estimates an autoregressive model of order one, AR(1), using the changes in quarterly sales data for the industry from the first quarter of 2004 through the fourth quarter of 2018. He obtains the following results for his AR(1) model:

$$\Delta sales_t = b_0 + b_1 \Delta sales_{t-1} + e_t$$

Exhibit 2: AR(1) Model for Changes in Industry Sales

	Coefficient	Standard Error
Intercept	20.00	2.15
Lag 1	0.10	0.04

The autocorrelations for the first four lags from Shears's AR(1) model are provided in Exhibit 3:

Exhibit 3: Autocorrelations from the AR(1) Model

Lag	Autocorrelation	p-Value
1	−0.032	0.38
2	−0.200	0.16
3	−0.065	0.23
4	0.470	0.02

Shears also derives a regression using the residuals from the AR(1) model. He regresses the squared residuals (or estimated errors) against the lagged squared residuals. The results of this regression are reported in Exhibit 4.

Exhibit 4: Squared Residuals Regression

	Coefficient	Standard Error	p-Value
Intercept	3.00	0.577	0.01
Lagged residual squared	0.28	0.185	0.31

Quarterly sales for the Specialty Retail Industry during 2018 were:

Exhibit 5: 2018 Quarterly Industry Sales

Quarter	Sales (in millions)
Quarter 1, 2018	900
Quarter 2, 2018	925
Quarter 3, 2018	950
Quarter 4, 2018	1,000

7. Shears's supervisor, Sam Kite, expresses concern that equation (1) might be misspecified. Specifically, Kite refers to the finding that "sales have been increasing at a fairly constant rate over time."

   Which of the following data transformations should be applied to the dependent variable in equation (1) to best address Kite's concern?
   A. Lagged transformation.
   B. Logarithmic transformation.
   C. First difference transformation.

8. Using the results for the linear trend equation in Exhibit 1, the specialty retail industry sales forecast for Quarter 1 of 2019 is *closest* to:
   A. $26 million.
   B. $976 million.
   C. $986 million.

9. Assuming the AR(1) model in Exhibit 2 is appropriate, Shears should conclude that the Quarter 1, 2019, change in sales is *most likely* to:
   A. fall from Quarter 4, 2018, change in sales.
   B. rise from Quarter 4, 2018, change in sales.
   C. remain unchanged from Quarter 4, 2018, change in sales.

10. Regarding seasonality, given a 5% level of significance, Shears should use Exhibit 3 to conclude he should add the following lag to his autoregressive model:
    A. no lag.
    B. the 3rd lag.
    C. the 4th lag.

11. From the data provided in Exhibit 4, for a 5% level of significance, Shears should conclude that his AR(1) model exhibits:
    A. no autocorrelation.
    B. no autoregressive conditional heteroskedasticity (ARCH).
    C. no multicollinearity.

12. Using the historical data provided in Exhibit 5, the two-period-ahead forecast of the change in industry sales is *closest* to:
    A. $5 million.
    B. $22.5 million.
    C. $120 million.

Use the following information to answer Questions 13 through 18.

Tristanya is a developed country with three states, West Tristanya (West), Central Tristanya (Central), and East Tristanya (East). Tristanya is a stable democracy with elected representatives, appointed judges, and an elected prime minister. All three states have approximately the same population and geographical area. Tristanya's savings rates are above the global average, and economic development has been mostly financed with domestic savings. The currency in Tristanya is the Tristanya dollar with a symbol of T$. The financial markets are highly liquid and function efficiently. Tristanya's foreign trade is a significant part of the economy, and because of this, Tristanya has continued to push for lower trade barriers. Similar to other developed nations, population growth rate in Tristanya is low and capital stock is high.

The three states adhere to all federal regulations but differ significantly on some policies that are not covered by federal laws. The states also have their own agencies for regional administration of state-specific regulations. Any jurisdictional issue is resolved in federal courts.

The government of Tristanya is increasing its efforts to boost labor productivity. Some of the proposals under consideration include:

1. Increased education funding for elementary and middle schools.

2. Increased tax credits for private research and development expenditures.

3. Increased depreciation allowances for tax purposes.

At a recent congressional hearing, Mr. Adel Mahi, the chief economic adviser to the prime minister, stated that Tristanya's capital accumulation affects the size of the Tristanyan GDP but not its growth rate.

All commercial and financial market regulations are the domain of federal agencies and government recognized self-regulatory organizations (SROs). In this regard, the federal government tends to set minimum standards and allows each state to create agencies to enforce their regulations.

Fuel costs have become an issue in Tristanya as demand for gasoline is expected to increase. Mandated fuel additives, specifically corn ethanol, are used to increase supply, and minimum fuel economy standards have been imposed to curtail demand.

East has the highest obesity rates among the three states. To control the state government's health care expenditure, East's government is implementing an additional tax on all sweet snack foods manufactured in the state. The tax is also known as the "sweet tax." Another regulation, the "supersize drinks ban," will prohibit restaurants in East from selling large portion sizes of carbonated beverages.

The most common form of sweetener in Tristanya is corn syrup. The agricultural industry has benefited from excess demand for corn to produce corn syrup and ethanol. Even after implementation of the "sweet tax", the demand for corn is expected to remain high.

West has the highest gasoline usage per capita, and reducing gasoline consumption is a policy goal for that state's government. West also has the most stringent environmental regulations and has recently raised their standards for minimum fuel economy for automobiles.

Juanita Estrada, an analyst, is assigned to assess the impact of all the regulatory changes on economic growth. Estrada lists the following findings from her analysis:

Finding 1: The snack food industry is in the process of relocating manufacturing of sweet snack foods to West and Central and relocating manufacturing of salty snack foods to East.

Finding 2: After West raised that state's fuel economy standards, the average miles driven per capita increased.

13. Based on finding 1, the snack food industry is engaging in regulatory:
   A. capture.
   B. arbitrage.
   C. competition.

14. Which Tristanyan industry is *most likely* to shrink due to the regulatory changes in the East?
   A. Snacks.
   B. Agriculture.
   C. Carbonated beverages.

15. The cost associated with finding 2 is a:
   A. component of the regulatory burden.
   B. component of the implementation cost.
   C. justification for sunset provisions.

16. The government proposal that would *most likely* lead to the highest increase in labor productivity is:
   A. Proposal 1.
   B. Proposal 2.
   C. Proposal 3.

17. Mahi's statement is consistent with:
   A. classical growth theory.
   B. endogenous growth theory.
   C. neoclassical growth theory.

18. The objectives of regulators in financial markets is *least likely* to include:
    A. low inflation.
    B. prudential supervision.
    C. promotion of economic growth.

Use the following information to answer Questions 19 through 24.

Viper Motor Company, a publicly traded automobile manufacturer located in Detroit, Michigan, periodically invests its excess cash in low-risk fixed-income securities. At the end of 2009, Viper's investment portfolio consisted of two separate bond investments: Pinto Corporation and Vega Incorporated.

On January 2, 2009, Viper purchased $10 million of Pinto's 4% annual coupon bonds at 92% of par. The bonds were priced to yield 5%. Viper intends to hold the bonds to maturity. At the end of 2009, the bonds had a fair value of $9.6 million.

On July 1, 2009, Viper purchased $7 million of Vega's 5% semiannual coupon mortgage bonds at par. The bonds mature in 20 years. At the end of 2009, the market rate of interest for similar bonds was 4%. Viper intends to sell the securities in the near term in order to profit from expected interest rate declines.

Neither of the bond investments were sold by Viper in 2009.

On January 1, 2010, Viper purchased a 60% controlling interest in Gremlin Corporation for $900 million. Viper paid for the acquisition with shares of its common stock.

Exhibit 1 contains Viper's and Gremlin's preacquisition balance sheet data.

Exhibit 1: Preacquisition Balance Sheet Data

in millions	Viper		Gremlin	
	Book Value	Fair Value	Book Value	Fair Value
Current assets	$9,000	$9,000	$500	$700
Noncurrent assets	7,500	7,800	900	950
	$16,500		$1,400	
Current liabilities	$3,000	$3,000	$250	$250
Long-term debt	7,700	7,500	400	300
Stockholders' equity	5,800		750	
	$16,500		$1,400	

Exhibit 2 contains selected information from Viper's financial statement footnotes.

Exhibit 2: Selected Footnote Information—Viper Motor Company

In millions
At the end of 2010, the carrying value of Viper's investment in Gremlin was $1,425, including goodwill. On that date, the fair value of Gremlin was $1,475, and the fair value of Gremlin's identifiable net assets was $1,350. The recoverable amount was estimated at $1,430.

19. The carrying value of Viper's investment portfolio as of December 31, 2009, is *closest* to:
    A. $16.6 million.
    B. $17.2 million.
    C. $17.5 million.

20. If Viper had initially classified its Vega bond investment as available for sale, which of the following *best* describes the *most likely* effect for the year ended 2009?
    A. Lower asset turnover.
    B. Higher return on equity.
    C. Lower net profit margin.

21. What is the appropriate adjustment, if any, if the Pinto bonds are reclassified as available-for-sale securities during 2010?
    A. The difference between the fair value and the carrying value on the date of reclassification is recognized in Viper's other comprehensive income.
    B. Any unrealized gain or loss, as of the date of reclassification, is immediately recognized in Viper's net income.
    C. No adjustment is necessary because reclassification to/from available for sale is strictly prohibited under U.S. GAAP and IFRS.

22. The amount of goodwill Viper should report in its consolidated balance sheet immediately after the acquisition of Gremlin is *closest* to:
    A. $250 million under the partial goodwill method.
    B. $350 million under the pooling method.
    C. $400 million under the full goodwill method.

23. According to U.S. GAAP, Viper's long-term debt-to-equity ratio, calculated immediately after the acquisition, is *closest* to:
    A. 1.07.
    B. 1.10.
    C. 1.12.

24. Using only the information contained in Exhibit 2, which of the following statements is *most* accurate when presenting Viper's consolidated income statement for the year ended 2010?
    A. An impairment loss of $5 million should be recognized under IFRS.
    B. An impairment loss of $275 million should be recognized under U.S. GAAP.
    C. No impairment loss is recognized under U.S. GAAP or IFRS.

Use the following information to answer Questions 25 through 30.

Delicious Candy Company (Delicious) is a leading manufacturer and distributor of quality confectionery products throughout Europe and Mexico. Delicious is a publicly traded firm located in Italy and has been in business over 60 years. Delicious complies with International Financial Reporting Standards (IFRS).

Caleb Scott, an equity analyst with a large pension fund, has been asked to complete a comprehensive analysis of Delicious in order to evaluate the possibility of a future investment.

Scott compiles the selected financial data found in Exhibit 1 and learns that Delicious owns a 30% equity interest in a supplier located in the United States. Delicious uses the equity method to account for its investment in the U.S. associate. The associate prepares its financial statements in accordance with U.S. Generally Accepted Accounting Principles (GAAP).

Exhibit 1: Selected Financial Data—Delicious Candy Company

In millions	2017	2016
Income Statement		
Revenue	€60,229	€55,137
Earnings before interest and tax	7,990	7,077
Earnings before tax	7,570	6,779
Income from associate[a]	354	270
Net income	6,501	5,625
Balance sheet		
Total assets[b]	€56,396	€53,111
Investment in associate	5,504	5,193
Stockholders' equity[c]	30,371	29,595

[a] Not included in EBIT or EBT.

[b] Total assets were €45,597 at the end of 2015.

[c] Stockholders' equity was €27,881 at the end of 2015.

Scott reads the Delicious's revenue recognition footnote found in Exhibit 2.

©2017 Kaplan, Inc.

Exhibit 2: Revenue Recognition Footnote

In millions

Revenue is recognized, net of returns and allowances, when the goods are shipped to customers and collectibility is assured. Several customers remit payment before delivery in order to receive additional discounts. Delicious reports these amounts as unearned revenue until the goods are shipped. Unearned revenue was €7,201 at the end of 2017 and €5,514 at the end of 2016.

Delicious operates two geographic segments: Europe and Mexico. Selected financial information for each segment is found in Exhibit 3.

Exhibit 3: Selected Financial Information by Segment

In millions	EBIT	Revenue	Total CapEx	Total Assets
Europe	€7,203	€50,463	€4,452	€36,642
Mexico	€787	€9,766	€8,269	€14,250

At the beginning of 2017, Delicious entered into an operating lease for manufacturing equipment. At inception, the present value of the lease payments, discounted at an interest rate of 10%, was €300 million. The lease term is six years, and the annual payment is €69 million. Similar equipment owned by Delicious is depreciated using the straight-line method and no residual values are assumed.

Scott gathers the information in Exhibit 4 to determine the implied "stand-alone" value of Delicious without regard to the value of its U.S. associate.

Exhibit 4: Selected 2017 Market Capitalization Data

In millions except exchange rates	Delicious	Associate
Market capitalization	€97,525	$32,330
Current exchange rate (€ per $)	€0.70	
Average exchange rate (€ per $)	€0.73	

Associate financial statements include an investment of $60 million in debt securities, which are reported as designated at fair value.

25. When applying the financial analysis framework to Delicious, which of the following is the *best* example of an input Scott should use when establishing the purpose and context of the analysis?
    A. The audited financial statements of Delicious prepared in conformance with either U.S. GAAP or IFRS.
    B. Ratio analysis adjusted for differences between U.S. accounting standards and international accounting standards.
    C. Review of the pension fund's guidelines related to developing the specific work product.

26. If the associate reported the investment in debt securities as held for trading instead of designated at fair value, the impact on Delicious's financial statement would be:
    A. to decrease total assets.
    B. to increase total assets.
    C. no change to total assets.

27. Using the data found in Exhibit 1 and Exhibit 2, which of the following *best* describes the impact on Delicious's financial leverage in 2017 as compared to 2016?
    A. Financial leverage increased, but the true nature of the leverage decreased.
    B. Financial leverage increased, and the true nature of the leverage increased.
    C. Financial leverage and the true nature of the leverage were unchanged.

28. The data found in Exhibit 3 indicates that Delicious may be over-allocating resources to the:
    A. Europe segment.
    B. Mexico segment.
    C. Europe segment and the Mexico segment.

29. If Delicious were to treat the operating lease as a finance lease, its interest coverage ratio for 2017 would be *closest* to:
    A. 16.9.
    B. 17.8.
    C. 19.0.

30. Using the data found in Exhibit 1 and Exhibit 4, Delicious's implied P/E multiple without regard to its U.S. associate is *closest* to:
    A. 14.0.
    B. 14.8.
    C. 15.1.

Use the following information to answer Questions 31 through 36.

George Armor, CFA, is a new stock analyst for Pedad Investments. One tool that Pedad uses to compare stock valuations is the dividend discount model (DDM). In particular, the firm evaluates stocks in terms of "justified" multiples of sales and book value. These multiples are based on algebraic manipulation of the DDM. Over time, these multiples seem to provide a good check on the market valuation of a stock relative to the company's fundamentals. Any stock that is currently priced below its value based on a justified multiple of sales or book value is considered attractive for purchase by Pedad portfolio managers. Exhibit 1 contains financial information from the year just ended for three stable companies in the meatpacking industry: Able Corporation, Baker, Inc., and Charles Company, from which Armor will derive his valuation estimates.

Exhibit 1: Selected Financial Information

	Able Corporation	Baker, Inc.	Charles Company
Revenue/share	$115.00	$52.80	$25.75
EPS	$2.50	$4.80	$4.00
DPS	$1.00	$1.60	$2.50
ROE	25%	15%	8%
Book value per share	$10.00	$32.00	$50.00
Stock price per share (current)	$60.00	$70.00	$35.50
Required return	20%	12%	10%

One of Pedad's other equity analysts, Marie Swift, CFA, recently held a meeting with Armor to discuss a relatively new model the firm is implementing to determine the P/E ratios of companies that Pedad researches. Swift explains that the model utilizes a cross-sectional regression using the previous year-end data of a group of comparable companies' P/E ratios against their dividend payout ratios (payout ratio), sustainable growth rates (g), and returns on equity (ROE). The resulting regression equation is used to determine a predicted P/E ratio for the subject company using the subject company's most recent year-end data. Swift has developed the following model, which has an R-squared of 81%, for the meatpacking industry (16 companies):

Predicted P/E = 2.74 + 8.21(payout ratio) + 14.21(g) + 2.81(ROE)

(STD error)   (2.11) (6.52)   (9.24)   (2.10)

After Swift presents the model to Armor, she points out that models of this nature are subject to limitations. In particular, multicollinearity, which appears to be present in the meatpacking industry model, can create great difficulty in interpreting the effects of the individual coefficients of the model. Swift continues by stating that in spite of this limitation, models of this nature generally have known and significant predictive power across different periods, although not across different stocks.

31. Based on Exhibit 1, select the stock that is the *most* undervalued by applying the justified price-to-book value method.
    A. Able Corporation.
    B. Baker, Inc.
    C. Charles Company.

32. Based on Exhibit 1, the justified price-to-sales ratio of Baker, Inc. is *closest* to:
    A. 1.5.
    B. 1.7.
    C. 1.9.

33. If valuation is based on the justified price-to-sales ratio, Armor should conclude that Able Corporation is:
    A. overvalued; the stock trades at more than double its value based on a justified price-to-sales ratio.
    B. overvalued relative to Baker, but undervalued relative to Charles.
    C. undervalued; the stock trades at less than half its value based on a justified price-to-sales ratio.

34. Armor has been asked to identify the relative valuation merits of the three stocks. Which of the following statements is correct?
    A. Able Corporation is the best investment because it has the highest ROE.
    B. Charles Company is the best investment because the stock is priced below book value.
    C. Able Corporation's earnings should grow the fastest due to its high ROE and retention ratio.

35. Based on Exhibit 1, indicate the company that has the lowest predicted P/E utilizing the meatpacking industry model presented by Swift.
    A. Able Corporation.
    B. Baker, Inc.
    C. Charles Company.

36. Evaluate Swift's comments regarding multicollinearity and predictive power. Which of the following comments is correct?
    A. Only the comment about multicollinearity is correct.
    B. Only the comment about predictive power is correct.
    C. Both comments are correct.

Use the following information to answer Questions 37 through 42.

Ande Lindstrom is currently in the final year of his undergraduate degree in finance and is preparing to take the Level I CFA exam in December. To keep on top of the material, Lindstrom runs a website for his peers who are also planning to sit for the CFA exam.

Lindstrom is currently reviewing several submissions from classmates on the subject of fixed-income instruments. These submissions are especially topical because the U.S. central bank raised target rate in the previous month. Lindstrom intends to post the spot rate curve shown in Exhibit 1, which is derived from U.S. Treasuries, along with any articles he agrees with.

Exhibit 1: U.S. Treasuries Spot Curve

Maturity (years)	1	2	3	5	7	10	20	30
Spot Rate (%)	0.25	0.36	0.90	1.49	2.27	2.94	3.52	4.00

Joe Hellens, a fellow Level I candidate, has submitted an article claiming that some banks are still offering forward rates that do not fully account for the new spot curve. As a result, Hellens claims that there are arbitrage opportunities. Upon analyzing a particular bank's offering of a two-year forward contract on a risk-free, 5-year, zero coupon bond, Hellens states that "the quoted forward price of $0.8608 per $1 is higher than it should be under the forward pricing model and, hence, arbitrage profits could be made."

Lindstrom is always wary of posting articles on to the website that could be interpreted as investment advice. Instead, he prefers instructional articles that allow the reader to carry out their own research. In place of Hellens's article on potential arbitrage opportunities (the profits of which he feels would be eliminated by transaction costs), Lindstrom intends to use the comment addressing active bond management shown in Exhibit 2.

Exhibit 2: Active Bond Management

"Active bond managers will seek to outperform the market by anticipating interest rate movements that are not in line with current spot and forward rates. For example, the price of a one-year forward contract on a one-year, zero coupon, risk-free bond will remain unchanged if the future one-year spot rate in one year is equal to the current two-year spot rate. If it is not, there may be an opportunity for active managers to outperform the market."

Dan Gorman has submitted an article for Lindstrom's review on the topic of the swap curve. Lindstrom is aware of the curve but unsure about how it is used in computing swap spreads and in bond valuation generally. Extracts from Gorman's article are shown in Exhibit 3.

Exhibit 3: Swap Curves and Spreads

"Swap spreads make use of the swap curve. Swap curves are a popular benchmark for the time value of money as they have at least two key advantages over the government yield curve:

Advantage One: Some countries do not have a liquid government bond market for maturities over one year. In those markets, the swap curve is an essential benchmark.

Advantage Two: Retail banks generally have familiarilty with the swap market because they hedge assets and liabilities on their balance sheet with swaps. For this reason, the swap rate makes a useful benchmark for the time value of money for them."

Swap curves can also be used to calculate the swap spread, which is an increasingly popular indicator of credit spreads in the markets. The swap spread is defined as:

"The spread paid by the floating-rate payer of an interest rate swap over the rate of the on-the-run government security with the same maturity."

The swap spread is a useful indicator of credit risk in the markets and can be used in conjunction with the TED, LIBOR-OIS, and Z-spreads to get an in-depth view of the state of the fixed-income markets. An investor can use these other three spreads as follows:

Z-spread: Calculated as the constant basis point spread added to the implied spot yield curve so that the discounted cash flows of a bond equal its market price. For a risky bond, the Z-spread is a more accurate measure of compensation for credit and liquidity risk than the swap spread.

TED spread: Calculated as the difference between LIBOR and the yield on a maturity-matched T-bill. TED spread gives better insight into the supply and demand conditions in the market at a given maturity as opposed to the swap spread, which focuses more on the risks in the banking system.

LIBOR-OIS spread: Calculated as the difference between LIBOR and the overnight indexed swap rate. It is considered a good indicator of the risk and liquidity inherent in the money markets.

Finally, Lindstrom has received an email from one of his professors praising his work on the website but also offering some constructive criticism. An extract from the email is shown in Exhibit 4.

Exhibit 4: Email

"...I would suggest one area you could look at improving is the portion on term structure theories. Personally I would remove the theory stating that lenders and borrowers influence the shape of the yield curve and that the yield of each maturity sector is determined independently.

I suggest instead that you take a look at the following equilibrium term structure model, which calculates the change in the short term interest rate (dr) over small increments of time (dt):

$$dr = a(b - r)dt + \sigma\sqrt{r}dz$$

It is a formula I personally use when modelling rates, typically with r = 3%, b = 8%, a = 0.40, σ = 20%.

37. Hellens's claim regarding the two-year forward contract on the five-year, risk-free, zero coupon bond is *most accurately* described as:
    A. incorrect, as the quoted price is roughly in line with the forward pricing model.
    B. incorrect, as the quoted price is much lower than the forward pricing model would suggest.
    C. correct.

38. Lindstrom's comment in Exhibit 2 on active bond management is *most likely*:
    A. correct.
    B. incorrect, as the forward price will be unchanged if the one-year spot rate occurring in one year is equal to the current one-year forward rate one year from now [$f(1,1)$].
    C. incorrect, as the forward price will be unchanged if the one-year spot rate occurring in one year is equal to the current one-year spot rate.

39. Which of the advantages of swap curves listed in Exhibit 3 is accurate?
    A. Advantage one only.
    B. Advantage two only.
    C. Both advantages one and two are accurate.

40. Gorman's definition of the swap spread in Exhibit 3 is *best* described as:
    A. correct.
    B. incorrect, as the spread is compared to the corporate bond being valued, not a government security.
    C. incorrect, as the spread uses the fixed-rate paid in the swap, not the floating rate.

41. With regards to the discussion of spreads in Exhibit 3, Gorman is *least accurate* in his:
    A. definition of the LIBOR-OIS spread.
    B. assertion that the *z*-spread is a more accurate measure of credit risk than the swap spread.
    C. assertion that the TED spread gives better insight into supply and demand conditions than does the swap spread.

42. The professor who sent the email in Exhibit 4 is *most likely* advocating the exclusion of the:
    A. segmented markets theory in favor of the Cox-Ingersoll-Ross model, with a mean reverting, short-term interest rate of 8%.
    B. preferred habitat theory in favor of the Vasicek model, with a mean reverting, short-term interest rate of 3%.
    C. segmented markets theory in favor of the Cox-Ingersoll-Ross model, with a mean reverting, short-term interest rate of 2%.

Use the following information to answer Questions 43 through 48.

Jon Garton, CFA, is an equity analyst covering several industry sectors for a boutique U.S. investment firm. Currently Garton is reviewing a reply that he received from the CFO of TorkSpark, Inc., a manufacturer of automotive parts.

Garton had noticed that the most recent quarterly filing by TorkSpark showed an increase in the volume of derivative transactions that showed gains and losses either in the income statement or in other comprehensive income. This is the third quarter in a row that Garton has observed such an increase, and in a recent analyst call, Garton asked the CFO to give some explanation for such an increase.

Extracts from the CFO's reply are shown in Exhibit 1.

Exhibit 1: TorkSpark CFO comments

"TorkSpark currently has a $68 million bond outstanding that is not due to mature until 2028. The coupon payments are fixed at 6.25% and paid quarterly. A decision was taken recently to try to reduce the interest rate risk on the bond.

The board also identified a need to address the financing of TorkSpark Plc., our wholly owned subsidiary in the UK. In order to raise the 175 million GBP needed to fund an expansion of the operations, the board leveraged its relationship with the Lobman Starn banking group here in the United States.

TorkSpark borrowed 250 million USD and set up a USD-GBP currency swap with a swap dealer based in Europe. Unfortunately, the dealer experienced some issues trying to hedge their position, so TorkSpark agreed to settle the swap at the PV of future payments only 170 days after origination.

The only other currency derivative TorkSpark used in the period was a currency forward contract that was used to hedge the risk on an unusually large EUR receipt. Due to TorkSpark discontinuing a product line, Redaux SA, a frequent customer, agreed to pay a large sum for all remaining stock. Due to continued political turbulence in the Eurozone, TorkSpark opted to hedge 60% of the EUR receivable."

Garton is familiar with Torkspark's euro currency forward contract because it was discussed in detail in the analyst call. The currency forward lead to a large loss that was offset by a gain on the receivable in other comprehensive income in the financial statements. Details of the contract are shown in Exhibit 2.

Exhibit 2: Currency Forward Contract

Contract Length:	90 days
90-day forward rate at origination:	€/$ 0.89239
Spot rate at origination:	€/$ 0.89298
90-day forward rate at expiry:	€/$ 0.84256
Spot rate at expiry:	€/$ 0.84487
Loss at settlement date:	$189,083

Garton is not convinced that all the derivatives transactions reflected in TorkSpark's financial statements are purely for hedging. He believes that there are significant exposures to both interest rate and currency risk for the next six quarters. As a result, Garton intends to suggest that his firm hedge their holding of TorkSpark stock using exchange-traded options.

Garton's strategy is to reduce the downside risk of the stock using a put option, and offset some of the put cost by using a call option at a higher exercise price.

Garton has experience using options to boost portfolio performance from his previous role as a portfolio manager at a small investment house. Garton feels that a particular stock he is currently covering, Toutoos, Inc., is poised for a modest gain in the next quarter, based on speculation that import tariffs into a country that Toutoos trades heavily with are to be abolished. Garton's firm does not hold any Toutoos stock, so to take advantage of a potential price increase, he intends to set up a bull call spread using the options shown in Exhibit 3.

Exhibit 3: Information about Toutoos, Inc., Stock and Options

Current stock price = $38.20

Option	Call Price	Call Delta	Put Price	Put Delta
Jun 36	$2.64	0.87	$0.15	−0.13
Jun 37	$1.84	0.76	$0.34	−0.24
Jun 38	$1.19	0.60	$0.68	−0.40
Jun 39	$0.70	0.43	$1.19	−0.57
Jun 40	$0.38	0.27	$1.86	−0.73
Jun 41	$0.18	0.16	$2.65	−0.84
Jun 42	$0.08	0.08	$3.54	−0.92

Note: Options expire on the third Friday of each month

Garton would like to construct a bull call spread that meets the following two criteria:

1. The strategy must at least break even if the stock price moves up by 3.5% from its current level by the maturity of the options

2. The maximum profit must be at least $2.30 per pair

Garton's colleague, Hans Robinson, informs Garton that bull spreads can also be constructed using put options. Robinson sends the following email to Garton with a suggested strategy using puts:

"Jon, here's the strategy I mentioned earlier: to take advantage of an increase in the price of Toutoos, sell Jun 41 puts and buy Jun 39 puts. This is a bull put spread that will generate an initial cash inflow. The maximum potential loss is equal to the net premium."

43. Which of the following positions is *most likely* to achieve the CFO's objective for the $68 million bond outstanding?
    A. Pay fixed interest rate swap with quarterly settlement.
    B. Pay floating interest rate swap with quarterly settlement.
    C. Long FRA on 90-day LIBOR.

44. In order to hedge exposure to the currency swap described by the CFO, the swap dealer would *least appropriately*:
    A. borrow GBP.
    B. borrow USD.
    C. lend USD.

45. The value of the euro receivable due from Redaux is *closest* to:
    A. € 1,800,000.
    B. € 3,000,000.
    C. € 5,000,000.

46. Garton's strategy to hedge the risk of the TorkSpark holding using options is *most likely* to require a:
    A. long call option and be referred to as a long collar.
    B. short call option and be referred to as a long straddle.
    C. short call option and be referred to as a collar.

47. The option combination Garton is *most likely* to use in setting up a bull call spread that meets both of his criteria is:
    A. a Jun 38 call and a Jun 42 call.
    B. a Jun 39 call and a Jun 42 call.
    C. a Jun 39 call and a Jun 41 call.

48. Robinson's statement outlining his option strategy is *most likely* inaccurate because:
    A. it would involve an initial cash outflow.
    B. to take advantage of a modest price rise, Robinson would sell the put option with the lower price and buy the option with the higher price.
    C. the maximum loss would not be equal to the net premium.

Use the following information to answer Questions 49 through 54.

Karen Westin, Kei Shinoya, and Carlos Perez, partners at PacRim Investment Consultants, are advising a client, the West Lundia Government Employees Pension Plan (WLGE), a large public pension fund. In a previous meeting with the pension board of WLGE, the PacRim team made a recommendation to increase the fund's exposure to domestic real estate. Because of the WLGE plan's large size and in-house expertise, the pension fund has the capacity to invest in and manage a wide variety of real estate investments. The currency in West Lundia is the West Lundian Dollar (WL$).

West Lundian Commercial Real Estate Market Expectations

Commercial real estate prices have experienced a moderate increase over the past year after a decade of unusually slow growth. Demand is expected to exceed supply over the next 10 years. The current average commercial mortgage rate of 3.75% is low by historical standards and is expected to stay relatively low for at least seven more years. The West Lundian economy is expected to enjoy an above average growth rate.

Exhibit 1: West Lundia's Economic Outlook

	Expected Annual Growth Rate	Relative to Other Developed Countries
Job Creation	3.0%	High
Population	1.8%	High
Retail Sales	1.5%	Low
Inflation	0.5%	Low

Because of the favorable real estate conditions, the consensus was to consider equity investments in real estate. Three options under consideration are:

Option 1: Direct investment, in an existing office building.

Option 2: Investment in a public equity REIT.

Option 3: Equity investment in a public REOC.

Option 1: Direct Investment	
Expected NOI Years 1–7	WL$ 7.0 MM
Expected NOI Year 8	WL$ 8.5 MM
Required return on equity investment	10%
NOI growth rate after 8 years	3.25%

Option 2: REIT	
Recent NOI	WL$ 140.0 MM
Non-cash rents	WL$ 5.0 MM
Full year adjustment for acquisition	WL$ 5.0 MM
Other assets	WL$ 50.0 MM
Total liabilities	WL$ 300.0 MM
Current market price per share	WL$ 125.00
Shares outstanding	15 MM
Going-in cap rate	7.00%
NOI growth rate	2.50%

Option 3: REOC	
Expected AFFO in Year 7	WL$ 13.5 MM
Holding Period	7 years
Present value of all dividends for 7 years	WL$ 39.7 MM
Shares outstanding	1.0 MM
Cap rate	7.0%
Growth rate (from Year 8)	2.50%

Additional Information:

1. The office building under consideration has existing tenants with long-term leases that will expire in seven years.

2. The REOC terminal value at the end of seven years is to be based on a price-to-AFFO multiple of 12x.

49. Based on the information in Exhibit 1, the REIT sector that represents the *least desirable* investment is:
    A. industrial.
    B. office.
    C. apartments.

50. The estimated value of the office building (Option 1) using the discounted cash flow approach is *closest* to:
    A. WL$ 89 million.
    B. WL$ 93 million.
    C. WL$ 99 million.

51. Based on its estimated value using the asset value approach, the REIT identified in Option 2 is:
    A. fairly priced.
    B. selling at a discount.
    C. selling at a premium.

52. The *most appropriate* reason to choose Option 1 (direct investment) over Options 2 and 3 is that Option 1 is likely to have the ability to:
    A. use higher leverage.
    B. provide greater tax advantages.
    C. avoid structural conflicts of interest.

53. The estimated value per share of Option 3, REOC, using the discounted cash flow approach is *closest* to:
    A. WL$ 125.50.
    B. WL$ 140.60.
    C. WL$ 162.00.

54. Option 3 would be preferred over Option 2 if:
    A. liquidity of the investment is critical.
    B. the investment must be efficient in terms of corporate taxes.
    C. capital appreciation is more highly valued than current income.

Use the following information to answer Questions 55 through 60.

Sally Sishek, CFA, works as a freelance risk management consultant in the United States. Recently, she was contacted by BlueCanopy Investments (BCI), an asset management firm that recently experienced a significant financial loss after what it described as a "serious failure in multiple risk management processes."

Sishek has had an initial meeting with Jon Bagwell, the chief investment officer of BCI, who is leading the review of risk management following the resignation of BCI's chief risk officer (CRO) last month.

Bagwell has concerns that the CRO relied too heavily on VaR as a risk measure, rather than also implementing other complimentary controls.

Sishek is reviewing the VaR analysis carried out by the recently departed CRO. Some of the calculations involved are shown in Exhibit 1.

Exhibit 1: VaR Calculations

Portfolio EGF Internal Ref:0300201 5% VaR

Inputs: Mean annual return   9.4%
          Annual volatility   14.2%

Assumptions:

- 250 trading days per year.
- Risk factors are normally distributed.
- Mean and volatility calculated using historical data over a three-year lookback period.
- The historical standard deviation has been adjusted upward to reflect the long-term expectations relative to the lookback period.

5% Annual VaR = [9.4% − (1.65 × 14.2%] = −14%
5% Daily VaR = [(0.0376% − (1.65 × 0.0568%)] = −0.056%

Sishek has some concerns about the calculations as well as the firm's use of VaR. Bagwell admits that he has very little idea how the VaR calculations were currently used to manage risk. Sishek suggests that in the short term, the firm should immediately implement at least the following recommendation:

Risk Management Recommendation
Impose a daily 1% VaR limit of (for example) $2,000,000 on a portfolio. Monitor the portfolio for any signs of trending and liquidate the portfolio if cumulative monthly losses exceed $7,500,000.

She also intends to provide a list of typical risk management measures that traditional asset managers employ and agreed to put together a case study on how each of these measures could be implemented. The list she will provide is shown in Exhibit 2.

Exhibit 2: Risk Management Measures

Typical risk measures employed by traditional asset managers include:

1. **Beta sensitivity:** useful for equity only

2. **Active share:** a measure of similarity to a benchmark

3. **Surplus-at-risk:** an application of VaR

4. **Maximum drawdown:** percentage of portfolio redeemed at peak times

Bagwell also revealed that he has some concerns over the trading methods authorized (and, in some cases, used) by the outgoing CRO. A recent internal audit of transactions carried out under his authorization revealed several instances of high frequency trading that auditors were uncomfortable with.

Multiple instances of trading patterns were flagged in an audit report as having a "high risk of inviting regulatory scrutiny." Two cases in particular concern Bagwell, and these are outlined in Exhibit 3.

Exhibit 3: High Frequency Trading Patterns

Case One
Trader [A] executed numerous transactions in rapid succession, taking the best offer price for security [XYZ] each time, but purchasing small quantities. This was followed by a sell order for a large quantity of the same security.

Case Two
The pattern of trading by Trader [B] over the period 8th June to 12th June suggests strongly that Trader [B] may be wash trading.

55.   In Exhibit 1, the annual VaR is *most accurately* described as being calculated using:
       A. a historical simulation.
       B. the parametric method.
       C. a Monte Carlo simulation.

56.   The calculated percentage value for daily VaR in Exhibit 1 is *most likely*:
       A. correct given the assumptions and method described.
       B. too high given the assumptions and method described.
       C. too low given the assumptions and method described.

57. Sishek's short-term risk management recommendation is *best* described as an example of:
    A. risk budgeting.
    B. a stop loss limit.
    C. a position limit.

58. The description of measures given by Sishek in Exhibit 2 is inaccurate with respect to:
    A. active share because it does not require the use of a benchmark.
    B. surplus-at-risk because it is not an application of VaR.
    C. maximum drawdown because it is not a measure of redemptions.

59. The activity described in case one of Exhibit 3 is *most likely* to be referred to as:
    A. front running.
    B. painting the tape.
    C. quote stuffing.

60. The activity described in case two of Exhibit 3 is *most likely* to involve:
    A. placing a legitimate trade on one side of the market and several illegitimate orders at different prices on the other side.
    B. executing simultaneous buy and sell orders on the same financial instrument.
    C. entering large quantities of fictitious orders into the market and instantaneously cancelling them.

End of Morning Session

EXAM 1
AFTERNOON SESSION

Question	Topic	Minutes (Points)
61 to 66	Ethical and Professional Standards	18
67 to 72	Quantitative Methods	18
73 to 78	Financial Reporting and Analysis	18
79 to 90	Corporate Finance	36
91 to 102	Equity Valuation	36
103 to 108	Fixed Income	18
109 to 114	Derivatives	18
115 to 120	Portfolio Management	18

61.	Ⓐ	Ⓑ	Ⓒ		101.	Ⓐ	Ⓑ	Ⓒ
62.	Ⓐ	Ⓑ	Ⓒ		102.	Ⓐ	Ⓑ	Ⓒ
63.	Ⓐ	Ⓑ	Ⓒ		103.	Ⓐ	Ⓑ	Ⓒ
64.	Ⓐ	Ⓑ	Ⓒ		104.	Ⓐ	Ⓑ	Ⓒ
65.	Ⓐ	Ⓑ	Ⓒ		105.	Ⓐ	Ⓑ	Ⓒ
66.	Ⓐ	Ⓑ	Ⓒ		106.	Ⓐ	Ⓑ	Ⓒ
67.	Ⓐ	Ⓑ	Ⓒ		107.	Ⓐ	Ⓑ	Ⓒ
68.	Ⓐ	Ⓑ	Ⓒ		108.	Ⓐ	Ⓑ	Ⓒ
69.	Ⓐ	Ⓑ	Ⓒ		109.	Ⓐ	Ⓑ	Ⓒ
70.	Ⓐ	Ⓑ	Ⓒ		110.	Ⓐ	Ⓑ	Ⓒ
71.	Ⓐ	Ⓑ	Ⓒ		111.	Ⓐ	Ⓑ	Ⓒ
72.	Ⓐ	Ⓑ	Ⓒ		112.	Ⓐ	Ⓑ	Ⓒ
73.	Ⓐ	Ⓑ	Ⓒ		113.	Ⓐ	Ⓑ	Ⓒ
74.	Ⓐ	Ⓑ	Ⓒ		114.	Ⓐ	Ⓑ	Ⓒ
75.	Ⓐ	Ⓑ	Ⓒ		115.	Ⓐ	Ⓑ	Ⓒ
76.	Ⓐ	Ⓑ	Ⓒ		116.	Ⓐ	Ⓑ	Ⓒ
77.	Ⓐ	Ⓑ	Ⓒ		117.	Ⓐ	Ⓑ	Ⓒ
78.	Ⓐ	Ⓑ	Ⓒ		118.	Ⓐ	Ⓑ	Ⓒ
79.	Ⓐ	Ⓑ	Ⓒ		119.	Ⓐ	Ⓑ	Ⓒ
80.	Ⓐ	Ⓑ	Ⓒ		120.	Ⓐ	Ⓑ	Ⓒ
81.	Ⓐ	Ⓑ	Ⓒ					
82.	Ⓐ	Ⓑ	Ⓒ					
83.	Ⓐ	Ⓑ	Ⓒ					
84.	Ⓐ	Ⓑ	Ⓒ					
85.	Ⓐ	Ⓑ	Ⓒ					
86.	Ⓐ	Ⓑ	Ⓒ					
87.	Ⓐ	Ⓑ	Ⓒ					
88.	Ⓐ	Ⓑ	Ⓒ					
89.	Ⓐ	Ⓑ	Ⓒ					
90.	Ⓐ	Ⓑ	Ⓒ					
91.	Ⓐ	Ⓑ	Ⓒ					
92.	Ⓐ	Ⓑ	Ⓒ					
93.	Ⓐ	Ⓑ	Ⓒ					
94.	Ⓐ	Ⓑ	Ⓒ					
95.	Ⓐ	Ⓑ	Ⓒ					
96.	Ⓐ	Ⓑ	Ⓒ					
97.	Ⓐ	Ⓑ	Ⓒ					
98.	Ⓐ	Ⓑ	Ⓒ					
99.	Ⓐ	Ⓑ	Ⓒ					
100.	Ⓐ	Ⓑ	Ⓒ					

EXAM 1
AFTERNOON SESSION

Use the following information to answer Questions 61 through 66.

Chester Brothers, LLC, is an investment management firm with $200 million in assets under management. Chester's equity style is described to clients as a large-cap core strategy. One year ago, Chester instituted a new compensation plan for its equity portfolio managers. Under this new plan, each portfolio manager receives an annual bonus based upon that manager's quarterly performance relative to the S&P 500 index. For each quarter of out-performance, the manager receives a bonus in the amount of 20% of his regular annual compensation. Chester has not disclosed this new plan to clients. Portfolio managers at Chester are not bound by non-compete agreements.

James Rogers, CFA, and Karen Pierce, CFA, are both portfolio managers affected by the new policy. Rogers out-performed the S&P 500 index in each of the last three quarters, largely because he began investing his clients' funds in small-cap securities. Chester has recently been citing Rogers's performance in local media advertising, including claims that "Chester's star manager, James Rogers, has outperformed the S&P 500 index in each of the last three quarters." The print advertising associated with the media campaign includes a photograph of Rogers, identifying him as James Rogers, CFA. Below his name is a quote apparently attributable to Rogers saying "as a CFA charterholder, I am committed to the highest ethical standards."

A few weeks after the advertising campaign began, Rogers was approached by the Grumpp Foundation, a local charitable endowment with $3 billion in assets, about serving on its investment advisory committee. The committee meets weekly to review the portfolio and make adjustments as needed. The Grumpp trustees were impressed by the favorable mention of Rogers in the marketing campaign. In making their offer, they even suggested that Rogers could mention his position on the advisory committee in future Chester marketing material. Rogers has not informed Chester about the Grumpp offer, but he has not yet accepted the position.

Pierce has not fared as well as Rogers. She also shifted into smaller-cap securities, but due to two extremely poor performing large-cap stocks, her performance lagged the S&P 500 index for the first three quarters. After an angry confrontation with her supervisor, Pierce resigned. When she left, Pierce took a copy of a computer model with the permission of the co-worker who developed the model, as well as the most recent list of her buy recommendations, which was created from the output of the computer model. Pierce soon accepted a position at a competing firm, Cheeri Group. On her first day at Cheeri, she contacted each of her five largest former clients, informing them of her new employment and asking that they consider moving their accounts from Chester to Cheeri. During both telephone conversations and e-mails with her former clients, Pierce mentioned that Chester had a new compensation program that created incentives for managers to shift into smaller-cap securities.

Cheeri has posted Pierce's investment performance for the past five years on its Web site, excluding the three most recent quarters. The footnotes to the performance information include the following two statements:

Statement 1: Includes large capitalization portfolios only.

Statement 2: Results reflect manager's performance at previous employer.

61. Chester's new compensation plan for awarding bonuses to individual portfolio managers:
    A. is consistent with CFA Institute Standards and does not require disclosure.
    B. is consistent with CFA Institute Standards only if fully disclosed to clients.
    C. is consistent with CFA Institute Standards, but any bonuses awarded under the plan must be fully disclosed to clients.

62. Assuming Rogers would like to accept the offer to serve on the Grumpp investment advisory committee, Rogers's obligations under the CFA Institute Standards require that he:
    A. refuse to serve on the Grumpp committee.
    B. accept the Grumpp committee position only after disclosing the offer to his supervisor.
    C. accept the Grumpp committee position and disclose his acceptance as soon as possible to his supervisor.

©2017 Kaplan, Inc.

63. Chester's advertising campaign includes claims about Rogers's investment performance, as well as Rogers's use and reference to the CFA charter. Is Chester's advertising campaign consistent with the CFA Institute Standards?
    A. Chester's performance claims are inconsistent with CFA Institute Standards, but his use and reference to the CFA designation is appropriate.
    B. Both the performance claim and the reference to the CFA charter are violations.
    C. Neither the performance claims nor the use and reference to the CFA designation are violations.

64. Under the CFA Institute Standards, Pierce taking the computer model when leaving her position at Chester would be *best* described as a violation:
    A. because she should have obtained written permission from her co-worker.
    B. unless she obtained permission from both her co-worker as well as from Chester.
    C. unless she obtained permission from Chester Brothers, LLC.

65. Pierce's behavior upon assuming her new position at Cheeri can *best* be described as violating CFA Institute Standards because she:
    A. encouraged her former clients to leave Chester.
    B. should not have contacted her former clients at all.
    C. disclosed Chester's new compensation program.

66. Cheeri's presentation of Pierce's investment performance is inconsistent with CFA Institute Standards because:
    A. the results were not calculated under GIPS.
    B. performance from a previous employer should not be included.
    C. the results misrepresent Pierce's large cap performance.

Use the following information to answer Questions 67 through 72.

Austin Clark, CFA, has been asked to analyze White Goods Corporation, a $9 billion company that owns a nationwide chain of stores selling appliances and other electronic goods. As part of his analysis of the White Goods Corporation, Clark's supervisor, David Horvath, asks Clark to forecast White Goods' 2009 sales using multiple regression analysis. The following model was developed:

$$\text{sales} = 20.1 + 0.001\ \text{GDP} + 1{,}000.6\ \text{TR} + 0.1\ \text{CC} - 3.2\ \text{PC} - 40.3\ \text{UR}$$
$$t\text{-values:} (1.1)\ (2.3) \qquad (1.75) \qquad (3.2) \quad (-0.48)\ (-0.9)$$

Number of observations:	76
Standard error estimate:	15.67
Unadjusted R^2:	0.96
Regression sum of squares:	412,522
Error sum of squares:	17,188

Independent Variable Descriptions

GDP = gross domestic product
TR = average rate on 5-year U.S. Treasury securities
CC = most recent quarter end consumer confidence index value
PC = previous year's sales of personal computers
UR = most recent quarter end unemployment rate

Variable Estimates for 2009

GDP = 8,000
TR = 0.05
CC = 97
PC = 60,000
UR = 0.055

Critical Values For Student's *t*-Distribution

Degrees of Freedom	Level of Significance for One-Tailed Test			
	10%	5%	2.5%	1%
	Level of Significance for Two-Tailed Test			
	20%	10%	5%	2%
5	1.476	2.015	2.571	3.365
15	1.341	1.753	2.131	2.602
25	1.316	1.708	2.060	2.485
50	1.299	1.676	2.009	2.403
60	1.296	1.671	2.000	2.390
70	1.294	1.667	1.994	2.381

Clark's supervisor asks him to prepare a report explaining the implications of the regression analysis results. Clark writes the following conclusions concerning regression analysis in his report:

Interpreting the results of regression analysis can be problematic if certain assumptions of the ordinary least squares framework are violated. The regression output for White Goods Corporation is unreliable for the following reasons:

Finding 1: The correlation between regression errors across time is very close to 1.

Finding 2: There is a strong relationship between the regression error variance and the regression independent variables.

67. Using his multiple linear regression, Clark's sales forecast for 2009 is *closest* to:
    A. –$191,914.
    B. $18.
    C. $192,090.

68. Is the regression coefficient of the 5-year U.S. Treasury interest rate statistically significantly different from zero at the 10% level of significance?
    A. Yes, because 1.75 > 1.29.
    B. Yes, because 1.75 > 1.67.
    C. No, because 1.75 < 1.99.

69. In this multiple regression equation, a potential statistical issue is:
    A. the coefficient of determination indicates a weak model.
    B. that sales cannot be statistically modeled.
    C. the PC variable is not a statistically significant variable.

70. What is the *F*-value that tests the hypothesis that all of the coefficients are equal to zero?
    A. 42.0.
    B. 101.0.
    C. 336.0.

71. In his report to his supervisor, Clark's test of serial correlation indicates that the *t*-statistics for the regression estimates likely are:
    A. biased upward.
    B. biased downward.
    C. unbiased.

72. Clark's two documented findings related to his examination of the regression errors should lead to the conclusion that Clark's regression equation exhibits strong evidence of:
    A. conditional heteroskedasticity.
    B. multicollinearity.
    C. unit roots.

Use the following information to answer Questions 73 through 78.

Curtis Fox, an equity analyst for Altex Investments, is reviewing financial statements for Hope Manufacturing and Levitt Industries. Hope Manufacturing has recently stated its intention to acquire a 20% stake in Levitt Industries for $185 million cash. Both companies are U.S. companies that follow U.S. GAAP.

Fox wants to consolidate his pro-forma financial statements for the two companies to see the effects of the proposed acquisition. Following are the most recent balance sheets and the pro-forma income statements developed by Fox before taking into account the acquisition.

Pre-Acquisition Balance Sheets (in million $) December 31, 2010	Hope	Levitt
Current assets	13,900	716
PP&E	26,977	108
Total assets	40,877	824
Current liabilities	10,363	220
Other liabilities	11,121	8
Common stock	6,127	108
Retained earnings	13,266	488
Total liabilities and equity	40,877	824

Pro-Forma Income Statements (in million $) for Year Ending December 31, 2011	Hope	Levitt
Revenue	66,176	2,176
Expenses	63,515	2,068
Net income	2,661	108
Dividends	1,525	0

Fox is concerned about the effect that the choice of accounting method will have on the earnings and financial ratios of Hope. Fox consults with Jeffery Gordon, who tells him, "Since Levitt is profitable and pays no dividends, the equity method will result in higher net income than the acquisition method. Additionally, the equity method will result in lower return on assets (ROA) than the acquisition method with partial goodwill."

73. Assuming the acquisition goes through at the beginning of 2011, and that Hope will have a significant influence on Levitt, Hope's total assets after acquisition would be *closest* to:
    A. $40,877.
    B. $41,062.
    C. $41,701.

74. Fox estimates that the fair value of Levitt's PP&E is $250 million. The amount allocated to goodwill would be *closest* to:
    A. $20.2 million.
    B. $37.4 million.
    C. $65.8 million.

75. For this question only, assume that as a result of the acquisition, Hope must depreciate an additional $50 million (Hope's share of the FMV adjustment) over a 10-year period to zero salvage value. Levitt's contribution to Hope's EBT for 2011 is projected to be *closest* to:
    A. $16.6 million.
    B. $18.8 million.
    C. $21.6 million.

76. For this question only, assume the acquisition occurs on December 31, 2010, and that there is no additional depreciation expense as a result of the acquisition. Compared to its beginning of year investment balance, the balance for Hope's investment in Levitt on December 31, 2011, will be:
    A. lower.
    B. higher.
    C. unchanged.

77. Is Gordon's statement regarding the effects of the choice of accounting method on net income and ROA correct?
    A. Yes.
    B. No, he is incorrect regarding the effect on ROA.
    C. No, he is incorrect regarding the effect on net income and ROA.

78. If Fox were to follow IFRS instead of U.S. GAAP, the accounting method prescribed for this type of investment would *most likely* be:
    A. the equity method.
    B. the acquisition method.
    C. proportionate consolidation.

Use the following information to answer Questions 79 through 84.

Fashion, Inc., is a major U.S. distributor of high-quality women's jewelry and accessories. The company's growth in recent years has been moderately above the industry average. However, competition is intensifying as a number of overseas competitors have entered this mature market. Although Fashion has been a publicly held company for many years, members of senior management and their families control 20% of the outstanding common stock. Martin Silver, the chief executive officer, has been under intense pressure from both internal and external large shareholders to find ways to increase the company's future growth.

Silver has consulted with the company's investment bankers concerning possible merger targets. The most promising merger target is Flavoring International, a distributor of a broad line of gourmet spices in the United States and numerous other countries. In recent years, Flavoring's earnings growth rate has been above competitors' and also has exceeded Fashion's experience. Superior income growth is projected to continue over at least the next five years. Silver is impressed with the appeal of the company's products to upscale customers, its strong operating and financial performance, and Flavoring's dynamic management team. He is contemplating retirement in three years and believes that Flavoring's younger, more aggressive senior managers could boost the combined company's growth through increasing Fashion's operating efficiency and expanding Fashion's product line in countries outside the United States. Alan Smith, who is Silver's key contact at the investment banking firm, indicates that a key appeal of this merger to Flavoring would be Fashion's greater financial flexibility and access to lower cost sources of financing for expansion of its products in new geographic areas. Fashion has a very attractive performance based stock option plan. Flavoring's incentive plan is entirely based on cash compensation for achieving performance goals. Additionally, the 80% of Fashion's stock not controlled by management interests is very widely held and trades actively. Flavoring became a publicly held company three years ago and doesn't trade as actively.

Silver has asked Smith to prepare a report summarizing key points favoring the acquisition and an acceptable acquisition price. In preparing his report, Smith relies on the following financial data on Fashion, Flavoring, and four recently acquired food and beverage companies.

Exhibit 1: Financial and Market Data for Fashion, Inc. and Flavoring International

Financial/Price Data	Fashion	Flavoring
Sales	$400 million	$105 million
Net income	$80 million	$22 million
Cash flow	$140 million	$42 million
Book value	$320 million	$72 million
Number of common shares outstanding	50 million	20 million
Current market price of common stock	$30.50	$20.00
Recent market price range	$34–26	$22–18

Exhibit 2: Transaction Data for Food and Beverage Industry

Valuation Variables	Jones Foods	Dale, Inc.	Hill Brands	Lane Co.	Mean Multiple
Acquisition stock price	$24	$32	$40	$46	—
Price/sales per share	5.0	3.7	4.0	3.8	4.13
Price/book value per share	6.9	5.5	5.8	5.6	5.95
Price/earnings per share	20.0	22.1	18.0	19.0	19.78
Price/cash flow per share	11.8	13.0	10.5	11.0	11.58

79. The strongest motivations for Fashion to acquire Flavoring would *most likely* be:
    A. the potential to increase Fashion's growth and market power.
    B. the potential to create synergies and increase market power.
    C. Fashion management's incentives and diversification.

80. The *least likely* reason that Flavoring's management would favor an acquisition by Fashion would be:
    A. Flavoring management's incentives.
    B. opportunities to utilize Fashion's larger financial resources to increase market share of both companies.
    C. opportunities to utilize Fashion's financial resources to expand the combined company's product line into the higher volume moderately priced market segment.

81. If Fashion issues common stock at the current market price and uses the proceeds to acquire Flavoring's outstanding common stock, the bootstrap earnings effect on post merger earnings would *most likely* occur if Flavoring's acquisition price:
    A. is $20 or lower.
    B. is $20 or higher.
    C. is $20 or lower and Fashion's post merger P/E remains at the current level.

82. Using the comparable transaction approach based on the four recently acquired companies, Smith determines an estimated takeover value based on equally weighted key valuation variables. The estimated takeover value would be *closest* to:
    A. $20.27.
    B. $21.76.
    C. $22.30.

83. Based on pre-acquisition prices of $20 for Jones Foods, $26 for Dale, Inc., $35 for Hill Brands, and $40 for Lane Co., the mean takeover premium for Flavoring would be *closest* to:
    A. 12.50%.
    B. 15.25%.
    C. 18.10%.

84. To justify his use of the comparable transaction approach to establish a fair acquisition for Flavoring, Smith would like to conclude his report with the most important reason for choosing this approach. Which of the following rationales would Smith *most likely* use?
    A. The fair acquisition price developed for Flavoring reflects a market based valuation approach, an advantage compared to discounted cash flow valuations, which are based on assumptions that do not incorporate market valuations.
    B. The acquisition prices for recently acquired companies provide a reasonable approximation of their realistic intrinsic values.
    C. The fair acquisition price developed for Flavoring is a realistic estimate of potential value to Fashion given that forecasts of future performance are unavailable.

Use the following information to answer Questions 85 through 90.

James Kelley is the CFO of X-Sport, Inc., a manufacturer of high-end outdoor sporting equipment. Using both debt and equity, X-Sport has been acquiring small competitor companies rather rapidly over the past few years, leading Kelley to believe that the firm's capital structure may have drifted from its optimal mix. Kelley has been asked by the board of directors to evaluate the situation and provide a presentation that includes details of the firm's capital structure as well as a risk assessment. In order to assist with his analysis, Kelley has collected information on the current financial situation of X-Sport. He has also projected the financial information for alternative financing plans. This information is presented in Exhibit 1.

Exhibit 1

	X-Sport, Inc.					Industry Average
	Current	*Plan A*	*Plan B*	*Plan C*	*Plan D*	
Debt/equity	1.50	2.33	1.86	1.22	0.82	1.27
K_d (after-tax)	5.0%	8.5%	6.2%	4.4%	3.9%	5.9%
K_e	12.0%	16.0%	13.5%	11.2%	10.9%	12.8%
Expected EPS	$5.67	$6.00	$6.33	$5.47	$4.89	$6.31
Payout ratio	45%					42%
Growth rate	6.1%					5.9%
Stock price	$43					

After carefully analyzing the data, Kelley writes his analysis and proposal and submits the report to Richard Haywood, the chairman and CEO of X-Sport. Excerpts from the analysis and proposal follow:

- In selecting a refinancing plan, we must not push our leverage ratio too high. An overly aggressive leverage ratio will likely cause debt rating agencies to downgrade our debt rating from its current Baa rating, causing our cost of debt to rise dramatically. This effect is explained using the static trade-off capital structure theory, which states that if our debt usage becomes high enough, the marginal increase in the interest tax shield will be more than the marginal increase in the costs of financial distress. However, using some additional leverage will benefit the company by reducing the net agency costs of equity required to align the interests of X-Sport management with its shareholders.
- In the event that X-Sport decides to proceed with a recapitalization plan, I recommend Plan D because it is the most consistent with the shareholders' interests.

Haywood reviews the report and calls Kelley into his office to discuss the proposal. Haywood suggests that Plan B would be the most appropriate choice for adjusting X-Sport's capital structure. Before Kelley can argue, however, the two are interrupted by a previously scheduled meeting with a supplier.

Haywood takes Kelley's data and proposes to the board of directors that X-Sport pursue one of three alternatives to restructure the company. The first alternative is Plan B from Kelley's analysis. The second alternative involves separating GearTech, one of the companies acquired over the last few years, from the rest of the company by issuing new GearTech shares to X-Sport common shareholders. The third alternative involves creating a new company, Euro-Sport, out of the firm's European operations and selling 35% of the new Euro-Sport shares to the public while retaining 65% of the shares within X-Sport. After some persuading, Haywood convinces the 7-member board (two of whom were former executives at GearTech) to accept the second alternative, which he had favored from the beginning. The board puts together an announcement to its shareholders as well as the general public, detailing the terms and goals of the plan.

One of the board members, Michael Ponting, points out that there are several theories of optimal capital structure. Ponting makes the following statements:

Statement 1: Miller and Modigliani Proposition II (without taxes) states that cost of equity is not affected by capital structure changes.

Statement 2: Pecking order theory states that debt financing is preferable to all equity financing.

Statement 3: Static trade-off theory states that all firms have an optimal level of debt.

A group of shareholders, upset about the board's plan, submit a formal objection to X-Sport's board as well as to the SEC. In the objection, the shareholders state that the independence of the board has been compromised to the detriment of the company and its shareholders. The objection also states that:

- The value of X-Sport's common stock has been impaired as a result of the poor corporate governance system.
- The liability risk of X-Sport has increased due to the increased possibility of future transactions that benefit X-Sport's directors, without regard to the long-term interests of shareholders.
- The asset risk of X-Sport has increased due to the inability of investors to trust the GearTech financial disclosures necessary to value the division.

85. Using the information in Exhibit 1, calculate X-Sport's weighted average cost of capital for the optimal capital structure.
    A. 7.46%.
    B. 7.75%.
    C. 8.76%.

86. Determine whether Kelley's report is correct with regard to the statements made about the static trade-off theory of capital structure and the net agency costs of equity.
    A. Kelley is only correct with respect to the static trade-off theory.
    B. Kelley is only correct with respect to the net agency cost of equity.
    C. Kelley is incorrect with respect to the static trade-off theory and the net agency cost of equity.

87. Which of the following *best* explains the difference between X-Sport's current cost of debt and the cost of debt associated with Plan A?
    A. Decreased tax advantage with Plan A.
    B. Increased liquidity risk for Plan A bond purchasers.
    C. Increased probability of bankruptcy with Plan A.

88. Which of the statements made by Ponting is correct?
    A. Only Statement 1 is correct.
    B. Only Statement 2 is correct.
    C. Only Statement 3 is correct.

89. Which of the following statements with regard to the alternative plans proposed to X-Sport's board of directors by Haywood is correct?
    A. The GearTech plan is an example of a spin-off transaction, while the Euro-Sport plan is an example of a carve-out transaction.
    B. The GearTech plan is an example of a carve-out transaction, while the Euro-Sport plan is an example of a spin-off transaction.
    C. Both the GearTech plan and the Euro-Sport plans are examples of spin-off transactions.

90. Evaluate the three statements in the shareholders' formal objection submitted to X-Sport's board of directors. The objection is correct with regard to:
    A. asset risk.
    B. liability risk.
    C. the value impact.

Use the following information to answer Questions 91 through 96.

Marie Williams, CFA, and David Pacious, CFA, are portfolio managers for Stillwell Managers. Williams and Pacious are attending a conference held by Henri Financial Education on the fundamentals of valuation for common stock, preferred stock, and other assets.

During the conference, the presenter uses an example of four different companies to illustrate the valuation of common stock from the perspective of a minority shareholder.

- Firm A is a noncyclical consumer products firm with a 50-year history. The firm pays a $1.80 dividend per share and attempts to increase dividends by 4% a year. Earnings and dividends have steadily increased for the past 20 years.
- Firm B is a technology firm. It has never paid a dividend and does not expect to in the near future. Furthermore, due to large investments in new factories and equipment, the firm is not expected to generate positive free cash flow in the foreseeable future.
- Firm C is an industrial firm with currently very little competition and a dividend growth rate of 9% a year. However, the profits in its product market have started to attract competitors and it is expected that Firm C's profits will slowly decline such that the dividend growth steadily falls each year until it reaches a growth rate of 4% a year.
- Firm D is a pharmaceutical firm that is currently enjoying high profits and paying dividends. However, the firm's strongest selling drug is coming off patent in three years. With no other drugs in the pipeline, the firm's dividend growth rate is expected to drop abruptly in three years and settle at a lower growth rate.

The next day, Pacious decides to put what he learned into practice. The stock he is valuing, Maple Goods and Services, currently pays a dividend of $3.00. The dividend growth rate is 25% and is expected to steadily decline over the next eight years to a stable rate of 7% thereafter. Given its risk, Pacious estimates that the required return is 15%.

Williams analyzes the value of Mataka Plastics stock. Its dividend is expected to grow at a rate of 18% for the next four years, after which it will grow at 4%. This year's dividend is $5.00 and Williams estimates the required return at 15%.

From the seminar, Pacious learned that a firm's health can be gauged by the present value of its future investment opportunities (PVGO). Tackling a calculation, he uses the following example for Wood Athletic Supplies:

Stock price	$90.00
Current earnings	$5.50
Expected earnings	$6.00
Required return on stock	15%

Pacious and Williams discuss the characteristics of firms in various stages of growth, where firms experience an initial growth phase, a transitional phase, and a maturity phase in their life. They both agree that the Gordon Growth Model is not always appropriate. Pacious makes the following statements.

Statement 1: For firms in the initial growth phase, earnings are rapidly increasing, there are little or no dividends, and there is heavy reinvestment. The return on equity is, however, higher than the required return on the stock, the free cash flows to equity are positive, and the profit margin is high.

Statement 2: When estimating the terminal value in the 3-stage dividend growth model, it can be estimated using the Gordon Growth Model or a price-multiple approach.

91. Which of the following *best* describes the appropriate valuation models for the Henri presentation scenarios?
   A. Firm A should be valued using a free cash flow model. Firm B should be valued using a free cash flow model.
   B. Firm A should be valued using a dividend discount model. Firm B should be valued using a residual income model.
   C. Firm A can be valued using either a free cash flow model or a dividend discount model. Firm B should be valued using a residual income model.

92. Which of the following *best* describes the appropriate valuation techniques for the Henri presentation scenarios?
   A. Firm C should be valued using a 2-stage dividend discount model. Firm D should be valued using an H dividend discount model.
   B. Firm C should be valued using an H dividend discount model. Firm D should be valued using a 2-stage dividend discount model.
   C. Both Firms C and D should be valued using the H dividend discount model.

93. Which of the following is *closest* to the current value for Maple Goods and Services stock?
    A. $15.90.
    B. $49.13.
    C. $67.13.

94. Which of the following is *closest* to the current value for Mataka Plastics stock?
    A. $62.49.
    B. $73.73.
    C. $81.60.

95. Which of the following is *closest* to the percent of Wood Athletic Supplies leading P/E related to PVGO?
    A. 56%.
    B. 59%.
    C. 69%.

96. Regarding Pacious's statements on the stages of growth and the Gordon Growth Model, are both statements correct?
    A. Yes.
    B. No, only Statement 2 is correct.
    C. No, both statements are incorrect.

Use the following information to answer Questions 97 through 102.

Asante Bizou is an equity analyst for Alpha, Inc., a boutique consulting firm in San Jose, CA. Alpha is providing consulting services to Prizm's board in evaluating the performance of Prizm's management. Bizou reviews Prizm's key financial data for the past three years.

Selected information from Prizm's financial statements is given in Exhibit 1.

Exhibit 1: Selected Prizm Financial Data

Income Statement	20X4	20X5	20X6
	$m	$m	$m
Sales	40.2	42.3	43.9
Cost of goods sold	(11.6)	(12.3)	(12.8)
Gross profit	28.6	30.0	31.1
Administrative expenses	(10.0)	(10.0)	(3.0)
Earnings before interest and tax	18.6	20.0	28.1
Interest	(6.3)	(6.3)	(4.2)
Earnings before tax	12.3	13.7	23.9
Tax	(5.1)	(5.6)	(11.4)
Net income	7.2	8.1	12.5
Dividends	(3.0)	(3.1)	(3.2)
Retained income	4.2	5.0	9.3

Exhibit 1: Selected Prizm Financial Data (continued)

Balance Sheet at 31 December	20X3	20X4	20X5	20X6
	$m	$m	$m	$m
Working capital	24.0	25.6	27.2	32.4
Fixed assets	76.0	78.6	82.0	78.1
Total assets	100.0	104.2	109.2	110.5
Liabilities	24.0	24.0	24.0	16.0
Common stock	20.0	20.0	20.0	20.0
Additional paid up capital	10.0	10.0	10.0	10.0
Retained income	46.0	50.2	55.2	64.5
	100.0	104.2	109.2	110.5
Market value of equity (31 December)	167	203	199	145

Other information:

- Beta of firm = 1.
- Debtholders' required rate of return: 5%.
- Equityholders' required rate of return: 15%.
- After tax WACC: 12.5%.
- Tax rate: 45%.

Notes:

1. Depreciation included in cost of goods sold and administrative expenses is 12m, 10.5m, and 9.6m for 20X6, 20X5, and 20X4, respectively.

2. $8m of debt was redeemed at the end of 20X6.

3. Other than the debt redeemed in 20X6, Prizm's liabilities consist mostly of long-term debt valued approximately at book value.

4. Replacement value of assets is roughly equal to book value minus 4%.

97. In computing EVA®, which of the following adjustments made by an analyst would be *least appropriate*?
    A. Add LIFO reserve to total capital.
    B. Expense R&D instead of capitalizing it.
    C. Eliminate deferred taxes and consider only cash taxes as an expense.

98. Prizm's EVA® for 20X6 is *closest* to:
    A. Negative $1.3 million.
    B. Negative $1.2 million.
    C. Positive $1.8 million.

99. Prizm's residual income for 20X6 is *closest* to:
    A. −$0.3 million.
    B. $0.7 million.
    C. $2.5 million.

100. Prizm's Market Value Added (MVA) as of fiscal year-end 20X6 is *closest* to:
    A. $9.3 million
    B. $12.5 million
    C. $50.5 million

101. Prizm's free cash flow to equity (FCFE) for 20X6 is *closest* to:
    A. 3 million.
    B. 13 million.
    C. 15 million.

102. For this question only, assume that the chairman has drawn up budgetary forecasts for 20X7 that suggest that residual income will be $5m for the year ahead. You believe that this will increase by 5% per year for the foreseeable future.

    Using the residual income method, the value of Prizm's equity as of 31st December 20X6 is *closest* to:
    A. $144.5 million.
    B. $147.0 million.
    C. $177.2 million.

Use the following information to answer Questions 103 through 108.

Juanita Joplin has just begun her summer internship in the bond trading department of Bearclaw Bank NA. Joplin is assigned to Suzanne Thomas who specializes in AA-rated corporate bonds. Thomas explains to Joplin that she relies on binomial interest rate trees to value bonds with embedded options. Thomas provides Joplin with a binomial interest rate tree derived from current swap rates using an interest rate volatility assumption of 10% as shown in Exhibit 1.

Exhibit 1: Binomial Interest Rate Tree ($\sigma = 10$ %, annual pay)

1 year	2 years	3 years

Thomas then illustrates valuation of two bonds issued by Dxon Corp. Thomas states that the credit risk of the two bonds is similar to the credit risk premium embedded in the swap rate. Selected data for the two bonds is provided in Exhibit 2.

Exhibit 2: Selected Data on Two Dxon Bonds

Bond	A	B
Coupon	5%, annual pay	5% annual pay
Par Value	$100	$100
Type	Option-Free	Extendible*
Maturity	3 years	2 years

*Bond B has an investor option to extend its maturity for an additional year at the same coupon rate.

Thomas states that pathwise valuation can also be used for the bonds instead of the binomial tree approach. She highlights one of the interest rate paths (labeled Path X) as 2.50% in year 1, 4.9445% in year 2 and 6.6821% in year 3.

Joplin feels that the default risk of Dxon Corp. is higher than the default risk of the surveyed banks reflected in the rates used to generate the interest rate tree in Exhibit 1. Accordingly, a spread should be added to the interest rate tree used in Exhibit 1. She learns that such a spread is called the OAS.

During lunch, Joplin sits next to Rex Briar, another intern. Briar notes that Bond B has an OAS of 28 basis points. Another bond, issued by Geneva Inc., has the same credit quality and other features as Bond B, except it is option free. The OAS for the Geneva Inc., bond is 24 basis points.

Joplin read a report prepared by Thomas for the risk management department of the bank. She underlines the following statement in the report:

"The effective duration of a callable bond is greater than the effective duration of a comparable option-free bond. Furthermore, a bond with an embedded at- or near-the-money call option would have a lower one-sided down duration as compared to the one-sided down duration for a comparable option-free bond."

103. Using the information in Exhibits 1 and 2, the value of bond A is *closest* to:
    A. $98.96.
    B. $100.16.
    C. $101.39.

104. The value of Bond A under path X is *closest* to:
    A. $98.02
    B. $99.63
    C. $101.02

105. Using the information in Exhibits 1 and 2, the value of bond B is *closest* to:
    A. $98.96.
    B. $101.16.
    C. $102.91.

106. For this question only, assume that Joplin is right about the credit risk of Dxon bonds. If the volatility estimate used in generating the interest rate tree is less than the true volatility, which of the following choices *most accurately* describes the impact on the calculated value of bond B and the estimated OAS of bond B?

	Value of bond B	Estimated OAS of bond B
A.	Underestimated	Too low
B.	Underestimated	Too high
C.	Overestimated	Too high

107. Relative to Bond B, the Geneva Inc. bond is *most likely* to be:
      A. underpriced.
      B. overpriced.
      C. correctly priced.

108. Thomas's statement in the report to the risk management department is *most likely*:
      A. correct.
      B. incorrect about effective duration only.
      C. incorrect about effective duration and about one-sided duration.

Use the following information to answer Questions 109 through 114.

Michelle Norris, CFA, manages assets for individual investors in the United States as well as in other countries. Norris limits the scope of her practice to equity securities traded on U.S. stock exchanges. Her partner, John Witkowski, handles any requests for international securities. Recently, one of Norris's wealthiest clients suffered a substantial decline in the value of his international portfolio. Worried that his U.S. allocation might suffer the same fate, he has asked Norris to implement a hedge on his portfolio. Norris has agreed to her client's request and is currently in the process of evaluating several futures contracts. Her primary interest is in a futures contract on a broad equity index that will expire 240 days from today. The closing price as of yesterday, January 17, for the equity index was 1,050. The expected dividends from the index yield 2% (continuously compounded annual rate). The continuously compounded risk-free rate is 4%. Norris decides that this equity index futures contract is the appropriate hedge for her client's portfolio and enters into the contract.

Sixty days after entering into the futures contract, the equity index reached a level of 1,015. The futures contract that Norris purchased is now trading on the Chicago Mercantile Exchange for a price of 1,035. Interest rates have not changed. After performing some calculations, Norris calls her client to let him know of an arbitrage opportunity related to his futures position. Over the phone, Norris makes the following comments to her client:

> "We have an excellent opportunity to earn a riskless profit by engaging in arbitrage using the equity index, risk-free assets, and futures contracts. My recommended strategy is as follows: We should sell the equity index short, buy the futures contract, and pay any dividends occurring over the life of the contract. By pursuing this strategy, we can generate profits for your portfolio without incurring any risk."

Sixty days ago when the Swiss franc/euro exchange rate was SF1.12 per euro, Witkowski entered into (on behalf of a client) a one-year, quarterly settlement euro-Swiss franc swap paying €1 million at inception. The fixed-for-fixed swap had the franc fixed rate at 0.96% and the euro fixed rate at 0.78%. Currently, the euro position has a value of €1.0014 per €1 notional and the exchange rate is SF 1.10 per euro. Exhibit 1 provides information about Swiss interest rates.

Exhibit 1: Swiss Interest Rates

Term	Rate	PV of $1
30	0.50%	0.9996
60	0.54%	0.9991
90	0.48%	0.9988
120	0.65%	0.9978
180	0.77%	0.9962
210	0.67%	0.9961
300	0.82%	0.9932
360	1%	0.9901

109. The price of the futures contract on the equity index as of the inception date, January 18, is *closest* to:
    A. 1,064.
    B. 1,071.
    C. 1,078.

110. Which of the following *best* describes the movement of the futures price on the 240-day equity index futures contract as the contract moves toward the expiration date?
    A. The futures price will move toward zero as expiration nears.
    B. The futures price will move toward the (at inception) expected spot price as expiration nears.
    C. The futures price will move toward the spot price as expiration nears.

111. Sixty days after the inception of the futures contract on the equity index, Norris has suggested an arbitrage strategy. Regarding the appropriateness of the strategy, the strategy is *best* described as:
    A. appropriate since the futures contract is underpriced.
    B. inappropriate since the futures contract is overpriced.
    C. inappropriate since the futures contract is properly priced in the market.

112. If the expected growth rate in dividends for stocks increases by 75 basis points, which of the following would benefit the most? An investor who:
    A. is short futures contracts on the equity index.
    B. is long futures contracts on the equity index.
    C. has a long position in put options on the equity index.

113. Sixty days after entering into the equity index futures contract, the value to the short party under the futures contract as compared to the value under an otherwise identical forward contract would *most likely* be:
A. lower.
B. the same.
C. higher.

114. Sixty days after inception, the value of the currency swap to Witkowski's client is *closest* to:
A. −€19,633
B. −€141,584
C. −€1,021,033

Use the following information to answer Questions 115 through 120.

Tamara Ogle, CFA, and Isaac Segovia, CAIA, are portfolio managers for Lucas Investment Management (Lucas). Ogle and Segovia both manage large institutional investment portfolios and are working together to research portfolio optimization strategies. Ogle mentions the Premier fund. Exhibit 1 shows the Premier fund's exposures and expected return, as well as benchmark specifications.

Exhibit 1: Premier Fund Characteristics

Security (i)	Portfolio Weight (w_{Pi})	Benchmark Weight (w_{Bi})	Return $E(R_i)$
X	35%	40%	11.20%
Y	20%	25%	4.25%
Z	45%	35%	14.00%
Total	100%	100%	

Ogle states that the information ratio for a manager is a good indicator of relative performance. Ogle also makes the following statements:

Statement 1:   "Unlike the Sharpe ratio, the information ratio can be affected by the addition of cash or leverage."

Statement 2:   "The information ratio of an unconstrained portfolio is unaffected by aggressiveness of the active weights."

Statement 3:   "Among active portfolios, the portfolio with the highest information ratio need not have the highest Sharpe ratio."

Statement 4:   "The optimal active risk for an unconstrained portfolio is less than the optimal active risk for a constrained portfolio."

Ogle then considers the Dena and Orient funds. Exhibit 2 shows selected data for the two funds.

Exhibit 2: Selected Information for Dena and Orient Funds

	Dena	Orient
Information coefficient	0.20	0.25
Transfer coefficient	0.99	0.80
Independent bets/year	12	X

Segovia also considers three funds that specialize in market timing. Information about the funds is given in Exhibit 3.

Exhibit 3: Selected Fund Data

	A	B	C
Frequency of bets per year	12	4	2
Number of independent stocks followed	2	3	2
Probability of correct call	0.52	0.58	0.59

115. Based on the information in Exhibit 1, the ex-ante active return for the Premier fund is *closest* to:
    A. 0.63%.
    B. 1.05%.
    C. 2.92%.

116. Regarding Ogle's Statements 1 and 2:
    A. both statements are incorrect.
    B. one statement is correct and one is incorrect.
    C. both statements are correct.

117. Assuming that Dena Fund and Orient Fund both have the same information ratio, the value of "X" in Exhibit 2 must be *closest* to:
    A. 10.
    B. 12.
    C. 16.

118. Based on the information in Exhibit 3, an investor that wishes to construct a portfolio with an active risk of 4% would *most appropriately* choose to combine the benchmark with:
    A. fund A.
    B. fund B.
    C. fund C.

119. Regarding Ogle's Statements 3 and 4:
    A. both statements are incorrect.
    B. one of the statements is correct and the other is incorrect.
    C. both statements are correct.

120. As the uncertainty of the information coefficient increases, we are *most likely* to observe an increase in the:
    A. expected active return.
    B. ex-ante information ratio.
    C. active risks.

End of Afternoon Session

Exam 2
Morning Session

Question	Topic	Minutes (Points)
1 to 6	Ethical and Professional Standards	18
7 to 12	Economics	18
13 to 24	Financial Reporting and Analysis	36
25 to 36	Equity Valuation	36
37 to 42	Fixed Income	18
43 to 48	Derivatives	18
49 to 60	Portfolio Management	36

Test Answers

1.	(A)	(B)	(C)		41.	(A)	(B)	(C)
2.	(A)	(B)	(C)		42.	(A)	(B)	(C)
3.	(A)	(B)	(C)		43.	(A)	(B)	(C)
4.	(A)	(B)	(C)		44.	(A)	(B)	(C)
5.	(A)	(B)	(C)		45.	(A)	(B)	(C)
6.	(A)	(B)	(C)		46.	(A)	(B)	(C)
7.	(A)	(B)	(C)		47.	(A)	(B)	(C)
8.	(A)	(B)	(C)		48.	(A)	(B)	(C)
9.	(A)	(B)	(C)		49.	(A)	(B)	(C)
10.	(A)	(B)	(C)		50.	(A)	(B)	(C)
11.	(A)	(B)	(C)		51.	(A)	(B)	(C)
12.	(A)	(B)	(C)		52.	(A)	(B)	(C)
13.	(A)	(B)	(C)		53.	(A)	(B)	(C)
14.	(A)	(B)	(C)		54.	(A)	(B)	(C)
15.	(A)	(B)	(C)		55.	(A)	(B)	(C)
16.	(A)	(B)	(C)		56.	(A)	(B)	(C)
17.	(A)	(B)	(C)		57.	(A)	(B)	(C)
18.	(A)	(B)	(C)		58.	(A)	(B)	(C)
19.	(A)	(B)	(C)		59.	(A)	(B)	(C)
20.	(A)	(B)	(C)		60.	(A)	(B)	(C)
21.	(A)	(B)	(C)					
22.	(A)	(B)	(C)					
23.	(A)	(B)	(C)					
24.	(A)	(B)	(C)					
25.	(A)	(B)	(C)					
26.	(A)	(B)	(C)					
27.	(A)	(B)	(C)					
28.	(A)	(B)	(C)					
29.	(A)	(B)	(C)					
30.	(A)	(B)	(C)					
31.	(A)	(B)	(C)					
32.	(A)	(B)	(C)					
33.	(A)	(B)	(C)					
34.	(A)	(B)	(C)					
35.	(A)	(B)	(C)					
36.	(A)	(B)	(C)					
37.	(A)	(B)	(C)					
38.	(A)	(B)	(C)					
39.	(A)	(B)	(C)					
40.	(A)	(B)	(C)					

Exam 2
Morning Session

Use the following information to answer Questions 1 through 6.

Charles Connor, CFA, is a portfolio manager at Apple Investments, LLC. Apple is a U.S.-based firm offering a wide spectrum of investment products and services. Connor manages the Biogene Fund, a domestic equity fund specializing in small capitalization growth stocks. The Biogene Fund generally takes significant positions in stocks, commonly owning 4.5–5% of the outstanding shares. The fund's prospectus limits positions to a maximum of 5% of the shares outstanding. The performance of the Biogene Fund has been superior over the last few years, but for the last two quarters the fund has underperformed its benchmark by a wide margin. Connor is determined to improve his performance numbers going forward.

The Biogene prospectus allows Connor to use derivative instruments in his investment strategy. Connor frequently uses options to hedge his fund's exposure as he builds or liquidates positions in his portfolio since Biogene's large positions often take several weeks to acquire. For example, when he identifies a stock to buy, he often buys call options to gain exposure to the stock. As he buys the stock, he sells off the options or allows them to expire. Connor has noticed that the increased volume in the call options often drives the stock price higher for a few days. He has seen a similar negative effect on stock prices when he buys large amounts of put options.

The end of the quarter is just a few days away, and Connor is considering three transactions:

Transaction A: Buying Put Options on Stock A

The Biogene Fund owns 4.9% of the outstanding stock of Company A, but Connor believes the stock is fully valued and plans to sell the entire position. He anticipates that it will take approximately 45 trading days to liquidate the entire Biogene position in Stock A.

Transaction B: Buying Call Options on Stock B

The Biogene Fund owns 5% of the outstanding stock of Company B. Connor believes there is significant appreciation potential for Stock B, but the stock price has dropped in recent weeks. Connor is hoping that by taking an option position, there will be a carryover effect on the stock price before quarter end.

Transaction C: Selling the Biogene Fund's Entire Position in Stock C

Connor believes that Stock C is still attractive, but he is selling the stock with the idea that he will repurchase the position next month. The motivation for the transaction is to capture a capital loss that will reduce the Biogene Fund's tax expense for the year.

Apple has an investment banking department that is active in initial public offerings (IPOs). George Arnold, CFA, is the senior manager of the IPO department. Arnold approached Connor about Stock D, a new IPO being offered by Apple. Stock D will open trading in two days. Apple had offered the IPO to all of its clients, but approximately 20% of the deal remained unsold. Having read the prospectus, Connor thinks Stock D would be a good fit for his fund, and he expects Stock D to improve his performance in both the short and long term. Connor is not aware of any information related to Stock D beyond that provided in the prospectus. Connor asked to purchase 5% of the IPO, but Arnold limited Biogene's share to 2%, explaining:

> "With Biogene's reputation, any participation will make the unsold shares highly marketable. Further, we may need Biogene to acquire more Stock D shares at a later date if the price does not hold up."

Connor is disappointed in being limited to 2% of the offering and suggests to Arnold in an e-mail that, given the 2% limitation, Biogene will not participate in the IPO. Arnold responded a few hours later with the following message:

> "I have just spoken with Ms. D, the CFO of Stock D. Although it is too late to alter the prospectus, management believes they will receive a large contract from a foreign government that will boost next year's sales by 20% or more. I urge you to accept the 2%—you won't be sorry!"

After reviewing Arnold's e-mail, Connor agrees to the 2% offer.

1. By executing Transaction A, Connor is:
    A. violating the Standards because his option trading can be reasonably expected to affect the price of Stock A.
    B. violating the Standards because the option position creates a profit opportunity in conflict with Biogene's clients.
    C. not violating the Standards.

2. By executing Transaction B, Connor is:
    A. violating the Standards because his option trading can be reasonably expected to affect his quarterly performance.
    B. not violating the Standards because the option position creates a profit opportunity consistent with Biogene's clients' interests.
    C. not violating the Standards because he believes there is significant appreciation potential in Stock B.

3. By executing Transaction C, Connor is:
   A. violating the Standards by executing a transaction for tax reasons only.
   B. violating the Standards by executing a transaction that provides tax benefits to the Biogene Fund.
   C. not violating the Standards.

4. By offering Biogene the opportunity to participate in the IPO of Stock D, Apple Investments has violated CFA Institute Standards relating to:
   A. priority of transactions but not independence and objectivity.
   B. independence and objectivity but not priority of transactions.
   C. neither priority of transactions nor independence and objectivity.

5. Arnold's arguments for limiting Biogene's share to 2% suggest that Apple:
   A. may engage in a liquidity pumping strategy that would be acceptable given that Biogene is a related entity.
   B. may engage in transaction-based manipulation of Stock D in the future, in violation of Standards relating to market manipulation.
   C. is violating Standards related to priority of transactions by offering the IPO to Biogene before it is fully subscribed.

6. Based upon Connor's acceptance of the 2% limitation after receiving the e-mail from Arnold:
   A. Connor has violated Standards relating to material nonpublic information, and Arnold has violated Standards relating to preservation of confidentiality.
   B. Connor has not violated Standards relating to material nonpublic information, but Arnold has violated Standards relating to preservation of confidentiality.
   C. Connor has not violated Standards relating to material nonpublic information, but Arnold has violated Standards relating to preservation of confidentiality and material nonpublic information.

Use the following information to answer Questions 7 through 12.

Alfred Farias, fixed income analyst for BNF, Inc., is analyzing the economic prospects of Procken, Krosse, Weira, and Toban, four countries in the same region. He collects the following economic and demographic statistics for the countries:

	Procken	*Krosse*	*Weira*	*Toban*
Current real GDP (in $ billions)	$250.0	$250.0	$4,500.00	$4,800.00
Projected real GDP in 5 years (in $ billions) based on potential GDP growth rate	$306.0	$315.0	$5,262.00	$5,778.00
Long-term growth rate of capital	4.0%	4.2%	3.2%	3.8%
Current capital base ($billions)	$782.9	$699.2	$18,750	$19,750
Imports (in $ billions)	$30.00	$60.00	$1,500.00	$900.00
Exports (in $ billions)	$32.00	$80.00	$1,000.00	$900.00
Population (in millions)	20.4	20.0	101.0	100.0
Labor growth rate	1.9%	2.9%	0.4%	0.8%
Cost of capital relative to total factor cost	32.5%	35.0%	25.0%	22.5%
Average real annual appreciation in equities (past five year)	4.0%	4.7%	4.5%	3.8%

A GDP per capita below $25,000 is considered a developing country, and a GDP per capita greater than $25,000 is considered a developed country.

Farias concludes that Weira and Toban have reached steady-state growth.

In the latest round of trade negotiations, representatives from each country discussed their efforts to foster their countries' economic development and benefit from the growth of world trade.

Procken's Representative: "We are wary of the potential for loss of domestic industries if we remove trade barriers. Given the state of our economy, I'm not certain that we can lower our trade barriers any further."

Krosse's Representative: "We in Krosse are not investing enough in infrastructure and education to increase the level of productivity and technology in our economy. We also need foreign direct investment and hence we welcome foreign investors."

Weira's Representative: "We are concerned about my country's negative trade balance. Weira needs more exports to sustain our growth."

Toban's Representative: "We seem to be at a point in Toban where the growth rate of my country's labor force may be insufficient to support our GDP growth rate."

7. Which country is *most likely* to benefit from capital deepening?
    A. Weira.
    B. Krosse.
    C. Procken.

8. For this question only, assume that the population growth rate is the same for Krosse and Procke. A possible cause for the difference in growth rate of labor is that relative to Procken, Krosse has:
    A. stricter immigration policies.
    B. a lower labor participation rate.
    C. experienced an increase in average hours worked.

9. The long-term growth rate of technology (TFP) for Toban is *closest* to:
    A. 0.4%.
    B. 2.1%.
    C. 2.3%.

10. Going forward, which country is *most likely* to experience lower stock market appreciation than that experienced over the past five years?
    A. Weira.
    B. Toban.
    C. Procken.

11. The rental price of capital in Weira is *closest* to:
    A. 6%.
    B. 12%.
    C. 25%.

12. Based on the information provided, which developing country is *most likely* to achieve convergence in growth rates and standard of living with their developed counterparts?
    A. Toban.
    B. Krosse.
    C. Procken.

Use the following information to answer Questions 13 through 18.

Lyle Kreiger, CFA, has recently taken an analyst role at Rockway Stone, a small private equity firm based in the United States. As part of his role, he has been asked to review the most recent unaudited financial statements from several private companies that have been identified as potential investments for the firm.

Rockway Stone has a strict policy of only investing in companies that demonstrate a high level of financial reporting quality. The firm has developed an internal scoring system to rank the quality of a target company's financial statements. The scoring system awards points for each incident of low reporting quality; any company that reaches 40 points is not considered for potential investment. The scoring system is shown in Exhibit 1.

Exhibit 1: Rockway Stone FR Quality Score Sheet

1.	Any instance of a change in policy year-to-year or reclassification of assets, liabilities, revenues, or expenses	**5 points**
2.	Any instance from 1. that also results in an increase in total assets	**Additional 5 points**
3.	Any instance from 1. that also results in an increase in revenue	**Additional 10 points**
4.	Any indication that earnings are not persistent	**5 points**

The first report Kreiger is reviewing is from Tolston Conductors, a firm providing highly polished metals to the technology industry. Kreiger's supervisor has instructed Kreiger to focus on the inventory note shown in Exhibit 2.

Exhibit 2: Tolston Conductors Extract

Note 8 – Inventories

	2014	2013
Raw Materials ($'000)	481	409
WIP ($'000)	1,392	894
Finished Goods ($'000)	508	496

Finished goods are classified as goods that are complete in all respects except packaging. Of the amount of inventory reported as work-in-progress in 2013, $342,000 has been reclassified as "other current assets." This WIP consisted primarily of highly polished metals that are now to be further reworked and are not expected to be ready for sale for two years.

Kreiger is also reviewing financial statements from Resonator Wellness, a firm producing health and wellness products in the U.K. Extracts from the pro forma financial statement recently released, along with 2013 and 2012 comparables, is shown in Exhibit 3.

Exhibit 3: Resonator Wellness financial Statement – Extract

Headline Operating Profit: Quarter Ending 31 December 2014 (£000)			
	2014	**2013**	**2012**
Stockholders' Equity	8,380	7,980	7,450
Revenue Retail Outlet Sales	1,402.2	3,543.9	3,501.6
Online Sales	3,086.2	398.9	389.4
Headline Net Income (Note A)	1,262.7	1,104.4	1,086.0

Note A: Headline net income excludes settlement costs and network costs. Settlement costs are one-off payments to settle legal procedures; these costs totaled (in £000) 20.0, 22.1, and 24.8 in 2012, 2013, and 2014, respectively. Network costs related to running the online business totaled (in £000) 202.0, 325.0, and 885.5 in 2012, 2013, and 2014, respectively. The financial accounts submitted to our bank in accordance with our loan covenants shows net income after charging both settlement and network costs in accordance with local GAAP.

Kreiger notes that the financial statements submitted to the firm's bankers did indeed report net income correctly in accordance with local GAAP. However, this figure was much less prominent than headline net income, as the GAAP income was disclosed only in the footnotes rather than on the face of the income statement. Kreiger believes that the legal settlements are payments made to dissatisfied customers and are a normal part of business. Kreiger also believes that the increase in network cost is consistent with increased focus on online operations. Resonator's required return on stockholders' equity is 5%.

Kreiger's final task is to analyze a set of financial statements for AltoJib Plc., a manufacturing and engineering company that is considering delisting. The company has a large number of investments in associates that Kreiger would like to isolate. Rockway Stone's approach to isolating the impact of investment in associates is to perform some classic DuPont analysis to calculate ROE. In doing so, net margin and asset turnover (but not financial leverage) are adjusted for the impact of investment in associates.

The information Kreiger has to work with is shown in Exhibit 4 along with Rockway Stone's method of isolating the impact of investment in associates on ROE using DuPont analysis.

Exhibit 4: AltoJib Plc. Financial Statements (Extracts)

	2014	2013	2012	2011
	(£000)	(£000)	(£000)	(£000)
Revenue	998.5	918.6	817.6	
Net Income	44.4	31.2	26.7	
Income from Associates	17.8	11.2	8.4	
Total Assets	1,260.8	1,166.6	1,043.2	1012.1
Investment in Associates	101.6	83.8	72.6	64.2
Equity	638.4	569.8	542.5	524.2
Financial leverage	2.01	1.99	1.93	

Calculation of ROE excluding associates
- Net margin is based on net income excluding income from associates.
- Asset turnover is calculated using average total assets excluding investments in associates.
- Financial leverage is calculated using average assets and average equity including investments in associates.

Calculation of total ROE
- Net margin is based on net income including income from associates.
- Asset turnover is calculated using average total assets including investments in associates.
- Financial leverage is calculated using average assets and average equity including investments in associates.

13. Due to the reclassification described in Exhibit 2, inventory turnover will *most likely*:
    A. increase.
    B. remain the same.
    C. decrease.

14. Under the scoring system described in Exhibit 1 and taking into account the inventory note in Exhibit 2, Tolston Conductors should *most accurately* be assigned:
    A. 5 points.
    B. 10 points.
    C. 20 points.

15. Which of the following statements is the *least accurate* regarding
    Resonator Wellness information shown in Exhibit 3?
    A. The financial statements submitted to analysts are not as decision-
       useful as they could be due to biased accounting choices.
    B. The financial statements submitted to the bank are not as decision-
       useful as they could be due to biased accounting choices.
    C. The financial statements submitted to the bank are decision-useful
       as they exhibit no evidence of biased accounting choices.

16. Which of the following conclusions is Kreiger *most likely* to draw
    about the earnings quality of Resonator Wellness? 2014 net income
    after correctly including network and settlement costs shows:
    A. compound annual growth of over 7%, and earnings that are of high
       quality as they are correctly calculated under GAAP.
    B. negative compound annual growth of over 35%, and earnings that
       are of low quality.
    C. negative compound annual growth of over 35%, and earnings that
       are of high quality as they are correctly calculated under GAAP.

17. Treating an investment as an investment in associate rather than in a
    subsidiary is *least likely* to:
    A. overstate net profit margins.
    B. understate fixed assets.
    C. understate net income.

18. Using the Rockway Stone approach to calculating ROE measures
    outlined in Exhibit 4, Kreiger is *most likely* to conclude that:
    A. ROE excluding the effects of investment in associates has
       decreased from 2012 to 2014.
    B. ROE excluding the effects of investment in associates in 2014 was
       approximately 35% lower than the total ROE in 2014.
    C. total ROE was higher than the ROE excluding the effects of
       investment in associates for 2012 and 2014, but lower in 2013.

Use the following information to answer Questions 19 through 24.

In 2009, Continental Supply Company was formed to provide drilling equipment and supplies to contractors and oilfield production companies located throughout the United States. At the end of 2013, Continental Supply created a wholly owned foreign subsidiary, International Oilfield Incorporated, to begin servicing customers located in the North Sea. International Oilfield maintains its financial statements in a currency known as the local currency unit (LCU). Continental Supply follows U.S. GAAP and its presentation currency is the U.S. dollar.

For the years 2013 through 2016, the weighted-average and year-end exchange rates, stated in terms of local currency per U.S. dollar, were as follows:

LCU/$US	2013	2014	2015	2016
Average	0.90	1.05	1.05	1.25
Year-end	1.00	1.10	1.00	1.50

International Oilfield accounts for its inventory using the lower-of-cost-or-market valuation method in conjunction with the first-in, first-out, cost flow assumption. All of the inventory on hand at the beginning of the year was sold during 2016. Inventory remaining at the end of 2016 was acquired evenly throughout the year.

At the beginning of 2014, International Oilfield purchased equipment totaling LCU 975 million when the exchange rate was LCU 1.00 to $1. During 2015, equipment with an original cost of LCU 108 million was totally destroyed in a fire. At the end of 2015, International Oilfield received a LCU 92 million insurance settlement for the loss. On June 30, 2016, International Oilfield purchased equipment totaling LCU 225 million when the exchange rate was LCU 1.25 to $1.

For the years 2015 and 2016, Continental Supply reported International Oilfield revenues in its consolidated income statement of $375 million and $450 million, respectively. There were no inter-company transactions. Following are International Oilfield's balance sheets at the end of 2015 and 2016:

LCU in millions	2016	2015
Cash and receivables	120.0	216.0
Inventory	631.3	650.4
Equipment	820.7	693.6
Liabilities (all monetary)	600.0	600.0
Capital stock	350.0	350.0
Retained earnings	622.0	610.0

At the end of 2016, International Oilfield's retained earnings account was equal to $525 million and, to date, no dividends have been paid. All of International Oilfield's capital stock was issued at the end of 2013.

19. Assuming International Oilfield is a significantly integrated sales division and virtually all operating, investing, and financing decisions are made by Continental Supply, foreign currency gains and losses that arise from the consolidation of International Oilfield should be reported in:
    A. shareholders' equity.
    B. operating cash flow.
    C. net income.

20. Assuming that International Oilfield's equipment is depreciated using the straight-line method over ten years with no salvage value, calculate the subsidiary's 2016 depreciation expense under the temporal method.
    A. $95.7 million.
    B. $104.7 million.
    C. $114.7 million.

21. Compute the cumulative translation adjustment reported on Continental Supply's consolidated balance sheet at the end of 2016, assuming International Oilfield is a relatively self-contained and independent operation of Continental Supply.
    A. –$227 million.
    B. –$200 million.
    C. $298 million.

22. Compared to the temporal method, which of the following *best* describes the impact of the current rate method on International Oilfield's gross profit margin percentage for 2016 when stated in U.S. dollars? The gross profit margin would be:
    A. lower.
    B. higher.
    C. the same.

23. When remeasuring International Oilfield's 2016 financial statements into the presentation currency, which of the following ratios is NOT affected by changing exchange rates under the temporal method?
    A. Current ratio.
    B. Total asset turnover.
    C. Quick ratio.

24. Assume the country where International Oilfield is operating has been experiencing 30% annual inflation over the past three years. Which of the following *best* describes the effect on Continental's consolidated financial statements for the year ended 2016?
   A. A gain is recognized in the income statement.
   B. A loss is recognized in the income statement.
   C. A gain is recognized as a direct adjustment to the balance sheet.

Use the following information to answer Questions 25 through 30.

Sampson Aerospace is a publicly traded U.S. manufacturer. Sampson supplies communication and navigation control systems to manufacturers of airplanes for commercial and government use. The company operates two divisions: (1) Commercial Operations, and (2) Government Operations. Revenues from the Government Operations division comprise 80% of Sampson's total company revenues. Revenues for other companies in the industry are also driven primarily by sales to the U.S. government.

Sampson has gained a reputation for offering unique products and services. Sampson's market share has been increasing, and its net profit margin is among the highest in its industry.

Zone, Inc., ("Zone") is a small privately held network solutions company in the southwestern United States. Zone is profitable, and almost entirely equity financed. Drew Smith, Sampson's CFO, is evaluating a potential acquisition of Zone in a leveraged buyout. In his analysis, Smith makes several adjustments to Zone's financial statements as detailed below:

Adjustment 1: Zone's owner/CEO received a compensation package of $1.2 million including bonus. This is consistent with CEO compensation packages at other firms. Smith considers the current management team to be very competent and does not anticipate any major changes; however, he increases the estimate for compensation expense to $1.5 million.

Adjustment 2: Zone has long-term leases on all of its facilities. The lease rates were negotiated before the real estate market collapsed recently. Smith adjusts the leasing cost downward by $3 million.

Adjustment 3: Zone has purchased fractional ownership in a corporate jet for its CEO. The benefit, with an annual cost of $350,000, is deemed to be excessive by market standards and Smith adjusts the cost estimate by that amount.

Exhibit 1 shows projections of selected financial data for Zone for the next year.

Exhibit 1: Selected Financial Information (Estimates) for Zone, Inc.

Item	$ Millions
Normalized EBITDA	32
Depreciation	11
SG&A expense	8
Net income	15
Capital expenditure	6
Working capital expense	5
Interest expense	2

Note: Zone's tax rate is expected to be 25%.

Sampson Aerospace recently announced that it is reducing its investment return assumption on its pension assets from 6% to 5%, and that it has entered negotiations to possibly acquire controlling equity interests in communications software firms, NavTech and Aerospace Communications. NavTech recently has decided to capitalize a significant portion of its research and development expense, and Aerospace Communications has restructured and reclassified many of its leases from operating to financial leases. Smith recently announced that Sampson had dropped out of negotiations with Knowledge Technologies, claiming it was likely not a sustainable business model.

Consensus forecasts for NavTech and Aerospace Communications are presented in Exhibit 2.

Exhibit 2: Selected Financial Data for NavTech and Aerospace Communications

	NavTech	Aerospace Comm.
Expected year-end dividend per share	$1.07	$0.55
Expected year-end free cash flow to equity per share	$0.80	$1.25
Weighted average cost of capital	10%	9%
Required return on equity	12%	12%
Current stock price	$21.40	$25

25. Regarding Smith's adjustments to Zone's financial statements, the *most appropriate* adjustment is:
    A. Adjustment 1.
    B. Adjustment 2.
    C. Adjustment 3.

26. For valuation purposes, Zone's expected (first year) FCFF is *closest* to:
   A. $14 million.
   B. $15 million.
   C. $16 million.

27. The *most* appropriate approach for Sampson Aerospace's valuation of NavTech and Aerospace Communications is the:
   A. dividend discount model.
   B. free cash flow model.
   C. relative value model.

28. Regarding the financial statement information provided in the analyst's report, the quality of financial statements has improved *least* for:
   A. Sampson.
   B. NavTech.
   C. Aerospace Communications.

29. By claiming that Knowledge Technologies is "not a sustainable business model," Sampson CEO Drew Smith would *most likely* estimate Knowledge Technologies's value using:
   A. balance sheet value.
   B. going concern value.
   C. liquidation value.

30. Assuming that NavTech is valued according to the constant growth dividend model, the market expectation of dividend growth implied by NavTech's current stock price is *closest* to:
   A. 3%.
   B. 5%.
   C. 7%.

Use the following information to answer Questions 31 through 36.

Ivan Johnson is reviewing the investment merits of BioTLab, a fast-growing biotechnology company. BioTLab has developed several drugs, which are being licensed to major drug companies. BioTLab also has several drugs in phase III trials (phase III trials are the last testing stage before FDA approval). Johnson notes that two drugs recently received approval which should provide BioTLab solid revenue growth and generate predictable cash flow well into the future. Based on the potential for the two drugs, BioTLab's estimated annual cash flow growth rate for the next two years is 25%, and long-term growth is expected to be 12%. Because of BioTLab's attractive investment opportunities, the company does not pay a dividend. BioTLab's current weighted average cost of capital is 15% and its stock is currently trading at $50 per share. Financial information for BioTLab for the most recent 12 months is provided below:

- Net working capital excluding cash increased from $7,460,000 to $9,985,000.
- Book value increased from $81,250,000 to $101,250,000.
- BioTLab currently has no debt.
- Research facilities and production equipment were purchased for $8,450,000.
- BioTLab held non-operating assets in the amount of $875,000.
- Net income for the 12 months was $20,000,000.
- BioTLab has a marginal tax rate of 40%.
- Noncash charges for depreciation and restructuring for the 12 months were $1,250,000.

BioTLab's management has indicated an interest in establishing a dividend and will fund new drug research by issuing additional debt.

Johnson also reviews a competitor to BioTLab, Groh Group, which has a larger segment operating in a highly cyclical business. The Groh Group has a debt to equity ratio of 1.0 and pays no dividends. In addition, Groh Group plans to issue bonds in the coming year.

31. Johnson prefers to use free cash flow analysis to value investments. Which of the statements below is *least* accurate in describing the advantages of free cash flow valuation models?
    A. Accounting issues limit the usefulness of reported earnings, while free cash flow is adjusted for these issues.
    B. Determining free cash flow is easier than dividends.
    C. A company must generate free cash flow to grow in the long run.

32. Using a two-stage, free cash flow to the firm model, determine which of the following is *closest* to the value of BioTLab.
    A. $419 million.
    B. $436 million.
    C. $477 million.

33. If BioTLabs establishes a dividend and issues additional debt, the *most likely* effect on FCFF will be:
    A. no effect.
    B. a decrease in FCFF.
    C. an increase in FCFF.

34. Which model would be *most* appropriate in valuing the Groh Group?
    A. FCFF model.
    B. FCFE model.
    C. Dividend Discount model.

35. Ten years have passed and BioTLab's drug pipeline has generated the expected growth. To support BioTLab's growth, the company levered its balance sheet to a debt-to-equity ratio of 35% by borrowing an additional $1.6 million during the last year, even as it paid total interest of $4 million. Still, the company generated $20 million in free cash flow to equity. The company's tax rate is 40% and pretax interest rate is 6%. The company's required rate of return on equity equals 13%. Using a single-stage FCFF model results in a value of $483,508,770. The expected growth rate in BioTLab's free cash flows is *closest* to:
    A. 6%.
    B. 8%.
    C. 10%.

36. Which of the following statements regarding free cash flow models is *least likely* correct?
    A. Sensitivity analysis indicates that the FCFE model's valuation of BioTLab's common stock is most sensitive to the company's growth rate.
    B. FCFE is net income plus depreciation minus net capital expenditures minus the increase in working capital plus net new debt financing.
    C. FCFF can be inflated by increasing capital expenditures relative to depreciation.

Use the following information to answer Questions 37 through 42.

Mike Diffle has been asked to evaluate the bonds of Hardin, Inc. The specific issue Diffle is considering has an 8% annual coupon and matures in two years. The bonds are currently callable at 101, and beginning in six months, they are callable at par. Bratton Corporation, Hardin's competitor, also has bonds outstanding which are identical to Hardin's except that they are not callable. Diffle believes the AA rating of both bonds is an accurate reflection of their credit risk. Diffle is wondering if the Bratton bonds might be a better investment than the Hardin bonds. Assume that the following 1-year interest rate tree is used to value bonds with a maturity of up to three years (this tree assumes interest rate volatility of 10%).

Today	Year 1	Year 2
		9.324%
	8.530%	
7.250%		7.634%
	6.983%	
		6.250%

Also, assume that the appropriate spot rates for securities maturing in one, two, and three years are 7.25%, 7.5%, and 7.80%, respectively.

Diffle believes he should begin his analysis with the option-free Bratton bonds. He decides to consider two different approaches to valuing the Bratton Bonds—one that uses the current spot rate curve and another that uses the interest rate tree given above.

For the next step in his analysis, Diffle has decided to calculate the value of the Hardin bonds using the interest rate tree. His assumption is that the bond will be called at any node of the tree where the calculated value exceeds the call price. Diffle summarizes the results of his bond valuation analysis in a memo to his supervisor, Luke Puldo. In this memo, Diffle makes the following statements:

Statement 1:   The value of the option embedded in the Hardin bonds can be derived by simply subtracting the interest rate tree value of the Hardin bonds from the interest rate tree value of the Bratton bonds.

Statement 2:   I am concerned that the 10% volatility assumption used to develop the interest rate tree might be too low. A higher volatility assumption would result in a lower value for the Hardin bonds.

After reviewing Diffle's analysis, Puldo notes that Diffle has not included any information on the option adjusted spread (OAS) for the Hardin bonds. Puldo suggests that Diffle should evaluate the OAS in order to get an idea of the liquidity risk of the Hardin bonds. Diffle counters that the OAS may not be very informative in this case, since he is uncertain as to the reliability of the interest rate volatility assumption.

To finish the analysis, Diffle would like to use his binomial model to evaluate the interest rate risk of both the Hardin bonds and the Bratton bonds. Diffle starts out with the benchmark interest rate tree and estimated OAS for both bonds. Then he shocks interest rates up and down by 25 basis points throughout the tree and adds the OAS estimated earlier. Using the tree and standard backward induction process, Diffle calculates values for the bonds. He plans to use these values as inputs into the following formulas for duration and convexity:

$$\text{duration} = \frac{V_- - V_+}{2 \times V_0 \times \Delta y} \qquad \text{convexity} = \frac{V_+ + V_- - 2V_0}{V_0 \times (\Delta y)^2}$$

Puldo notes that the duration estimate for the two bonds is not directly comparable. Assuming that the underlying option is at- or near-the-money, the duration of one of the bonds will be lower than the other one.

37. Calculate the value of the Bratton bonds using the interest rate tree.
    A. 100.218.
    B. 100.378.
    C. 100.915.

38. Using the interest rate tree, and assuming that the bonds will be called at any node of the tree where the calculated value exceeds the call price, which of the following is *closest* to the value of the Hardin bonds?
    A. 100.472.
    B. 100.915.
    C. 101.358.

39. Indicate whether the statements made by Diffle in his memo regarding the value of the embedded option and the effect of the volatility assumption are correct.
    A. Only the statement regarding the value of the embedded option is correct.
    B. Only the statement regarding the effect of the volatility assumption is correct.
    C. Both statements are correct.

40. Which of the following *most* accurately critiques the OAS discussion between Diffle and Puldo? Puldo is:
    A. correct that the OAS will provide insight into the liquidity risk of the Hardin bonds, and Diffle is correct that different volatility assumptions would change the OAS.
    B. correct that the OAS will provide insight into the liquidity risk of the Hardin Bonds, but Diffle is incorrect since OAS implicitly adjusts for the volatility of interest rates.
    C. incorrect that the OAS will provide insight into the liquidity risk of the Hardin Bonds, but Diffle is correct that different volatility assumptions would change the OAS.

41. With regards to Puldo's statement about comparability of duration of the two bonds, which of the following statements is *most accurate*? Bratton bonds' duration would be:
    A. lower than the duration of Hardin bonds under a rising interest rate scenario.
    B. lower than the duration of Hardin bonds under a declining interest rate scenario.
    C. higher than the duration of Hardin bonds under a declining interest rate scenario.

42. Which of the following statements is *most* accurate regarding Diffle's calculation of duration and convexity?
    A. The duration estimate will be inaccurate since it does not account for any change in cash flows due to the call option embedded in the Hardin bond.
    B. The duration estimate for the Bratton bonds will reflect the projected percentage change in price for a 100-basis-point change in interest rates.
    C. The estimates for both duration and convexity will be inaccurate because the OAS was not estimated again after the rate shock.

Use the following information to answer Questions 43 through 48.

Charles Mabry manages a portfolio of equity investments heavily concentrated in the biotech industry. He just returned from an annual meeting among leading biotech analysts in San Francisco. Mabry and other industry experts agree that the latest industry volatility is a result of questionable product safety testing methodologies. While no firms in the industry have escaped the public attention brought on by the questionable safety testing, one company in particular is expected to receive further attention—Biological Instruments Corporation (BIC), one of several long biotech positions in Mabry's portfolio. BIC is not expected to pay dividends in the foreseeable future. Several regulatory agencies as well as public interest groups have heavily criticized the rigor of BIC's product safety testing.

In an effort to manage the risk associated with BIC, Mabry has decided to allocate a portion of his portfolio to options on BIC's common stock. After surveying the derivatives market, Mabry has identified the following European options on BIC common stock:

	BIC Call Options				BIC Put Options		
	Strike	Maturity	Premium		Strike	Maturity	Premium
Call A	40	October	3.51	Put D	30	November	2.31
Call B	50	October	1.98	Put E	40	November	4.14
Call C	60	October	1.42	Put F	50	November	9.21

Note: October options expire on the 21st of the month, while November options expire on the 18th.

Mabry wants to hedge the large BIC equity position in his portfolio, which closed yesterday (June 1) at $42 per share. Since Mabry is relatively inexperienced with utilizing derivatives in his portfolios, Mabry enlists the help of an analyst from another firm, James Grimell.

Mabry and Grimell arrange a meeting in Boston where Mabry discusses his expectations regarding the future returns of BIC's equity. Mabry expects BIC equity to make a recovery from the intense market scrutiny but wants to provide his portfolio with a hedge in case BIC has a negative surprise. Grimell makes the following suggestion:

"If you want to avoid selling the BIC position and are willing to earn only the risk-free rate of return, you should sell calls and buy puts on BIC stock with the same market premium. Alternatively, you could buy put options to manage the risk of your portfolio. I recommend waiting until the vega on the options rises, making them less attractive and cheaper to purchase."

43. Which of the following statements regarding the delta of the BIC options is correct? (Assume that the largest delta is defined as the delta furthest from zero.)
    A. Call C has the largest delta of all the BIC options.
    B. Put D has the smallest delta of all the BIC options.
    C. Put F has the largest delta of all the BIC options.

44. If the gamma of Put E is equal to 0.081, which of the following correctly interprets the option's gamma?
    A. The sensitivity of Put E's price to changes in BIC's stock price is very likely to change.
    B. A dynamic hedging strategy using Put E would require infrequent rebalancing.
    C. A $1.00 increase in BIC's stock price will increase Put E's premium by $0.081.

45. Assuming that on October 15, the closing price of BIC common stock is $40 per share, how would the delta of Put F have changed from June 1?
    A. The delta on Put F will move closer to –1.
    B. The delta on Put F will move closer to 0.
    C. The delta on Put F will move closer to 1.

46. If the premium on Put D on November 1 is $3.18, which of the following has *most likely* occurred?
    A. The price of BIC stock has decreased to $26.82.
    B. BIC had a negative earnings surprise.
    C. Volatility of BIC stock has decreased.

47. Given Mabry's assessment of the risks associated with BIC, which option strategy would be the *most* effective in delta-neutral hedging the risk of BIC stock?
    A. Add put options to the portfolio as the put option delta moves closer to zero.
    B. Add call options to the portfolio as the call option delta moves further away from zero.
    C. Add put options to the portfolio as the put option delta moves toward –1.

48. Which of the following correctly analyzes Grimell's comments regarding earning the risk-free rate by selling calls and buying puts, and regarding waiting for the option vegas to increase?
    A. Only Grimell's statement regarding earning the risk-free rate is correct.
    B. Only Grimell's statement regarding waiting for vega to rise is correct.
    C. Neither of Grimell's statements is correct.

Use the following information to answer Questions 49 through 54.

Gordon Stenton, CFA, works for a small investment management firm in the United States. Part of his role involves managing portfolios for high net worth individuals. Currently, Stenton is corresponding with Rachael Matten. Matten has withdrawn her assets from Altune, an asset management firm, and is considering allocating $2.5 million of those funds to Stenton's firm. Matten indicated that she was unhappy with the level of disclosure about trading methods and risk management that were employed at Altune.

Matten has sent Stenton a list of questions to assess the policies at Stenton's firm.

The first issue Matten wants clarification on pertains to the use of VaR. Among the documents that Altune sent Matten were two statements (shown in Exhibit 1). Matten was unsure of how to interpret either of these statements.

Exhibit 1: VaR

Statement 1
Your portfolio has a 5% monthly VaR of $225,000.

VaR is calculated using a parametric methodology and an assumption of normality for all risk factors.

Statement 2
The average loss once the VaR cutoff is exceeded is estimated to be $320,000.

Matten indicates that in statement 1, she understands that the $225,000 represents the loss that will occur 5% of the time. She would also like to confirm her suspicion that the maximum loss is impossible to calculate.

To provide Matten the risk management process employed at his firm, Stenton intends to send Matten the description shown in Exhibit 2.

Exhibit 2: Risk Management Measures

Primary Risk Management Measure – Steps
Step 1: Identify the top 10 exposures for the portfolio.
Step 2: Design a hypothetical global event that would simultaneously adversely affect each of the exposures.
Step 3: Assess the impact on the portfolio.

Matten has also raised an issue about the trading methods used by Stenton. She has read several negative comments in the financial press regarding the use of algorithms to trade and about the growing trend of high frequency trading. She has asked Stenton to comment on the trends she has noted in Exhibit 3.

Exhibit 3: Trading Concerns

Concern 1
The increase in the use of execution algorithms to take advantage of arbitrage opportunities.

Concern 2
The increase in market fragmentation resulting from an increase in high frequency trading.

49. Which of the following statements regarding statement 1 in Exhibit 1 is *least accurate*?
   A. The monthly VaR of $225,000 indicates an annual VaR of $2.7 million.
   B. The fund will lose more than $225,000 in a month, 5% of the time.
   C. The methodology described is not applicable to portfolios containing option positions.

50. Statement 2 in Exhibit 1 is *most accurately* described as:
   A. incremental VaR.
   B. conditional VaR.
   C. marginal VaR.

51. In her interpretation of VaR, Matten is *most likely*:
   A. correct regarding the $225,000 but incorrect regarding the maximum loss.
   B. incorrect regarding the $225,00 but correct regarding the maximum loss.
   C. incorrect regarding the $225,000 and the maximum loss.

52. The primary risk management measure discussed in Exhibit 2 is *most accurately* described as:
   A. sensitivity risk analysis.
   B. reverse stress testing.
   C. Monte Carlo simulation.

53. Stenton should *most accurately* respond to concern 1 in Exhibit 3 by saying that:
    A. The increase in the use of execution algorithms to profit from arbitrage opportunities has increased market efficiency.
    B. The increase in the use of execution algorithms to profit from arbitrage opportunities has decreased market stability.
    C. Execution algorithms are not used to profit from arbitrage opportunities.

54. Stenton should *most accurately* respond to concern 2 in Exhibit 3 by saying that:
    A. high frequency trading is only partly responsible for market fragmentation.
    B. only one specific type of high frequency trading algorithm, smart order routing, is responsible for market fragmentation.
    C. smart order routing was developed as a response to market fragmentation.

Use the following information to answer Questions 55 through 60.

Samuel Edson, CFA, portfolio manager for Driver Associates, employs a multifactor model to evaluate individual stocks and portfolios. Edson examines several possible risk factors and finds two that are priced in the marketplace. These two factors are investor sentiment (IS) risk and business cycle (BC) risk. Edson manages three equity portfolios (A, B, and C) and derives the following relationships for each portfolio, as well as for the S&P 500 stock market index:

$$R_A = 0.1750 + 2.0F_{IS} + 1.5F_{BC} \qquad (1)$$

$$R_B = 0.0940 + 0.5F_{IS} + 0.8F_{BC} \qquad (2)$$

$$R_C = 0.1550 + 1.25F_{IS} + 1.15F_{BC} \qquad (3)$$

$$R_{S\&P} = 0.1475 + 1.5F_{IS} + 1.25F_{BC} \qquad (4)$$

where:
R_A, R_B, R_C, and $R_{S\&P}$ = the returns for portfolios A, B, C, and the S&P 500 market index, respectively

Portfolios A and B are well-diversified, while C is a less than fully diversified, value-oriented portfolio. F_{IS} is the surprise in investor sentiment, and F_{BC} is the surprise in the business cycle. Surprises in the risk factors are defined as the difference between the actual value and the predicted value.

Exhibit 1 provides data for the actual and predicted values for the investor sentiment and business cycle risk factors.

Exhibit 1: Risk Factor Values

Factor	Actual Value	Predicted Value
Investor sentiment	1%	2%
Business cycle	2%	3%

Driver Associates also provides Edson with the following multifactor equations on three additional portfolios (D, E, and Z):

$$E(R_D) = R_F + 1.0F_{IS} + 0.0F_{BC} = 9\% \qquad (5)$$

$$E(R_E) = R_F + 0.0F_{IS} + 1.0F_{BC} = 8\% \qquad (6)$$

$$E(R_Z) = R_F + 1.5F_{IS} + 1.25F_{BC} = 16\% \qquad (7)$$

Driver Associates uses a two-factor Arbitrage Pricing Model to develop equilibrium expected returns for individual stocks and portfolios:

$$E(R) = \text{risk-free rate} + b_1\lambda_1 + b_2\lambda_2 \qquad (8)$$

where:
b_1 = sensitivity of the portfolio return to changes in risk factor 1
b_2 = sensitivity of the portfolio return to changes in risk factor 2
λ_1 = risk premium associated with risk factor 1
λ_2 = risk premium associated with risk factor 2

At the time of Edson's analysis, the long-term government bond yield was 5%.

55. Equations (1) through (4) are examples of:
A. macroeconomic factor models.
B. fundamental factor models.
C. statistical factor models.

56. Edson's supervisor, Rosemary Valry, asks Edson to interpret the intercept of the multifactor equation for Portfolio A (0.175). Edson should respond that the intercept equals:
A. the expected return for Portfolio A, assuming no surprises in the macroeconomic variables.
B. the expected return for Portfolio A, assuming the macroeconomic variables (investor sentiment and business cycle) equal zero.
C. the expected abnormal return for Portfolio A.

57. The firm-specific surprises contributed 1.20% to Portfolio A's return. Using the data in Exhibit 1, the actual return on Portfolio A is closest to:
A. 12.2%.
B. 13.7%.
C. 15.2%.

58. Driver Associates uses portfolios D, E, and Z as part of their risk management strategies. Which of these portfolios are factor portfolios?
A. Portfolios D and E.
B. Portfolios D and Z.
C. Portfolio Z only.

59. Valry instructs Edson to use the two-factor model to examine Driver Associates's well-diversified balanced Portfolio P, which has an Investor Sentiment factor sensitivity equal to 1.25 and a Business Cycle factor sensitivity equal to 1.10. According to Driver Associates's model, the expected return for Portfolio P equals:
    A. 8.3%.
    B. 10.8%.
    C. 13.3%.

60. Assuming Driver Associates uses the S&P 500 index as their performance benchmark, which of the following portfolios is expected to have the *least* active factor risk?
    A. Portfolio D.
    B. Portfolio E.
    C. Portfolio Z.

End of Morning Session

Exam 2
Afternoon Session

Question	Topic	Minutes (Points)
61 to 66	Ethical and Professional Standards	18
67 to 72	Quantitative Methods	18
73 to 78	Economics	18
79 to 84	Financial Reporting and Analysis	18
85 to 90	Corporate Finance	18
91 to 96	Corporate Finance	18
97 to 102	Equity Valuation	18
103 to 108	Fixed Income	18
109 to 114	Derivatives	18
115 to 120	Alternative Investments	18

Test Answers

61.	Ⓐ	Ⓑ	Ⓒ
62.	Ⓐ	Ⓑ	Ⓒ
63.	Ⓐ	Ⓑ	Ⓒ
64.	Ⓐ	Ⓑ	Ⓒ
65.	Ⓐ	Ⓑ	Ⓒ
66.	Ⓐ	Ⓑ	Ⓒ
67.	Ⓐ	Ⓑ	Ⓒ
68.	Ⓐ	Ⓑ	Ⓒ
69.	Ⓐ	Ⓑ	Ⓒ
70.	Ⓐ	Ⓑ	Ⓒ

71.	Ⓐ	Ⓑ	Ⓒ
72.	Ⓐ	Ⓑ	Ⓒ
73.	Ⓐ	Ⓑ	Ⓒ
74.	Ⓐ	Ⓑ	Ⓒ
75.	Ⓐ	Ⓑ	Ⓒ
76.	Ⓐ	Ⓑ	Ⓒ
77.	Ⓐ	Ⓑ	Ⓒ
78.	Ⓐ	Ⓑ	Ⓒ
79.	Ⓐ	Ⓑ	Ⓒ
80.	Ⓐ	Ⓑ	Ⓒ

81.	Ⓐ	Ⓑ	Ⓒ
82.	Ⓐ	Ⓑ	Ⓒ
83.	Ⓐ	Ⓑ	Ⓒ
84.	Ⓐ	Ⓑ	Ⓒ
85.	Ⓐ	Ⓑ	Ⓒ
86.	Ⓐ	Ⓑ	Ⓒ
87.	Ⓐ	Ⓑ	Ⓒ
88.	Ⓐ	Ⓑ	Ⓒ
89.	Ⓐ	Ⓑ	Ⓒ
90.	Ⓐ	Ⓑ	Ⓒ

91.	Ⓐ	Ⓑ	Ⓒ
92.	Ⓐ	Ⓑ	Ⓒ
93.	Ⓐ	Ⓑ	Ⓒ
94.	Ⓐ	Ⓑ	Ⓒ
95.	Ⓐ	Ⓑ	Ⓒ
96.	Ⓐ	Ⓑ	Ⓒ
97.	Ⓐ	Ⓑ	Ⓒ
98.	Ⓐ	Ⓑ	Ⓒ
99.	Ⓐ	Ⓑ	Ⓒ
100.	Ⓐ	Ⓑ	Ⓒ

101.	Ⓐ	Ⓑ	Ⓒ
102.	Ⓐ	Ⓑ	Ⓒ
103.	Ⓐ	Ⓑ	Ⓒ
104.	Ⓐ	Ⓑ	Ⓒ
105.	Ⓐ	Ⓑ	Ⓒ
106.	Ⓐ	Ⓑ	Ⓒ
107.	Ⓐ	Ⓑ	Ⓒ
108.	Ⓐ	Ⓑ	Ⓒ
109.	Ⓐ	Ⓑ	Ⓒ
110.	Ⓐ	Ⓑ	Ⓒ

111.	Ⓐ	Ⓑ	Ⓒ
112.	Ⓐ	Ⓑ	Ⓒ
113.	Ⓐ	Ⓑ	Ⓒ
114.	Ⓐ	Ⓑ	Ⓒ
115.	Ⓐ	Ⓑ	Ⓒ
116.	Ⓐ	Ⓑ	Ⓒ
117.	Ⓐ	Ⓑ	Ⓒ
118.	Ⓐ	Ⓑ	Ⓒ
119.	Ⓐ	Ⓑ	Ⓒ
120.	Ⓐ	Ⓑ	Ⓒ

EXAM 2
AFTERNOON SESSION

Use the following information to answer Questions 61 through 66.

Pat Wilson, CFA, is the chief compliance officer for Excess Investments, a global asset management and investment banking services company. Wilson is reviewing two investment reports written by Peter Holly, CFA, an analyst and portfolio manager who has worked for Excess for four years. Holly's first report under compliance review is a strong buy recommendation for BlueNote Inc., a musical instrument manufacturer. The report states that the buy recommendation is applicable for the next 6 to 12 months with an average level of risk and a sustainable price target of $24 for the entire time period. At the bottom of the report, an e-mail address is given for investors who wish to obtain a complete description of the firm's rating system. Among other reasons supporting the recommendation, Holly's report states that expected increases in profitability, as well as increased supply chain efficiency, provide compelling support for purchasing BlueNote.

Holly informs Wilson that he determined his conclusions primarily from an intensive review of BlueNote's filings with the SEC but also from a call to one of BlueNote's suppliers who informed Holly that their new inventory processing system would allow for more efficiency in supplying BlueNote with raw materials. Holly explains to Wilson that he is the only analyst covering BlueNote who is aware of this information and that he believes the new inventory processing system will allow BlueNote to reduce costs and increase overall profitability for several years to come.

Wilson must also review Holly's report on BigTime Inc., a musical promotion and distribution company. In the report, Holly provides a very optimistic analysis of BigTime's fundamentals. The analysis supports a buy recommendation for the company. Wilson finds one problem with Holly's report on BigTime related to Holly's former business relationship with BigTime Inc. Two years before joining Excess, Holly worked as an investment banker and received 1,000 restricted shares of BigTime as a result of his participation in taking the company public. These facts are not disclosed in the report but are disclosed on Excess Investment's Web site.

Just before the report is issued, Holly mentions to Wilson that BigTime unknowingly disclosed to him and a few other analysts who were waiting for a conference call to begin that the company is planning to restructure both its sales staff and sales strategy and may sell one of its poorly performing business units next year.

Three days after issuing his report on BigTime, which caused a substantial rise in the price of BigTime shares, Holly sells all of the BigTime shares out of both his performance fee-based accounts and flat-fee accounts and then proceeds to sell all of the BigTime shares out of his own account on the following day. Holly obtained approval from Wilson before making the trades.

Just after selling his shares in BigTime, Holly receives a call from the CEO of BlueNote who wants to see if Holly received the desk pen engraved with the BlueNote company logo that he sent last week and also to offer two front row tickets plus limousine service to a sold-out concert for a popular band that uses BlueNote's instruments. Holly confirms that the desk pen arrived and thanks the CEO for the gift and tells him that before he accepts the concert tickets, he will have to check his calendar to see if he will be able to attend. Holly declines the use of the limousine service should he decide to attend the concert.

After speaking with the CEO of BlueNote, Holly constructs a letter that he plans to send by e-mail to all of his clients and prospects with e-mail addresses and by regular mail to all of his clients and prospects without e-mail addresses. The letter details changes to an equity valuation model that Holly and several other analysts at Excess use to analyze potential investment recommendations. Holly's letter explains that the new model, which will be put into use next month, will utilize Monte Carlo simulations to create a distribution of stock values, a sharp contrast to the existing model which uses static valuations combined with sensitivity analysis. Relevant details of the new model are included in the letter, but similar details about the existing model are not included. The letter also explains that management at Excess has decided to exclude alcohol and tobacco company securities from the research coverage universe. Holly's letter concludes by stating that no other significant changes that would affect the investment recommendation process have occurred or are expected to occur in the near future.

61. According to CFA Institute Research Objectivity Standards (ROS), which of the following statements is *most* accurate with regard to the rating system used by Holly in his investment report on BlueNote Inc.? The rating system:
    A. has appropriately incorporated the three recommended rating system elements from the ROS.
    B. should not have included a price target as it makes an implicit guarantee of investment performance.
    C. should not have included a time frame, as it misrepresents the level of certainty of the recommendation.

62. Did Holly violate any CFA Institute Standards of Professional Conduct with respect to his report on BlueNote or BigTime, as it relates to potential use of material nonpublic information?
    A. Holly has violated Standard on material nonpublic information in the case of both reports.
    B. There is a violation regarding the BlueNote report, but no violation with the BigTime report.
    C. There is a violation regarding the BigTime report, but no violation with the BlueNote report.

63. According to CFA Institute Research Objectivity Standards (ROS), which of the following statements is *most* accurate with regard to Holly's disclosure of his ownership of BigTime restricted shares and past investment banking relationship with BigTime? The disclosure:
    A. is neither required nor recommended by the ROS since the shares are restricted.
    B. complies with the ROS recommended procedures for disclosing conflicts of interest.
    C. does not comply with the ROS recommended procedures because neither the disclosure nor a page reference to the disclosure appears on the front of the research report.

64. According to CFA Institute Standards of Professional Conduct, which of the following statements is *most likely* correct with regard to Holly's report and subsequent sale of his and his clients' shares of BigTime common stock? Holly has:
    A. violated the Standard by attempting to manipulate the market price of BigTime stock.
    B. not violated the Standard since he first obtained approval to make the trades from his compliance officer.
    C. not violated the Standard since he acted in the best interest of his clients by realizing gains on BigTime stock.

65. According to CFA Institute Standards of Professional Conduct, which of the following *best* describes the actions Holly should take with regard to the desk pen and the concert tickets offered to him by the CEO of BlueNote? Holly:
    A. must not accept the desk pen or the concert tickets.
    B. may accept both the desk pen and the concert tickets.
    C. may accept the desk pen but should not accept the concert tickets.

66. In his letter to clients explaining the change in the valuation model, did Holly violate any CFA Institute Standards of Professional Conduct?
    A. No.
    B. Yes, because he did not treat all clients fairly in his dissemination of the letter.
    C. Yes, because he failed to include details of the current valuation model to contrast with the new model.

Use the following information to answer Questions 67 through 72.

Lena Pilchard, research associate for Eiffel Investments, is attempting to measure the value added to the Eiffel Investments portfolio from the use of 1-year earnings growth forecasts developed by professional analysts.

Pilchard's supervisor, Edna Wilrus, recommends a portfolio allocation strategy that overweights neglected firms. Wilrus cites studies of the "neglected firm effect," in which companies followed by a small number of professional analysts are associated with higher returns than firms followed by a larger number of analysts. Wilrus considers a company covered by three or fewer analysts to be "neglected."

Pilchard also is aware of research indicating that, on average, stock returns for small firms have been higher than those earned by large firms. Pilchard develops a model to predict stock returns based on analyst coverage, firm size, and analyst growth forecasts. She runs the following cross-sectional regression using data for the 30 stocks included in the Eiffel Investments portfolio:

$$R_i = b_0 + b_1 COVERAGE_i + b_2 LN(SIZE_i) + b_3(FORECAST_i) + e_i$$

where:
R_i = the rate of return on stock i
$COVERAGE_i$ = one if there are three or fewer analysts covering stock i, and equals zero otherwise
$LN(SIZE_i)$ = the natural logarithm of the market capitalization (stock price times shares outstanding) for stock i, units in millions
$FORECAST_i$ = the 1-year consensus earnings growth rate forecast for stock i

Pilchard derives the following results from her cross-sectional regression:

Exhibit 1: Results of Pilchard's Cross-Sectional Regression

Variable	Coefficient	T-statistic
Constant	0.060	1.56
COVERAGE	0.050	3.20
LN(SIZE)	−0.003	−2.50
FORECAST	0.200	2.85

The standard error of estimate in Pilchard's regression equals 1.96 and the regression sum of squares equals 400.

Wilrus provides Pilchard with the following values for analyst coverage, firm size, and earnings growth forecast for Eggmann Enterprises, a company that Eiffel Investments is evaluating.

Exhibit 2: Coverage, Firm Size, and Earnings Growth Forecast for Eggmann Enterprises

Number of analysts	5
Firm size	$500 million
Earnings growth forecast	50%

Pilchard uses the following table to conduct some of her hypothesis tests.

Exhibit 3: Critical Values for Student t-Distribution

Degrees of Freedom	Area in Upper Tail				
	0.10	0.05	0.025	0.01	0.005
26	1.315	1.706	2.056	2.479	2.779
27	1.314	1.703	2.052	2.473	2.771
28	1.313	1.701	2.048	2.467	2.763
29	1.311	1.699	2.045	2.462	2.756
30	1.310	1.697	2.042	2.457	2.750

67. Wilrus asks Pilchard to derive the lowest possible value for the coefficient on the FORECAST variable using a 99% confidence interval. The appropriate lower bound for the FORECAST coefficient is *closest* to:
    A   0.0055.
    B. 0.0628.
    C. 0.1300.

68. Wilrus asks Pilchard to assess the overall significance of her regression. To address the question, Pilchard calculates the R-square. She also decides to run a test of the significance of the regression as a whole. Determine the appropriate test statistic she should use to test the overall significance of the regression.
    A. F-statistic.
    B. t-statistic.
    C. Chi-square statistic.

69. Pilchard is asked whether her regression indicates that small firms outperform large firms, after controlling for analyst coverage and consensus earnings growth forecasts. Pilchard determines the appropriate hypothesis test to answer the question. Eiffel Investments uses a 0.01 level of significance for all hypothesis tests. Given the results of her regression, Pilchard should make which of the following decisions after controlling for analyst coverage and consensus earnings forecasts?
    A. Not reject the hypothesis that $b_2 \geq 0$, and conclude that large firms significantly outperformed small firms.
    B. Reject the hypothesis that $b_2 \geq 0$, and conclude that large firms significantly outperformed small firms.
    C. Reject the hypothesis that $b_2 \geq 0$, and conclude that small firms significantly outperformed large firms.

70. Holding firm size and consensus earnings growth forecasts constant, the estimated average difference in stock returns between neglected and non-neglected firms equals:
    A. 1%.
    B. 3%.
    C. 5%.

71. Pilchard derives the ANOVA table for her regression. In her ANOVA table, the degrees of freedom for the regression sum of squares and total sum of squares should equal:
    A. 3 and 30, respectively.
    B. 4 and 29, respectively.
    C. 3 and 29, respectively.

72. Using the inputs for Eggmann Enterprises provided in Exhibit 2, the predicted stock return for Eggmann Enterprises is *closest* to:
    A. 4%.
    B. 9%.
    C. 14%.

Use the following information to answer Questions 73 through 78.

Debbie Angle and Craig Hohlman are analysts for a large commercial bank, Arbutus National Bank. Arbutus has extensive dealings in both the spot and forward foreign exchange markets. Angle and Hohlman are providing a refresher course on foreign exchange relationships for its traders.

Angle uses a three country example from North America to illustrate foreign exchange parity relations. In it, the Canadian dollar is expected to depreciate relative to the U.S. dollar and the Mexican peso. Nominal, 1-year interest rates are 7% in the United States and 13% in Mexico. From this data and using the uncovered interest rate parity relationship, Angle forecasts future spot rates.

During their presentation, Hohlman discusses the effect of monetary and fiscal policies on exchange rates. He cites a historical example from the United States, where the Federal Reserve shifted to an expansionary monetary policy to stimulate economic growth. This shift was largely unanticipated by the financial markets because the markets thought the Federal Reserve was more concerned with inflationary pressures. Hohlman states that the effect of this policy was an increase in economic growth and an increase in inflation. The cumulative effect on the dollar was unchanged, however, because, according to the Mundell-Fleming model, an expansionary monetary policy would strengthen the dollar whereas under relative purchasing power parity, an increase in inflation would weaken the dollar.

Regarding U.S. fiscal policies, Hohlman states that if these were unexpectedly expansionary, real interest rates would increase, which would produce an appreciation of the dollar. Hohlman adds that a sustained increase in the federal budget would attract foreign capital such that the long-run effect would be an increase in the value of the dollar.

Hohlman makes the following statements about parity conditions:

Statement 1:   If relative purchasing power parity holds, we can say that uncovered interest rate parity also holds under certain conditions.

Statement 2:   For uncovered interest rate parity to hold, the forward rate must be an unbiased predictor of the future spot rate.

Angle next discusses the foreign exchange expectations. While examining Great Britain and Japan, she states that it appears the 1-year forward rate, which is currently ¥200/£, is an accurate predictor of the expected future spot rate. Furthermore, she states that uncovered interest rate parity and relative purchasing power parity hold. In the example for her presentation, she uses the following figures for the two countries.

	Great Britain	*Japan*
Expected GDP growth	2.50%	1.80%
Nominal 1-year interest rates	9.70%	6.40%
Growth in exports	3.90%	5.70%

As a follow-up to Angle's example, Hohlman discusses the use and evidence for purchasing power parity. He makes the following statements.

Statement 3: Absolute purchasing power parity is based on the law of one price, which states that a good should have the same price throughout the world. Absolute purchasing power parity is not widely used in practice to forecast exchange rates.

Statement 4: Although relative purchasing power parity is useful as an input for long-run exchange rate forecasts, it is not useful for predicting short-run currency values.

73. Using Angle's analysis, what is the nominal 1-year interest rate in Canada?
    A. Less than 7%.
    B. Between 7% and 13%.
    C. Greater than 13%.

74. Are Hohlman's statements regarding the effect of monetary policies on the dollar correct?
    A. Yes, they are correct.
    B. No, under the Mundell-Fleming model, expansionary monetary policy in the U.S. would weaken the dollar.
    C. No, the dollar value would be unchanged, but under the asset market model and not the Mundell-Fleming model.

75. What additional condition must be satisfied for Hohlman's Statement 1 to be valid?
    A. Covered interest parity must hold.
    B. Fisher effect must hold.
    C. The international Fisher relation must hold.

76. Hohlman's Statement 2 is:
    A. correct.
    B. incorrect as uncovered interest rate parity holds only if real interest rate parity holds.
    C. incorrect as uncovered interest rate parity holds only if covered interest rate parity holds.

77. Which of the following is *closest* to the current ¥/£ spot rate?
    A. ¥194/£.
    B. ¥200/£.
    C. ¥206/£.

78. Regarding the statements made by Hohlman on purchasing power parity, are both statements correct?
    A. Yes.
    B. No, only Statement 4 is correct.
    C. No, both statements are incorrect.

Use the following information to answer Questions 79 through 84.

Engineered Packaging Inc. (EPI) is a manufacturer of industrial and consumer packaging products. The company's products include composite and plastic rigid packaging, flexible packaging, as well as metal and plastic ends and closures. In January 2018, EPI entered into a joint venture with BMI Enterprises. EPI contributed ownership of five plants, while BMI contributed a new manufacturing technology. The joint venture is known as EP/BM LLC. EPI owns 50% of EP/BM LLC and uses the equity method to account for its investment. The following information for 2018 is provided:

In Millions, Year-End 2018	EPI	EP/BM LLC
Revenue	$3,115	$421
Cost of goods sold	$2,580	$295
SG&A	$316	$50
Interest expense	$47	$8
Equity in earnings of EP/BM	$22	
Pretax income	$194	$68
Income tax	$60	$24
Net income	$134	$44

In Millions, December 31, 2018	EPI	EP/BM LLC
Assets		
Cash	$118	$13
Accounts receivable	$390	$50
Inventory	$314	$41
Property	$1,007	$131
Investment	$38	
Total	$1,867	$235

Liabilities and Equity	EPI	EP/BM LLC
Accounts payable	$274	$35
Long-term debt	$719	$125
Equity	$874	$75
Total	$1,867	$235

79. Had EPI used the proportionate consolidation method instead of the equity method to account for its investment, which of the following statements is the *most* accurate?
    A. Net profit margin would be the same.
    B. Return on assets would be the same.
    C. Return on equity would be the same.

80. Based on the acquisition method, EPI's current ratio at the end of 2018 (using the financial information provided) is *closest* to:
    A. 1.8.
    B. 2.6.
    C. 3.0.

81. Based on the acquisition method, EPI's interest coverage ratio for 2018 (using the financial information provided) is *closest* to:
    A. 3.6.
    B. 4.0.
    C. 5.4.

82. Had EPI used the acquisition method instead of the equity method to account for its investment, EPI's long-term debt-to-equity ratio would have been:
    A. higher.
    B. lower.
    C. the same.

83. For this question only, assume that EP/BM LLC sold inventory to EPI for $50 million during 2018. Of that inventory, $20 million was unsold at the end of the year. Compared to the equity method, the acquisition method would result in:
    A. higher net income.
    B. higher ending inventory.
    C. lower net income.

84. For this question only, assume that EPI accounts for its investment in EP/BM LLC using the acquisition method with partial goodwill. As compared to the acquisition method, the return on ending equity under proportionate consolidation will *most likely* be:

A. lower.

B. the same.

C. higher.

Use the following information to answer Questions 85 through 90.

GigaTech, Inc., is a large U.S.-based technology conglomerate. The firm has business units in three primary categories: (1) hardware manufacturing, (2) software development, and (3) consulting services. Because of the rapid pace of technological innovation, GigaTech must make capital investments every two to four years. The company has identified several potential investment opportunities for its hardware manufacturing division. The first of these opportunities, Tera Project, would replace a portion of GigaTech's microprocessor assembly equipment with new machinery expected to last three years. The current machinery has a book value of $120,000 and a market value of $195,000. The Tera Project would require purchasing machinery for $332,000, increasing current assets by $190,000, and increasing current liabilities by $80,000. GigaTech has a tax rate of 40%. Additional pro forma information related to the Tera Project is provided in the following table:

	Existing Equipment	Tera Project
Annual sales	$523,000	$708,000
Cash operating expenses	$352,000	$440,000
Annual depreciation	$40,000	$110,667
Accounting salvage value	$0	$0
Expected salvage value (after three years)	$90,000	$113,000

Analysts at GigaTech have noted that investment in the Tera Project can be delayed for up to nine months if managers at the company decide this is necessary. However, once the capital investment is made, the project will be necessary to maintain continuing operations. Tera Project can be scaled up with more equipment requiring less capital than the original investment if results are meeting expectations. In addition, the equipment used in Tera Project can be used in shift work if brief excess demand is expected.

GigaTech is also considering expanding its software development operations in India. Software development equipment must be continually replaced to maintain efficiency as newer and faster technology is developed. The company has identified two mutually exclusive potential expansion projects, Zeta and Sigma. Zeta requires investing in equipment with a 3-year life, while Sigma requires investing in equipment with a 2-year life. GigaTech has estimated real capital costs for the two projects at 10.58%. GigaTech expects inflation to be approximately 4.0% for the foreseeable future. Nominal cash flows and net present values for the Zeta and Sigma projects are provided in the following table:

| | Annual Cash Flows | | | | |
Project	0	1	2	3	NPV
Zeta	−$360,000	$250,000	$220,000	$190,000	$148,671
Sigma	−$470,000	$330,000	$390,000	$0	$111,853

Recently, GigaTech's board of directors has become concerned with the firm's capital budgeting decisions and has asked management to provide a detailed explanation of the capital budgeting process. After reviewing the report from management, the board makes the following comments in a memo:

- The capital rationing system being utilized is fundamentally flawed since, in some instances, projects that do not increase earnings per share are selected over projects that do increase earnings per share.
- The cash flow projections are flawed since they fail to include costs incurred in the search for projects or the economic consequences of increased competition resulting from highly profitable projects.
- We are making inappropriate investment decisions since the discount rate used to evaluate all potential projects is the firm's weighted average cost of capital.

85. Assuming that working capital will be recaptured at the end of the project, which of the following is *closest* to the final period after-tax cash flow for the Tera Project?
   A. $196,467.
   B. $210,267.
   C. $219,467.

86. Which of the following *best* describes how GigaTech should implement scenario analysis to analyze the Tera Project?
   A. Generate a base case, high, and low estimate of NPV by changing only the most sensitive cash flow variable.
   B. Generate a base case, high, and low estimate of NPV by changing only the discount rate applicable to the project.
   C. Generate a base case, high, and low estimate of NPV by simultaneously changing sales, expense, and discount rate assumptions for each case.

87. Which of the following is *least likely* to be a real option available to GigaTech with regard to the Tera Project?
   A. Abandonment option.
   B. Expansion option.
   C. Flexibility option.

88. Using the least common multiple of lives approach, determine whether the Zeta Project or the Sigma Project will increase the value of GigaTech by a greater amount.
    A. Zeta Project.
    B. Sigma Project.
    C. Both projects increase GigaTech's value by the same amount.

89. Determine whether the board of director's memo is correct with regard to its statements about GigaTech's capital rationing system and its method of projecting project cash flows.
    A. Only the statement regarding capital rationing is correct.
    B. Only the statement regarding cash flow projections is correct.
    C. Neither the statement regarding capital rationing nor the statement regarding cash flow projections is correct.

90. Which of the following would *best* correct GigaTech's discount rate problem described in the board of director's memo?
    A. Use the firm's marginal cost of capital to evaluate all potential projects.
    B. Use a beta specific to each potential project to determine the appropriate discount rate.
    C. Use the cost of the firm's equity capital to discount the cash flows of all potential projects.

Use the following information to answer Questions 91 through 96.

Broadstore Inc. is a retailer operating in urban areas in the eastern and mid-western United States. Currently, Broadstore operates 120 retail outlets, but its executives seek to expand significantly. In order to achieve the rapid expansion, the board has identified two acquisition targets they believe could add value for Broadstore's shareholders.

The first target is retailer Sagan Termett Inc., (Sagan). Sagan's store locations are geographically distributed in a way that would complement Broadstore without too much overlap; Sagan's stores are primarily on the west coast. Broadstore's board believes the company may be receptive to a bid at the right price.

Jackson Torrelle, CFA, works for Broadstore and has been asked to look at the details of a possible share-for-share exchange. The board believes that synergies of $2.3 million per year in perpetuity would be realized if the companies merged.

Broadstore currently has 20 million shares outstanding with a market price of $19.20 per share. Sagan Termett has 15.75 million shares outstanding with a market price of $16.20 per share. Torrelle has been asked to consider the following three scenarios for a possible merger:

Scenario 1: Broadstore offers to purchase 100% of Sagan Termett's shares in exchange for 13 million newly issued shares in the merged entity.

Scenario 2: Broadstore offers to purchase 100% of Sagan Termett's shares for $270 million.

Scenario 3: Broadstore offers to purchase approximately 30% of Sagan Termett's stores for cash.

Torrelle intends to calculate the present value of any synergies using a discount rate of 8%. However, he has concerns as to whether any synergies will be realized and has sent an email to the CFO outlining the consequences if they are not. An extract from the email is shown in Exhibit 1.

Exhibit 1: Torrelle Email (Extract)

"...the assumed synergies arise primarily from the synchronization of accounting systems. I believe the estimate of the annual savings excludes significant one-off costs of training and parallel running of the systems. I estimate that these costs would reduce the present value of synergies by $8 million."

The second target is Exellara Inc., a company that offers logistical solutions to retailers, and currently works with Broadstore, providing most of its distribution network.

Broadstore has only recently identified Exellara as a target and has yet to calculate a value for the company. As part of a preliminary review, the board has obtained a recently published research report that contains a comparable company analysis for Exellara. An extract from the report is shown in Exhibit 2.

Exhibit 2: Exellara Research Report (Extract)

Relative Valuation	Company I	Company II	Company III
Ratio			
P/E	12.3	15.8	9.9
P/S	1.2	1.9	1.3
P/BV	2.5	2.2	3.0
Exellara Metrics			
Earnings per share	$2.73		
Sales per share	$21.21		
Book value per share	$13.92		

The research report concluded that the likely price a potential acquirer would have to pay for Exellara would be $45.70. Torrelle is unsure how this conclusion was arrived at, as he does not have all the appendices to the report outlining its assumptions and calculation methods. He is particularly concerned that the price seems too high, as Broadstore has been criticized in the past for several acquisitions that shareholders did not feel were in their best long-term interests.

Specifically, eight years ago, a small online retailer, with no history of profits, was purchased by the company in an attempt to quickly gain an online presence. Several key staff members left the target company shortly after the acquisition, leaving the operations of the company in turmoil. In the aftermath of this episode, an outside consultant was called in to review what went wrong, and an extract of the report is shown in Exhibit 3.

Exhibit 3: Consultant Report (Extract)

> "...it is our conclusion that a failure in corporate governance at the board level led to a hastily constructed bid and, ultimately, a loss of value to shareholders. It appears that upper level management believed a fast entry into the growing online market would lead to large performance bonuses and, hence, a deal was pushed through before any acceptable level of due diligence was performed."

Torrelle is also concerned with the acquisition from an ethical standpoint. Exellara has long been a target of environmental protestors, as it consistently opposes fuel emissions legislation and continues to use some of the most fuel inefficient vehicles on the road today. It has also been in the news for picking and choosing where its distribution centers are located, based purely on local minimum wage legislation.

Torrelle believes that when considering options for its distribution network, Broadstore should carefully weigh the social benefits and costs involved. He believes the company should pursue the development of an electric fleet of vehicles, although the cost may be higher. It is clearly a policy that, in the long term, would produce the greatest good for the greatest number of people.

91. If Broadstore proceeded with Scenario 3, with regards to Sagan Termett, it is *most likely* that:
   A. Sagan Termett's shareholders would not have to pay tax on any capital gains on the transaction.
   B. the transaction may be subject to approval by Sagan Termett's shareholders.
   C. Broadstore would be required to assume the liabilities of Sagan Termett.

92. If Broadstore proceeded with Scenario 1, with regards to Sagan Termett, and the original estimate of synergies is realized, the gain to Broadstore's shareholders would be *closest* to:
   A. $5,000,000.
   B. $13,000,000.
   C. $21,000,000.

93. If Torrelle's concerns outlined in Exhibit 1 were correct, the *most likely* result is that the gain to:
   A. Broadstore would be reduced under Scenario 1 but not under Scenario 2.
   B. both Broadstore and Sagan Termett shareholders would be reduced under Scenario 1.
   C. both Broadstore and Sagan Termett shareholders would be reduced under Scenario 2.

94. The acquisition price for Exellara in the research report has *most likely* been calculated using:
   A. only the P/E metric and a takeover premium of 20%.
   B. an average of the three metrics and a takeover premium of 20%.
   C. an average of the three metrics and a takeover premium of 35%.

95.   The risk posed to shareholder value outlined in Exhibit 3 is *most accurately* described as:
        A. accounting risk.
        B. strategic policy risk.
        C. asset risk.

96.   Torrelle's suggested alternative for the establishment of a new distribution network *most closely* fits with:
        A. a Kantian approach to business ethics.
        B. a utilitarian approach to business ethics.
        C. the Friedman doctrine.

Use the following information to answer Questions 97 through 102.

Sentinel News is a publisher of more than 100 newspapers around the country, with the exception of the Midwestern states. The company's CFO, Harry Miller, has been reviewing a number of potential candidates (both public and private companies) that would provide Sentinel News entrance into the Midwestern market. Recently, the founder of Midwest News, a private newspaper company, passed away. The founder's family members are inclined to sell their 80% controlling interest. The family members are concerned that Midwest News's declining newspaper circulation is not cyclical, but rather permanent. The family members would reinvest the cash proceeds from the sale of Midwest News into a diversified portfolio of stocks and bonds. Miller's staff collects the financial information shown in Exhibit 1.

Exhibit 1: Midwest News's Financial Information

Total assets	$92.5 million
Total debt	$0
Total equity	$79.5 million
Shares outstanding	1.5 million
Revenues	$251.5 million
Net income (next year's forecast)	$19.5 million

Miller noted that Midwest News does not pay a dividend, nor does the company have any debt. The most comparable publicly traded stock is Freedom Corporation. Freedom, however, has significant radio and television operations. Freedom's estimated beta is 0.90, and 40% of the company's capital structure is debt. Freedom is expected to maintain a payout ratio of 40%. Analysts are forecasting the company will earn $3.00 per share next year and grow their earnings by 6% per year. Freedom has a current market capitalization of $15 billion and 375 million shares outstanding. Freedom's current market value equals its intrinsic value.

Miller's staff uses current expectations to develop the appropriate equity risk premium for Midwest News. The staff uses the Gordon growth model (GGM) to estimate Midwest's equity risk premium. The equity risk premium calculated by the staff is provided in Exhibit 2.

Miller believes the best method to estimate the required return on equity of Midwest News is the build-up method. All relevant information to determine Midwest News's required return on equity is presented in Exhibit 2.

Exhibit 2: Required Return Estimate Factors

Risk-free rate	3.5%
Equity risk premium	4.0%
Small size premium	3.5%
Specific-company premium	2.0%
Beta	1.2
Growth rate	3.0%

The specific-company premium reflects concerns about future industry performance and business risk in Midwest News. Miller makes two statements concerning the valuation methodology used to value Midwest News's equity.

Statement 1: The required return estimate that is calculated from Exhibit 2 reflects all adjustments needed to make an accurate valuation of Midwest News.

Statement 2: It is better to use the free cash flow model to value Midwest News than a dividend discount model.

Miller considered two different valuation models to determine the price of Midwest News's equity: a single-stage free cash flow model and a single-stage residual income model.

97. Using Freedom Corporation as a comparable, the estimated beta for Midwest News is *most likely*:
   A. greater than 0.90.
   B. less than 0.90.
   C. equal to 0.90.

98. The required return estimate of Freedom Corporation is *closest* to:
   A. 3%.
   B. 6%.
   C. 9%.

99. Which of the following is NOT an input used to estimate Midwest News's equity risk premium based on the Gordon growth model (GGM)?
   A. Dividend yield on the market index.
   B. Current long-term government bond yield.
   C. Expected growth in the market index's P/E ratio.

100. Based on Exhibit 2 and using the build-up method, Midwest News's required return on equity is *closest* to:
   A. 13.0%.
   B. 13.8%.
   C. 15.8%.

101. Using the single-stage residual income model and assuming the required return on equity is 15%, the value of Midwest News is *closest* to: (use information in Exhibits 1 and 2)
   A. $75 per share.
   B. $95 per share.
   C. $115 per share.

102. Miller has made two statements, one concerning the required return estimate and the other concerning the relative merits of the free cash flow model versus the dividend discount model. Are Miller's statements correct?
   A. Only Statement 1 is correct.
   B. Only Statement 2 is correct.
   C. Both Statements 1 and 2 are correct.

Use the following information to answer Questions 103 through 108.

CTT Credit Analysis provides fixed-income credit analysis to fund managers and high net worth individuals. Tam Lowenstadt, CFA, joined the firm recently; one of his first tasks is to provide a new client with an overview of the credit analysis models the firm uses. He begins by outlining some key underlying principles, as shown in Exhibit 1.

Exhibit 1: Key Underlying Principles

1. The probability of default multiplied by the recovery rate given default is equal to the expected loss.

2. To allow for differing states of the economy, both the probability of default and loss given default may be taken as weighted averages using the probabilities of each state of the economy.

3. The expected loss will be lower than the present value of expected loss as it is modified to take the time value of money and the risk premium into account.

Lowenstadt also provides an overview of the structural model approach to credit analysis. He starts off by explaining the basic approach of valuing the credit risk by using an option analogy. He makes two key statements regarding this analogy and how it can be used to value equity and debt:

Statement 1: Owning the company's debt with a face value of K and a maturity of T is economically equivalent to owning a riskless bond with face value of K and maturity of T and simultaneously purchasing a European put option on the assets of the company with a strike price equal to K and maturing at time T.

Statement 2: Holding the company's equity is economically equivalent to owning a European call option on the company's assets.

CTT Credit Analysis always includes an illustration of the term structure of yield spreads in any analysis it provides to clients. Lowenstadt demonstrates this calculation in his overview. He provided annualized yields for a zero-coupon, risk-free bond and a zero-coupon, corporate bond based on daily closing market prices over the last week as shown in Exhibit 2.

Exhibit 2: One Year Yields

Date	Risk-Free Bonds	Corporate Bond XVT
June 1	0.0124	0.0298
June 2	0.0124	0.0297
June 3	0.0125	0.0298
June 4	0.0126	0.0299
June 5	0.0126	0.0300
June 6	0.0127	0.0301
June 7	0.0128	0.0301

Lowenstadt demonstrates how the firm calculates the approximate expected loss per year using the given yields and assuming frictionless markets.

CCT does not recommend the use of reduced form models of credit analysis to its clients. Lowenstadt defended this decision based on the firm's standard response as shown in Exhibit 3.

Exhibit 3: CCT Firm View on Reduced Form Models

Point 1

Although the reduced form models used allow for the probability of default to vary with the state of the economy, they do not allow for systematic default across companies.

Point 2

Reduced form models can only be used under the assumption that the company has a zero-coupon bond that is actively traded.

Finally, Lowenstadt also discussed CCT's application of credit analysis to asset-backed securities. Lowenstadt is aware that the client has some collateralized debt obligations in her portfolio. His overview is shown in Exhibit 4.

Exhibit 4: ABS Overview

Section 1 – Key Calculations

- Probability of default.
- Probability of loss.
- Present value of expected loss.

Section 2 – Applicable Models

- Structural models.
- Reduced form models.

Section 3 – Valuing ABS Tranches

- Composition of collateral pool.
- Use of Monte Carlo models to analyze cash flow waterfall patterns.

103. In Exhibit 1, which of the underlying principles outlined by Lowenstadt is *most accurate*?
    A. Principle 1.
    B. Principle 2.
    C. Principle 3.

104. Lowenstadt's statement 1 is *most likely*:
    A. incorrect, as he should have instead stated *purchasing* a European call option.
    B. incorrect, as he should have instead stated selling a European *put* option.
    C. correct.

105. Lowenstadt's statement 2 is *best* described as:
    A. incorrect, as he should have instead stated *American* call option.
    B. incorrect, as he should have instead stated European *put* option.
    C. correct.

106. Based on the yields given in Exhibit 2, the expected loss per year is *closest* to:
    A. 1.25%.
    B. 1.32%.
    C. 1.73%.

107. Which of Lowenstadt's points in Exhibit 3 is *correct*?
    A. Only point 1 only is accurate.
    B. Only point 2 only is accurate.
    C. Neither point is accurate.

108. Lowenstadt's overview of asset-backed securities in Exhibit 4 *most likely* contains an error in:
A. section A, because the probability of default is not relevant for asset-backed securities.
B. section B, because structural models cannot be used for asset-backed securities.
C. section C, because Monte Carlo simulations cannot be applied to asset-backed securities.

Use the following information to answer Questions 109 through 114.

Rock Torrey, an analyst for International Retailers Incorporated (IRI), has been asked to evaluate the firm's swap transactions in general, as well as a 2-year fixed for fixed currency swap involving the U.S. dollar and the Mexican peso in particular. The dollar is Torrey's domestic currency, and the exchange rate as of June 1, 2009, was $0.0893 per peso. The swap calls for annual payments and exchange of notional principal at the beginning and end of the swap term and has a notional principal of $100 million. The counterparty to the swap is GHS Bank, a large full-service bank in Mexico.

The current term structure of interest rates for both countries is given in the following table:

Time Period	U.S. Interest Rates	Mexican Interest Rates
360 days	4.0%	5.0%
720 days	4.5%	5.2%

Torrey believes the swap will help his firm effectively mitigate its foreign currency exposure in Mexico, which stems mainly from shopping centers in high-end resorts located along the eastern coastline. Having made this conclusion, Torrey begins writing his report for the management of IRI. In the report, Torrey makes the following statements about interest rate derivative instruments:

Statement 1: A payer swap can be replicated using a long receiver swaption and a short payer swaption with the same exercise rates. If the exercise rate is set such that the premiums of the payer and receiver swaptions are equal, then the exercise rate must be equal to the market swap fixed rate.

Statement 2: A long callable bond can be replicated using a long option-free bond plus a short receiver swaption.

Torrey is also evaluating a two-year European interest rate call option with a strike rate of 5% and a notional principal of $2 million. Torrey wants to use a binomial tree as shown in Exhibit 1 to value the option.

Exhibit 1: Two-Period Interest Rate Tree

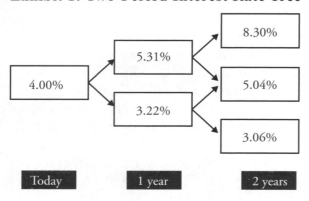

| Today | 1 year | 2 years |

Six months (180 days) have passed since Torrey issued his report to IRI's management team, and the current exchange rate is now $0.085 per peso. The new term structure of interest rates is as follows:

Time Period	U.S. Interest Rates	Mexican Interest Rates
180 days	4.2%	5.0%
540 days	4.8%	5.2%

109. For the currency swap that Torrey is evaluating, calculate the annual payments that will be required of International Retailers Incorporated.
    A. 29.1 million pesos.
    B. 40.7 million pesos.
    C. 56.8 million pesos.

110. Torrey's statement 1 is *most likely*:
    A. correct.
    B. incorrect about long receiver swaption and short payer swaption.
    C. incorrect about the exercise rate being equal to the market swap fixed rate if the premiums of the two swaptions are equal.

111. Torrey's statement 2 is *most likely*:
    A. correct.
    B. incorrect about the long option free bond.
    C. incorrect about the short receiver swaption.

112. The value of the two-year interest rate call option is *closest* to:
    A. $7,717.
    B. $15,434.
    C. $18,415.

113. Calculate the present value of the dollar fixed payments for the 2-year currency swap six months after Torrey's initial analysis.
    A. $93.28 million.
    B. $101.69 million.
    C. $108.80 million.

114. Calculate the value of the 2-year currency swap from the perspective of the counterparty paying dollars six months after Torrey's initial analysis.
    A. −$0.72 million.
    B. −$3.21 million.
    C. −$4.21 million.

Use the following information to answer Questions 115 through 120.

Bill Henry, CFA, is the CIO of IS University Endowment Fund located in the United States. The Fund's total assets are valued at $3.5 billion. The investment policy uses a total return approach to meet the return objective that includes a spending rate of 5%. In addition, the policy constraints established make tax-exempt instruments an inappropriate investment vehicle. The Fund's current asset mix includes an 18% allocation to private equity. The private equity allocation is shown in Exhibit 1.

Exhibit 1: IS University Endowment Fund's Private Equity Investments

Private Equity	Percentage Allocation
Venture capital	12%
Buyouts	56%
Special situations	32%

The private equity allocation is a mixture of funds with different vintages. For example, within the venture capital category, investments have been made in five different funds. Exhibit 2 provides details about the Alpha Fund with a vintage year of 2014 and committed capital of $195 million. The distribution waterfall calls for 20% carried interest when NAV before distributions exceeds committed capital.

Exhibit 2: $195 million Venture Capital Alpha Fund *($Millions)*

Year	Called-Down	Management Fees	Operating Results
2014	$30	$0.45	−$10
2015	$25	$0.83	$55
2016	$75	$1.95	$75

The Alpha Fund is considering a new investment in Targus Company. Targus is a start-up biotech company seeking $9 million of venture capital financing. Targus's founders believe that, based on the company's new drug pipeline, a company value of $300 million is reasonable in five years. Management at Alpha Fund views Targus Company as a risky investment (15% risk of failure) and is using a discount rate of 40%.

115. Which of the following risk factors will *most likely* impact the private equity portion of the IS University Endowment?
    A. Lack of diversification.
    B. Illiquid investments.
    C. Taxation risk.

116. Using Exhibit 2, calculate the 2016 percentage management fee of the Alpha Fund.
    A. 1.5%.
    B. 2.0%.
    C. 2.5%.

117. Alpha Fund's 2016 dollar amount of carried interest is *closest* to:
    A. $0 million.
    B. $10 million.
    C. $20 million.

118. Which of the following is *most likely* a characteristic of a venture capital investment?
    A. The typical investment uses leverage.
    B. Measureable risk.
    C. Increasing capital requirements.

119. Using the single period NPV method (venture capital method), the post-money valuation of Targus Company is *closest* to:
    A. $48 million.
    B. $50 million.
    C. $55 million.

120. For this question only, assuming that the founders will hold 2.5 million shares, and the post money valuation is $90 million, the price per share for the venture capital investor is *closest* to:
    A. $32.40.
    B. $34.12.
    C. $36.00.

End of Afternoon Session

Exam 3
Morning Session

Question	Topic	Minutes (Points)
1 to 6	Quantitative Methods	18
7 to 12	Financial Reporting and Analysis	18
13 to 18	Equity	18
19 to 24	Equity	18
25 to 30	Fixed Income	18
31 to 36	Fixed Income	18
37 to 42	Derivatives	18
43 to 48	Derivatives	18
49 to 54	Alternative Investments	18
55 to 60	Portfolio Management	18

Test Answers

1.	(A)	(B)	(C)
2.	(A)	(B)	(C)
3.	(A)	(B)	(C)
4.	(A)	(B)	(C)
5.	(A)	(B)	(C)
6.	(A)	(B)	(C)
7.	(A)	(B)	(C)
8.	(A)	(B)	(C)
9.	(A)	(B)	(C)
10.	(A)	(B)	(C)
11.	(A)	(B)	(C)
12.	(A)	(B)	(C)
13.	(A)	(B)	(C)
14.	(A)	(B)	(C)
15.	(A)	(B)	(C)
16.	(A)	(B)	(C)
17.	(A)	(B)	(C)
18.	(A)	(B)	(C)
19.	(A)	(B)	(C)
20.	(A)	(B)	(C)
21.	(A)	(B)	(C)
22.	(A)	(B)	(C)
23.	(A)	(B)	(C)
24.	(A)	(B)	(C)
25.	(A)	(B)	(C)
26.	(A)	(B)	(C)
27.	(A)	(B)	(C)
28.	(A)	(B)	(C)
29.	(A)	(B)	(C)
30.	(A)	(B)	(C)
31.	(A)	(B)	(C)
32.	(A)	(B)	(C)
33.	(A)	(B)	(C)
34.	(A)	(B)	(C)
35.	(A)	(B)	(C)
36.	(A)	(B)	(C)
37.	(A)	(B)	(C)
38.	(A)	(B)	(C)
39.	(A)	(B)	(C)
40.	(A)	(B)	(C)
41.	(A)	(B)	(C)
42.	(A)	(B)	(C)
43.	(A)	(B)	(C)
44.	(A)	(B)	(C)
45.	(A)	(B)	(C)
46.	(A)	(B)	(C)
47.	(A)	(B)	(C)
48.	(A)	(B)	(C)
49.	(A)	(B)	(C)
50.	(A)	(B)	(C)
51.	(A)	(B)	(C)
52.	(A)	(B)	(C)
53.	(A)	(B)	(C)
54.	(A)	(B)	(C)
55.	(A)	(B)	(C)
56.	(A)	(B)	(C)
57.	(A)	(B)	(C)
58.	(A)	(B)	(C)
59.	(A)	(B)	(C)
60.	(A)	(B)	(C)

Exam 3
Morning Session

Questions 1–6 relate to Goldensand Jewelry, Ltd.

Introduction

Rajesh Singh is the CFO of Goldensand Jewelry, Ltd, a London-based retailer of fine jewelry and watches. Singh has noticed that the price of gold has begun to increase. If economic activity continues to pick up, the price of gold is likely to accelerate its rate of increase as both the level of demand and inflation rates increase.

Implications of Rising Gold Price

Singh has become concerned about the cost implications for Goldensand if gold prices continue to rise. He has requested a meeting with Anita Biscayne, Goldensand's COO. In preparation for the meeting, Singh asked one of his staff, Yasunobu Hara, to prepare a regression analysis comparing the price of gold to the average cost of Goldensand's purchases of finished gold jewelry. Hara provides the regression results as shown in Exhibit 1.

Exhibit 1: 1979–2009 Annual Data (31 Observations)

Variable	Coefficient	Standard Error of the Coefficient
Intercept	11.06	7.29
Cost of gold	2.897	0.615
standard error of the forecast = 117.8		

Exhibit 2: Partial Student's *t*-distribution Table

	Level of Significance for One-Tailed Test					
df	**0.100**	**0.050**	**0.025**	**0.010**	**0.005**	**0.0005**
	Level of Significance for Two-Tailed Test					
df	**0.200**	**0.100**	**0.050**	**0.020**	**0.010**	**0.001**
29	1.311	1.699	2.045	2.462	2.756	3.659
30	1.310	1.697	2.042	2.457	2.750	3.646
31	1.309	1.696	2.040	2.453	2.744	3.636

Reviewing the regression results, Biscayne becomes concerned about the implications for the cost of finished jewelry to Goldensand if the price of gold continues to rise. To remain profitable, the cost of finished jewelry should not exceed $2,000.

Regression Concerns

Overall Concerns

Singh's principal concern about the regression is whether the time period chosen is a good predictor of the current situation. He makes the following statement:

Statement 1: We may have a problem with parameter instability if the relationship between gold prices and jewelry costs has changed over the past 30 years.

Singh also focuses on the value of the slope coefficient. He expected it to be 4.0 based on his experience in the industry. Hara computes the appropriate test statistic and reports the following:

Statement 2: We fail to reject the null hypothesis that the slope coefficient is equal to 4.0 at the 5% level of significance.

Testing for Heteroskedasticity

Biscayne remarks that the dramatic increase in the price level over the past 30 years leads her to suspect heteroskedasticity in the regression results. She suggests to Singh that they should conduct a Breusch-Pagan chi-square test for heteroskedasticity by calculating the following test statistic:

$n \times R^2$ with k degrees of freedom

where:
n = number of observations
R^2 = R^2 of the regression of jewelry prices on gold prices
k = number of independent variables

Model Misspecification

Biscayne and Singh have various views on the potential for model misspecification and the effect of any such misspecification.

- Biscayne worries that the regression model is misspecified because it does not include a variable to measure the cost of the highly specialized labor used by manufacturing jewelers. She points out that the effect of omitting an important variable in a regression analysis is that the regression coefficients will be unbiased and inconsistent.
- Singh adds that another common consequence of misspecifying a regression analysis is creating undesired stationarity.

Multiple Regression

Hara conducts a series of regression analyses using all possible combinations of the suggested independent variables based on their average quarterly values. He returns with the following regression results as shown in Exhibit 3 for the equation which uses all suggested independent variables.

Exhibit 3: 1999–2009 Quarterly Data (44 Observations)

Independent Variables	Coefficient	t-Statistic
Intercept	–3.9	3.7
Gold price	4.7	14.5
Silver price	1.2	7.8
Platinum price	3.5	3.1
Labor costs	0.82	2.4
GDP (EU)	0.000274	5.7
GDP (Middle East)	0.000049	3.6
Personal income (EU)	0.000314	2.1
Personal income (Middle East)	0.009876	2.2

R^2: 0.55

Durbin-Watson: 3.89

Hara is concerned about the equation described in Exhibit 3. He makes the following statement:

Statement 3: The model appears to suffer from multicollinearity. Dropping one or more independent variables will increase the coefficient of determination.

Biscayne responds with the following statement:

Statement 4: An autocorrelation problem can be addressed by using the Hansen method to adjust the R^2.

Exhibit 4: Partial Durbin-Watson Table

	Critical Values for the Durbin-Watson Statistic ($\alpha = 0.05$)					
	K = 3		K = 4		K = 5	
n	d_l	d_u	d_l	d_u	d_l	d_u
39	1.33	1.66	1.27	1.72	1.22	1.79
40	1.34	1.66	1.29	1.72	1.23	1.79
45	1.38	1.67	1.34	1.72	1.29	1.78

1. The per ounce price of gold that corresponds to the $2,000 cost of finished jewelry is *closest* to:
    A. $687.
    B. $712.
    C. $3,240.

2. Are Singh (Statement 1) and Hara (Statement 2) correct or incorrect regarding the usefulness of regression results described in Exhibit 1 and the value of the slope coefficient?
    A. Both are correct.
    B. One is correct, the other is incorrect.
    C. Both are incorrect.

3. Is Biscayne correct with regard to the specification of the Breusch-Pagan test?
    A. No, because it is an *F*-test.
    B. No, because the wrong R^2 is used.
    C. No, because the degrees of freedom are equal to k and n − k − 1.

4. Regarding the comments on the potential consequences of misspecification in the simple linear regression, is Singh correct or incorrect regarding his comment on his concern over stationarity, and is Biscayne correct or incorrect about the effect of omitting an important variable?
    A. Only Singh is incorrect.
    B. Only Biscayne is incorrect.
    C. Both are incorrect.

5. Is Hara's Statement 3 about multicollinearity accurate?
    A. Yes.
    B. No, because removal of independent variables is a remedy for residual autocorrelation.
    C. No, because the coefficient of determination would not increase.

6. Is Biscayne correct regarding his statement concerning how to correct for autocorrelation?
    A. No, because the White method is used to adjust the R^2.
    B. No, because the Hansen method adjusts the coefficient standard errors.
    C. No, because the Hansen method is used to address the problem of multicollinearity.

Questions 7–12 relate to Kay Longton, CFA.

Kay Longton, CFA, works as an equity analyst for BKJE Services, a small advisory firm Longton founded with three colleagues she previously worked with. BKJE offers a range of services to both institutional and retail investors and prides itself on its ability to service both clients with relatively shallow knowledge of the markets as well as experienced veterans.

Currently Longton is engaged with Coreblue, a buy-side client that has recently seen a significant downturn in the performance of several of its actively managed funds. As recently as 2014, Coreblue was featured in lists highlighting the best performing funds, but recent poor performance has resulted in a 24% drop in assets under management. A thorough in-house review revealed that several of the historically best-performing investments in one of Coreblue's biggest funds had not been subject to the mandatory screening process. Three of these investments subsequently saw decreases in market capitalization of more than 40% and were responsible for more than 70% of the drop in the fund's active return.

Longton is currently reviewing the investments in question in order to report to Coreblue whether any warning signs were evident from the financial statements. Longton hopes this report will lead to a much bigger project for BKJE involving redesign of Coreblue's screening and analysis process.

The first company Longton is reviewing, Reddyfast, Inc., rose to prominence in 2012 when it promised to deliver custom built kitchen/dining room extensions in customer backyards, which could be built on-site in a day. Longton intends to include in her report the following extracts from Reddyfast's financial statements shown in Exhibit 1.

Exhibit 1: Reddyfast Financial Statements and Notes (Extracts, $ '000s)

	2012	2013	2014
Revenue	14,000	13,720	15,915
Cost of Goods Sold	(11,340)	(10,976)	(12,891)
Gross Profit	2,660	2,744	3,024
Accounts Receivable *(note 1)*	1,789	1,907	2,610

Note 1: Accounts Receivable Securitization
In 2014, the company received $400,000 from the sale of accounts receivable. These balances are not shown in the accounts receivable figure in the balance sheet. An associated finance charge has been disclosed in operating profit for the year.

Longton has isolated these figures as she believes that analysis of the relationship between receivables and revenue should have revealed cause for concern over the period 2012–2014. She intends to restate the financial statements for accounts receivables sold, and then compute the trend in days of sales outstanding using end-of-year receivables.

Longton plans to make the following statements concerning inventory management trends that Coreblue should be on the lookout for:

Statement 1
A substantial and unexpected increase in sales in the final quarter may be a sign that a company is using bill-and-hold transactions to give a one-off boost to revenue and cash flows toward the end of a period.

Statement 2
Earnings are made up of a cash earnings component and an accrual earning component. The cash component of earnings is more persistent. A firm with a higher proportion of cash earnings will have a higher β in the following expression of earnings persistence:

$$\text{Earnings}_{t+1} = \alpha + \beta(\text{Earnings}_t) + \varepsilon$$

The second company in question is Ervington Boddan, Inc. (EB), a provider of heating solutions for recreational vehicles across the United States. Three board members of EB have also served as board members for Reddyfast since its inception in 2009.

Longton is concerned that EB's growth is fueled largely by income from associates, and, as a result, Longton intends to prepare a report showing the core ROE without including the results on such investments. In order to illustrate the driving forces behind ROE, she intends to perform a classic DuPont analysis that excludes the impact of associates from the margin and turnover ratios. One of Longton's interns has prepared the extracts shown in Exhibit 2 to assist with the analysis.

Exhibit 2: EB Financial Statements (Extracts, $ millions)

	2014	2015	2016
Revenue	**11,719**	**12,071**	**12,795**
Cost of Goods Sold	9,243	9,502	10,357
Research and Development	80	78	76
Depreciation and Amortization	831	839	864
Other Operating Expenses	590	625	675
Total Expenses	**10,744**	**11,045**	**11,973**
Operating Profit	**975**	**1,026**	**822**
Finance Costs	(178)	(183)	(194)
Finance Income	23	23	23
Income From Associates	56	63	94
Profit Before Tax	**876**	**929**	**745**
Tax	(157)	(159)	(160)
Profit After Tax	**719**	**770**	**585**
Non-Controlling Interest	(16)	(16)	(16)
Net Income Attributable to Shareholders of Parent	**703**	**754**	**568**
Balance Sheet			
Non-Current Assets			
PPE	8,120	8,193	8,203
Intangibles	982	980	992
Investment in Associates	1,733	1,890	2,014
Other Non-Current Assets	1,013	1,102	1,712
Total Non-Current Assets	**11,848**	**12,165**	**12,921**
Total Current Assets	**3,245**	**3,345**	**3,354**
Total Assets	**15,093**	**15,510**	**16,275**
Total Liabilities	**10,678**	**10,899**	**11,010**
Shareholders' Equity	**4,415**	**4,611**	**5,265**

The third company under review is Yopatta Solutions, Inc. The company provides marketing and advertising services to a variety of clients, promising to deliver a "one stop shop" solution for all client customer communication needs.

Due to the nature of its business, Yopatta (like its peers) has relatively few tangible assets on its balance sheet. However, on reviewing the notes to the balance sheet, Longton identifies that Yopatta has a significant operating lease commitment. Using end-of-year reported balance sheet data, Longton calculated Yopatta's debt-to-equity ratio to be 48%. She now intends to restate the ratio after capitalizing operating lease commitments using the information in Exhibit 3.

Exhibit 3: Yopatta Leverage

Balance Sheet 31 Dec 2015 As Reported	
Non-Current Assets	7,892
Current Assets	6,422
Total Assets	14,314
Debt	2,367
Other Liabilities	7,011
Total Liabilities	9,378
Shareholders' Equity	4,936

Notes:

Operating Lease Commitments

Yopatta is committed to making the following payments under non-cancellable operating leases:

	$ million
Year ended 31 December 2016	148
Year ended 31 December 2017	148
Year ended 31 December 2018	148
Year ended 31 December 2019	148
Year ended 31 December 2020	98
Years ending 31 December 2021–25	490

Longton assumes that all lease payments occur at the end of each year, and that the payments from 2021–25 are all equal. Yopatta recently went to the market and issued senior unsecured debt at a yield of 4%; Longton intends to apply this rate to capitalize the operating lease.

Longton believes that this recalculation is essential for all companies with operating leases as she believes that U.S. GAAP will very soon be updated to require the capitalization of all operating leases longer than one year. As a result, Longton will add the following comment on the impact on the income statement in her report:

Potential Accounting Policy Change

The requirement to capitalize operating leases will impact not only leverage ratios, but also coverage ratios based on the income statement. This lease capitalization will result in a decrease in operating profit, a decrease in interest expense, and a decrease in interest coverage ratios.

7. Using the information in Exhibit 1 and Longton's stated method of calculation, Longton is *most likely* to conclude that Reddyfast's:
    A. days of sales outstanding increased by approximately 28% between 2012 and 2014, possibly due to aggressive revenue recognition or quicker receivables collection.
    B. days of sales outstanding increased by approximately 47% between 2012 and 2104, possibly due to aggressive revenue recognition or poor receivables management.
    C. receivables turnover increased by approximately 21% between 2012 and 2014, possibly due to increased collection periods and aggressive revenue recognition policies.

8. Statement 1 by Longton is *most likely* to be:
    A. correct.
    B. incorrect with respect to revenue.
    C. incorrect with respect to cash flows.

9. Statement 2 by Longton is *most likely* to be:
    A. correct.
    B. incorrect, because accruals component of earnings is more persistent.
    C. incorrect, because in for formula given, a high α (not β) represents persistence.

10. Using Exhibit 2, Longton is *most likely* to conclude that EB's associates' contribution to ROE in 2016 was:
    A. more than in 2015.
    B. about the same as in 2015.
    C. less than in 2015.

11. Yopatta's restated debt-to-equity ratio will be *closest* to:
    A. 49%.
    B. 57%.
    C. 68%.

12. Longton's comment on the potential accounting policy change is *best* described as:
    A. correct.
    B. incorrect regarding the decrease in operating profit.
    C. incorrect regarding the decrease in interest coverage ratios.

Questions 13–18 relate to O'Connor Textiles, Part 1.

Emily De Jong, CFA, works for Charles & Williams Associates, a medium-sized investment firm operating in the northeastern United States. De Jong is responsible for producing financial reports to use as tools to attract new clients. It is now early in 2019, and De Jong is reviewing information for O'Connor Textiles and finalizing a report that will be used for an important presentation to a potential investor at the end of the week.

Following an acquisition of a major competitor in 2002, O'Connor went public in 2003 and paid its first dividend in 2009. Dividends are paid at the end of the year. After 2018, dividends are expected to grow for three years at 11%: $2.13 in 2019, $2.36 in 2020, and $2.63 in 2021. The average of the arithmetic and compound growth rates are given in Exhibit 1. Dividends are then expected to settle down to a long-term growth rate of 4%. O'Connor's current share price of $70 is expected to rise to $72.92 by the end of the year according to the consensus of analysts' forecasts.

O'Connor's annual dividend history is shown in Exhibit 1.

Exhibit 1: O'Connor Textiles Dividend History

Year	Dividend ($)	% Change		
2009	0.76			
2010	0.76	0.000		
2011	0.76	0.000		
2012	0.82	7.895		
2013	0.91	10.976		
2014	1.03	13.187		
2015	1.16	12.621	Arithmetic mean growth	11.1%
2016	1.34	15.517	Compound growth	10.9%
2017	1.52	13.433		
2018	1.92	26.316		

De Jong is also considering whether or not she should value O'Connor using a free cash flow model instead of the dividend discount model.

In addition, De Jong observes that the current return on 3-month T-bills is 3% and determines that the expected return on the market portfolio is 7%. She has gathered monthly data on company stock returns ($R_{i,t}$) and market returns ($R_{M,t}$) and has decided to run an ordinary least squares regression according to the model $R_{i,t} = \alpha_i + \beta_i R_{M,t} + \varepsilon_t$. De Jong uses the S&P 500 as the proxy for the market portfolio.

The output from the regression appears in Exhibit 2.

Exhibit 2: Summary Output

Dependent Variable = $R_{i,t}$

Regression Statistics	
Multiple R-Squared	0.6275
R-Squared	0.3938
Adjusted R-Squared	0.3891
Standard Error	0.0572
Observations	132

ANOVA

	df	SS	MS	F	Significance F
Regression	1	0.2764	0.2764	8.4437	<0.0001
Residual	130	0.4256	0.0033		
Total	131	0.7020			

	Coefficients	Adjusted Standard Error	t-Stat	P-value	Lower 95%	Upper 95%
Intercept	0.0062	0.0051	1.2067	0.2297	−0.0039	0.0163
$R_{M,t}$	1.0400	0.1136	9.1549	<0.0001	0.8190	1.2685

Charles Wang, De Jong's colleague, is of the opinion that O'Connor's growth rate will be 11% but will decline linearly to a long-term growth rate of 4% over the next six years. Wang also feels that the required rate of return for O'Connor should be 9.50%.

13. Based on information in Exhibit 2, the required return on equity (according to the CAPM) for O'Connor is *closest* to:
    A. 4.2%.
    B. 7.2%.
    C. 9.2%.

14. For this question only, assume that O'Connor's cost of equity is 10%. The value of one share of O'Connor stock in early 2019 using the two-stage dividend discount model (DDM) is *closest* to:
    A. $38.50.
    B. $40.00.
    C. $47.50.

15. For this question only, assume that De Jong's estimate of the value of O'Connor stock using a two-stage DDM is $75. Assuming the market has also applied a two-stage DDM, and the market's consensus estimate of dividend growth and required return are the same as De Jong's, the market's consensus estimate of the duration of the high-growth period is *most likely*:
    A. less than three years.
    B. equal to three years.
    C. greater than three years.

16. In what situation is it *most appropriate* for De Jong to employ a:

Dividend discount model?	FCFE model?
A. Non-control perspective	FCFE aligned with profitability
B. Control perspective	FCFE aligned with profitability
C. Non-control perspective	FCFE aligned with dividend policy

17. The value of O'Connor stock using Wang's assumptions is *closest* to:
    A. $43.65
    B. $48.75
    C. $52.35

18. For this question only, assume that the market price of O'Connor stock is $48.00 and the linearly declining high growth period is 5 years. The required rate of return implicit in the market price is *closest* to:
    A. 8.86%
    B. 9.22%
    C. 10.81%

Questions 19–24 relate to O'Connor Textiles, Part 2.

De Jong continues her analysis of O'Connor. She is concerned that along with a dividend discount model approach she would also like to get a measure of the contribution that the key managers, Melanie and Arthur O'Connor, have made to the company's apparent ongoing success.

She considers using NOPAT and EVA to assess management performance. She believes that increasing invested capital to take advantage of projects with positive net present values increases both NOPAT and EVA.

However, De Jong decides to use residual income analysis instead. She provides the following justification for using the residual income model:

- The calculation of residual income depends primarily on readily available accounting data.
- The residual income model can be used even when cash flow is difficult to forecast.
- The residual income model does not depend on dividend payments or on positive free cash flows in the near future.
- The residual income model depends on the validity of the clean surplus relation.

She also considers the following assumptions about continuing residual income:

Assumption 1:   Residual income is positive and continues at the same level year after year.

Assumption 2:   ROE declines over time to the cost of equity.

Assumption 3:   Residual income declines to zero immediately.

De Jong gathers recent financial information data on O'Connor, as shown in Exhibit 1.

Exhibit 1: O'Connor Textiles, Inc. Summary Income Statement (U.S. $ thousands, except per share data)

	2018	2019
	Actual	*Projection*
Sales	$509,447	$529,429
Cost of sales	398,100	405,068
Selling and administrative expenses	49,608	59,378
Depreciation and amortization	18,562	22,979
Total operating expenses	466,270	487,425
Earnings from operations	43,177	42,004
Interest expense	28,004	28,906
Earnings before income taxes	15,173	13,098
Provision for income taxes	5,138	4,453
Net earnings for the year	10,035	8,645
Earnings per share: basic	$0.59	$0.51
Fully diluted	$0.56	*

*Non-dilutive

De Jong has also determined that at the beginning of 2018, O'Connor had total capital of $324,000,000, of which $251,000,000 was debt and $73,000,000 was equity. The company's cost of debt before taxes is 7%, and the cost of equity capital is 8%. The company has a tax rate of approximately 34%. Weighted average cost of capital is 5.4%. Net operating profit after tax (before any adjustments) is $28,517,640.

De Jong is interested in obtaining the market's assessment of the implied growth rate in residual income and notes that the book value per share for O'Connor at the beginning of 2019 was $4.29, and the current market price is $70. She forecasts the return on equity (ROE) for 2019 to be 11.84%.

De Jong discusses her analyses with a colleague, who makes the following general statements:

Statement 1: It is usually the case that value is recognized later in the residual income model than in the dividend discount model.

Statement 2: When the present value of expected future residual income is negative, the justified P/B based on fundamentals is less than one.

19. Is De Jong correct about the *likely* effects on NOPAT and EVA from increasing invested capital to take advantage of projects with positive net present values?
    A. Yes in both cases.
    B. Yes in one case, and no in the other.
    C. No in both cases.

20. Are De Jong's justifications for using the residual income model correct?
    A. Yes.
    B. No, because the residual income model should be not be used when cash flows are difficult to forecast.
    C. No, because the residual income model depends on positive free cash flows in the near future.

21. Which of De Jong's assumptions about continuing residual income will lead to the highest persistence factor?
    A. Assumption 1.
    B. Assumption 2.
    C. Assumption 3.

22. O'Connor's residual income and economic value added (EVA) for 2018 are *closest* to:

Residual income	EVA
A. $6.1 million	$11.0 million
B. $4.2 million	$11.0 million
C. $4.2 million	$2.6 million

23. The implied residual income growth rate for 2019, based on the residual income model, is *closest* to:
    A. 7.75%.
    B. 8.16%.
    C. 8.82%.

24. Are the statements made by De Jong's colleague correct?
    A. Both statements are correct.
    B. Only Statement 1 is correct.
    C. Only Statement 2 is correct.

Questions 25-30 relate to Susan Evermore.

The Wyroman International Pension Fund includes a $65 million fixed-income portfolio managed by Susan Evermore, CFA, of Brighton Investors. Evermore is in the process of constructing a binomial interest-rate tree that generates arbitrage-free values for on-the-run Treasury securities. She plans to use the tree to value more complex bonds with embedded options. She starts out by observing that the yield on a one-year Treasury security is 3.50%. She determines in her initial attempt to price the two-year Treasury security that the value derived from the model is higher than the Treasury security's current market price.

After several iterations Evermore determines that the interest rate tree that correctly values the one and two-year Treasury securities has a rate of 4.50% in the lower node at the end of the first year and a rate of 7.0% in the upper node at the end of the first year. She uses this tree to value a two-year, 6% annual coupon bond with a par value of $100 that is callable in one year at $99.50. She determines that an OAS of 50bps is appropriate for this bond.

Evermore also uses the same interest rate tree to price a 2-year 6% coupon bond that is putable in one year, and value the embedded put option. She concludes that if the yield volatility decreases unexpectedly, the value of the putable bond will increase and the value of the embedded put option will also increase, assuming all other inputs are unchanged. She also concludes that the computed OAS for the bond would decrease as the estimated level of yield volatility decreases.

Evermore also uses the interest rate tree to estimate the option-adjusted spreads of two additional callable corporate bonds, as shown in the following figure.

Issuer	Option-Adjusted Spread
AA-rated issuer	53 basis points
BB-rated issuer	−18 basis points

Evermore concludes, based on this information, that the AA-rated issue is undervalued, and the BB-rated issue is overvalued.

At a subsequent meeting with the trustees of the fund, Evermore is asked to explain what a binomial interest rate model is and how it was used to estimate effective duration and effective convexity. Evermore is uncertain of the exact methodology because the actual calculations were done by a junior analyst, but she tries to provide the trustees with a reasonably accurate step-by-step description of the process:

Step 1: Given the bond's current market price, the on-the-run Treasury yield curve, and an assumption about rate volatility, create a binomial interest rate tree.

Step 2: Add 100 basis points to each of the 1-year rates in the interest rate tree to derive a "modified" tree.

Step 3: Compute the price of the bond if yield increases by 100 basis points using this new tree.

Step 4: Repeat Steps 1 through 3 to determine the bond price that results from a 100 basis point decrease in rates.

Step 5: Use these two price estimates, along with the original market price, to calculate effective duration and effective convexity.

Lucas Davenport, a trustee and university finance professor, immediately speaks up to disagree with Evermore. He claims that a more accurate description of the process is as follows:

Step 1: Given the bond's current market price, the Treasury yield curve, and an assumption about rate volatility, create a binomial interest rate tree and calculate the bond's option-adjusted spread (OAS) using the model.

Step 2: Impose a parallel upward shift in the on-the-run Treasury yield curve of 100 basis points.

Step 3: Build a new binomial interest rate tree using the new Treasury yield curve and the original rate volatility assumption.

Step 4: Add the OAS from Step 1 to each of the 1-year rates on the tree to derive a "modified" tree.

Step 5: Compute the price of the bond using this new tree.

Step 6: Repeat Steps 1 through 5 to determine the bond price that results from a 100 basis point decrease in rates.

Step 7: Use these two price estimates, along with the original market price, to calculate effective duration and effective convexity.

At the meeting with the trustees, Evermore also presents the results of her analysis of the effect of changing market volatilities on a 1-year convertible bond issued by Highfour Corporation. Each bond is convertible into 25 shares of Highfour common stock. The bond is also callable at 110 at any time prior to maturity. She concludes that the value of the bond will decrease if either (1) the volatility of returns on Highfour common stock decreases or (2) yield volatility decreases.

Davenport immediately disagrees with her by saying "changes in the volatility of common stock returns will have no effect on the value of the convertible bond, and a decrease in yield volatility will result in an increase in the value of the bond."

25.   The value of the 2-year 6% callable bond today using the interest rate tree is *closest* to:
        A. $95.24.
        B. $101.01.
        C. $102.21.

26.   Is Evermore correct in her analysis of the effect of a change in yield volatility?
        A. Incorrect on the puttable bond only.
        B. Incorrect on the put option only.
        C. Incorrect on both the bond and the option.

27.   Is Evermore correct about the effect of a decrease in estimated level of yield volatility on the computed OAS?
        A. Yes.
        B. No, OAS depends only on credit and liquidity risk and hence would be unchanged.
        C. No, the computed OAS would increase.

28.   Is Evermore correct in her analysis of the relative valuation of the bonds?
        A. Correct on both issues.
        B. Correct on the AA issue only.
        C. Correct on the BB issue only.

29.   Which of the following statements regarding the methodologies for estimating effective duration and convexity is *most accurate*?
        A. Davenport's description is a more accurate depiction of the appropriate methodology than Evermore's.
        B. The two methodologies will result in the same effective duration and convexity estimates only if the same rate volatility assumption is used in each.
        C. The two methodologies will result in the same effective duration and convexity estimates only if the same rate volatility assumption is used in each and the bond's OAS is equal to zero.

30.   For this question, analyze each effect separately. Is Davenport correct in disagreeing with Evermore's conclusions regarding the effect on the value of the convertible bond resulting from a change in volatility?
        A. Davenport is correct on both conclusions.
        B. Davenport is correct on stock return volatility only.
        C. Davenport is correct on yield volatility only.

Questions 31–36 relate to Natalia Berg.

Natalia Berg, CFA, has estimated the key rate durations for several maturities in three of her equally-weighted bond portfolios, as shown in Exhibit 1.

Exhibit 1: Key Rate Durations for Three Fixed-Income Portfolios

Key Rate Maturity	Portfolio 1	Portfolio 2	Portfolio 3
2-year	2.45	0.35	1.26
5-year	0.20	0.40	1.27
10-year	0.15	4.00	1.23
20-year	2.20	0.25	1.24
Total	5.00	5.00	5.00

At a fixed-income conference in London, Berg hears a presentation by a university professor on the increasing use of the swap rate curve as a benchmark instead of the government bond yield curve. When Berg returns from the conference, she realizes she has left her notes from the presentation on the airplane. However, she is very interested in learning more about whether she should consider using the swap rate curve in her work.

As she tries to reconstruct what was said at the conference, she writes down two statements about the swap rate curve:

Statement 1:   The swap rate curve typically has yield quotes at more maturities than government bond markets have.

Statement 2:   Retail banks are more likely to use the government spot curve as a benchmark as they have minimal exposure to swap markets.

Berg also obtains information on several bonds issued by Salant Enterprises as shown in Exhibit 2.

Exhibit 2: Selected Information on Salant Enterprises Bonds

Label	A	B	C
Bond type	Callable	Putable	Extendible
Option type	European	European	
Exercise date	2 years	3 years	
Maturity	3 years	4 years	3 years
Extension period	-	-	1 year
Coupon Rate	5%	5%	5%
Value	$99.50	$100.69	

Berg determines that to obtain an accurate estimate of the effective duration and effective convexity of a callable bond using a binomial model, the specified change in yield (i.e., Δy) must be equal to the OAS.

Berg also observes that the current Treasury bond yield curve is upward sloping. Based on this observation, Berg forecasts that short-term interest rates will increase.

31. If the spot-rate curve experiences a parallel downward shift of 50 basis points:
    A. all three portfolios will experience the same price performance.
    B. Portfolio 1 will experience the best price performance.
    C. Portfolio 3 will experience the best price performance.

32. If the 5- and 10-year key rates increase by 20 basis points, but the 2- and 20-year key rates remain unchanged:
    A. all three portfolios will experience the same price performance.
    B. Portfolio 1 will experience the best price performance.
    C. Portfolio 2 will experience the best price performance.

33. Are the two observations Berg records after the fixed income conference accurate?
    A. Both statements are accurate.
    B. Only Statement 1 is accurate.
    C. Only Statement 2 is accurate.

34. Based on the information in Exhibit 2, the value of Bond C is *most likely:*
    A. $99.50.
    B. between $99.50 and $100.69.
    C. $100.69.

35. Is Berg correct about the specified change in yield needed to obtain an accurate estimate of the effective duration and effective convexity of a callable bond using a binomial model?
    A. No, because the specified change in yield must be larger than the option-adjusted spread (OAS).
    B. No, because the specified change in yield must be smaller than the OAS.
    C. No, because the specified change in yield can be larger than, smaller than, or equal to the OAS.

36. Is Berg's short-term interest rate forecast consistent with the pure expectations theory and the liquidity premium theory?
    A. Consistent with both theories.
    B. Consistent with the pure expectations theory only.
    C. Consistent with the liquidity premium theory only.

Questions 37–42 relate to Jonathan Adams.

Jonathan Adams, CFA, is doing some scenario analysis on forward contracts. The process involves pricing the forward contracts and then estimating their values based on likely scenarios provided by the firm's forecasting and strategy departments. The forward contracts with which Adams is most concerned are those on fixed income securities, interest rates, and currencies.

The first contract he needs to price is a 270-day forward on a $100 par Treasury bond with ten years remaining to maturity. The bond has a 5% coupon rate, has just made a coupon payment, and will make its next two coupon payments in 182 days and in 365 days. It is currently selling for 98.25. The risk-free rate is 4%. Adams is also analyzing forward rate agreements (FRAs).

The LIBOR spot curve is as follows:

30-day: 3.12%	60-day: 3.32%	90-day: 3.52%
120-day: 3.72%	150-day: 3.92%	180-day: 4.12%

Adams determines the price of a 2×5 FRA from the spot yield curve using the following calculation:

$$\left[\frac{1+0.0352\left(\frac{90}{360}\right)}{1+0.0332\left(\frac{60}{360}\right)}-1\right]\left(\frac{360}{90}\right)$$

Finally, Adams wants to price a currency forward on euros and Swiss francs. The euro spot rate is $1.1854 and the Swiss franc spot rate is $1.0210. The dollar risk-free rate is 3%, the euro risk-free rate is 4%, and the Swiss risk-free rate is 2%.

37. The no-arbitrage price for the forward contract on the Treasury bond is *closest* to:
    A. 98.54.
    B. 98.57.
    C. 98.62.

38. If the Treasury bond price decreases to 98.11 (including accrued interest) over the next 60 days, the value of a short position in the 270-day forward contract on a $10 million bond is *closest* to:
    A. $76,500.
    B. $76,800.
    C. $78,000.

39.   How many of the following terms are correct in the calculation of the FRA price: 0.0352, 0.0332, 60/360, 90/360?
      A. Two.
      B. Three.
      C. Four.

40.   After 30 days, Adams wants to value a $10 million short position in the 2×5 FRA. The 90-day forward rate in 30 days is now 4.14%, and the original price of the FRA was 4.30%. 120-day LIBOR has changed to 3.92%. The current value of the $10 million FRA to the short position under this scenario is *closest* to:
      A. $15,794.
      B. $3,948.
      C. –$15,794.

41.   The no-arbitrage price for a 1-year forward contract on euros is *closest* to:
      A. $1.1401.
      B. $1.1740.
      C. $1.1969.

42.   If the Swiss franc is trading at a 1-year forward premium of $0.0301, the *most appropriate* arbitrage transaction would entail:
      A. borrowing the Swiss franc.
      B. lending the Swiss franc.
      C. buying the Swiss franc in the forward market.

Questions 43–48 relate to GD Barton, Inc.

GD Barton, Inc., (GD) is a large multinational company headquartered in the U.S. Through a series of subsidiaries around the world, GD operates in multiple sectors including retail, engineering, health care, and reinsurance. The company has a large treasury and risk management arm based in the U.K., and all responsibility for cash and risk management is centered in this London office.

Recently, a major breach of controls was discovered in the office; a junior employee had bypassed internal controls and opened large positions in several derivative contracts. The employee in question was only authorized to use such contracts for hedging purposes, but the company fears that it may have exposure in excess of $100 million on unhedged positions opened by the employee.

Following an internal investigation, Miguel Hernandez, CFA, has been assigned to review and value several contracts that were flagged during the audit.

Details of three of the contracts, confirmed as being unauthorized (i.e., not used for hedging), have been summarized in an email to Hernandez. Extracts of this email are shown in Exhibit 1.

Exhibit 1: Unauthorized Contracts

Contract 1 – Interest Rate Swap

Term:	2 years
Fixed rate:	3.50%
Settlement:	semi-annual (30/360)
Opened:	180 days ago (first settlement just occurred)
Notional:	$150 million
Position:	Fixed-rate payer
Current term structure:	$LIBOR_{180}$ 2.90%, $LIBOR_{360}$ 3.00%, $LIBOR_{540}$ 3.20%

Contract 2 – Equity Swap

Term:	1 year
Fixed rate:	3.70%
Equity index at last settlement:	1926.64
Settlement:	quarterly (30/360)
Opened:	120 days ago
Notional:	$250 million
Position:	Fixed-rate payer
Current term structure:	$LIBOR_{60}$ 2.70%, $LIBOR_{150}$ 2.85%, $LIBOR_{240}$ 2.95%
Current equity index:	1892.23

Contract 3 – Forward Rate Agreement

Contract:	90-day forward rate on 180-day LIBOR (i.e., 3 × 9 FRA)
Price:	3.8%
Opened:	50 days ago
Notional:	$125 million
Current term structure:	**NOTE:** Which LIBOR rates do you require here?

In addition to the confirmed breaches in Exhibit 1, the investigation also discovered a number of transactions related to credit default swaps (CDS). Hernandez has received an email from a member of the investigative team asking for his advice on GD's exposure as a result of these transactions. An extract from that email is shown in Exhibit 2.

Exhibit 2: Credit Default Swaps

"…without authorization, the employee sold $350 million notional of protection on the iTraxx Main[1] index, a position that remains open. GD has no exposure to debt instruments issued by any of the constituents of the index, and there appear to be no other transactions in any index CDS. There were, however, two other transactions in single-name CDS. On behalf of GD, the employee purchased $2.5 million of notional exposure on a single-name CDS protection on POPRT corporation debt and $3.5 million of notional exposure on TRTRS corporation debt.

POPRT is a constituent of the iTraxx Main index, but TRTRS is not. Since the single-name positions were opened, the credit spread on both POPRT and TRTRS has increased by over 250 basis points."

1   The iTraxx Main is an equally weighted CDS index consisting of 125 investment-grade entities.

Hernandez thinks the TRTRS transaction may actually be a legitimate contract undertaken by another employee of the firm, Dan Eagen. Hernandez recently spoke informally with Eagen, who stated that he believes that "TRTRS is currently preparing to undergo a leveraged buy-out at a significant premium to current market value." Eagen's intention was to make a gain by taking a position in the CDS and TRTRS stock.

43.   The value to GD of contract 1, as described in Exhibit 1, is *closest* to:
  A. −$8,400,000.
  B. −$2,990,000.
  C. −$770,000.

44.   The value to GD of contract 2, as described in Exhibit 1, is *closest* to:
  A. $2,510,000.
  B. −$2,510,000.
  C. −$6,500,000.

45.   Which of the following current LIBOR rates would Hernandez *most likely* require in order to value contract 3?
  A. 90-day LIBOR and 180-day LIBOR.
  B. 40-day LIBOR and 130-day LIBOR.
  C. 40-day LIBOR and 220-day LIBOR.

46.   As a result of the transactions described in Exhibit 2, GD's current net notional exposure to POPRT debt is *closest* to:
  A. $3.5 million.
  B. $0.3 million.
  C. zero.

47. If GD were to enter into an offsetting contract to hedge its exposure to TRTRS under the CDS described in Exhibit 2, this would *most likely* result in:
    A. a loss on the CDS position.
    B. a gain on the CDS position.
    C. no gain or loss on the CDS position.

48. Eagen is *most likely* to take advantage of his prediction for TRTRS by:
    A. purchasing CDS protection and selling the underlying stock.
    B. selling CDS protection and buying the underlying stock.
    C. buying CDS protection and buying the underlying stock.

Questions 49–54 relate to Jeff Markgraf, CFA.

Jeff Markgraf, CFA, is the managing director at Alpha Alternatives LLP. Markgraf has a successful track record of investing in real estate for his institutional clients. Markgraf is seeking to diversify his scope and is looking into investing in commodities and in private equity.

Markgraf reaches out to his college friend, Bill Small, who manages a private equity fund specializing in leveraged buyouts. Markgraf asks Small about ways in which private equity funds add value to their portfolio investments.

Markgraf concludes that futures contracts offer the best mechanism for him to gain exposure to the commodities market. He seeks to develop further understanding of the components of total return of a portfolio invested in commodity futures.

Markgraf is intrigued by the use of swaps to gain exposure to commodities. Upon investigation, Markgraf discovers that a swap (the "T-Z swap") is available from Alpha's brokers that has a variable payment based on the difference in price between two commodities.

Markgraf observes that cattle futures prices are greater than the spot prices while the corn futures prices are less than the spot prices. Markgraf also read that futures prices may be influenced by weather.

Markgraf wants some exposure to precious metals and expects to use silver futures contracts to accomplish this. Markgraf will roll over maturing contracts to the next shortest available contract. Markgraf believes that silver will help diversify his overall portfolio, especially since silver futures prices are less than silver spot prices.

49. Which of the following would be *least* appropriate as a part of Small's response to Markgraf's question?
    A. Optimizing financial leverage.
    B. Creating operational improvement.
    C. Incentivizing the general partner.

50. Relative to seasonality in the demand for natural gas, seasonality in demand for oil is *most likely* to be:
    A. about the same.
    B. greater.
    C. lower.

51. Early frost in some parts of the country has resulted in damage to corn crops and a temporary shortage in the supply of corn. Under the theory of storage, relative to the spot prices, futures prices are *most likely* to be:
    A. the same.
    B. higher.
    C. lower.

52. The "T-Z swap" that is available from Alpha's brokers is *most likely* a(n):
    A. excess return swap.
    B. basis swap.
    C. total return swap.

53. Which theory is *least likely* to explain the pricing relationship in the cattle futures market?
    A. The insurance perspective.
    B. The hedging pressure hypothesis.
    C. The theory of storage.

54. Markgraf's position in silver futures contracts is *most likely* to produce a roll return that is:
    A. zero.
    B. negative.
    C. positive.

Questions 55–60 relate to Terry Holt and Bill McGuire.

Terry Holt, CFA, is an investment consultant that advises several institutional clients, including pension funds and endowments. Holt is evaluating the performance of Magna Alpha fund. He obtains the fund's active weights and expected returns relative to the benchmark as shown in Exhibit 1.

Exhibit 1: Magna Alpha Fund

Asset Class (i)	Portfolio Return $E(R_{Pi})$	Benchmark Return $E(R_{Bi})$	Active Weight
Equities	13%	12%	10%
Bonds	7%	5%	−11%
Cash	3%	3%	1%

Bill McGuire, Holt's supervisor, makes the following statements:

1.   The optimal risky portfolio for any investor is the one with the highest Sharpe ratio irrespective of the risk tolerance of the client.

2.   The Sharpe ratio would be the same as the information ratio for a market-neutral long-short equity fund that has the risk-free asset as the portfolio's benchmark.

Holt then obtains data on three active funds specializing in commodities investing. Exhibit 2 presents data on these funds.

Exhibit 2: Fund Data

Fund	Prime	Redux	Optimus
Expected active return	2.40%	1.25%	1.28%
Active risk	6%	5%	4%

McGuire recommends that Holt investigate two other funds, run by active managers A and B, as well. Exhibit 3 shows the relevant information.

Exhibit 3: Active Managers A and B

Manager A: Invests in stocks and makes bets annually. Has an information coefficient of 0.20 and transfer coefficient of 0.4.

Manager B: Unconstrained optimization involving monthly bets on market timing (rotation between equity and cash). Manager B is correct 55% of the time.

©2017 Kaplan, Inc.

Holt mentions to McGuire that one has to be careful about actively managed funds that are actually closet index funds. These funds tend to be characterized by very low active risk, low information ratio, and a Sharpe ratio that is almost the same as the Sharpe ratio for the fund's benchmark.

55. Using the information in Exhibit 1, the expected active return from asset allocation for Magna Alpha fund is *closest* to:
A. 0.68%.
B. 1.25%.
C. 1.93%.

56. Regarding McGuire's statements:
A. both statements are correct.
B. only one statement is correct.
C. neither statement is correct.

57. Which component of the fundamental law of active management captures the relationship between risk-adjusted active weights and risk-adjusted forecasted returns?
A. Transfer coefficient.
B. Information coefficient.
C. Information ratio.

58. Using the information in Exhibit 2, which fund would be *most* suitable for an investor with a constraint of maximum active risk of 5%?
A. Prime.
B. Redux.
C. Optimus.

59. To achieve the same information ratio as Manager B, the number of stocks that Manager A must make independent bets on is *closest* to:
A. 14.
B. 19.
C. 22.

60. Holt is *least likely* to be correct about which factor as an indicator of a closet index fund?
A. Low active risk.
B. Low information ratio.
C. Same Sharpe ratio as the benchmark.

End of Morning Session

EXAM 3
AFTERNOON SESSION

Question	Topic	Minutes (Points)
61 to 66	Ethics	18
67 to 72	Ethics	18
73 to 78	Economics	18
79 to 84	Financial Reporting and Analysis	18
85 to 90	Financial Reporting and Analysis	18
91 to 96	Financial Reporting and Analysis	18
97 to 102	Corporate Finance	18
103 to 108	Corporate Finance	18
109 to 114	Equity	18
115 to 120	Equity	18

Test Answers

61.	(A)	(B)	(C)		101.	(A)	(B)	(C)
62.	(A)	(B)	(C)		102.	(A)	(B)	(C)
63.	(A)	(B)	(C)		103.	(A)	(B)	(C)
64.	(A)	(B)	(C)		104.	(A)	(B)	(C)
65.	(A)	(B)	(C)		105.	(A)	(B)	(C)
66.	(A)	(B)	(C)		106.	(A)	(B)	(C)
67.	(A)	(B)	(C)		107.	(A)	(B)	(C)
68.	(A)	(B)	(C)		108.	(A)	(B)	(C)
69.	(A)	(B)	(C)		109.	(A)	(B)	(C)
70.	(A)	(B)	(C)		110.	(A)	(B)	(C)
71.	(A)	(B)	(C)		111.	(A)	(B)	(C)
72.	(A)	(B)	(C)		112.	(A)	(B)	(C)
73.	(A)	(B)	(C)		113.	(A)	(B)	(C)
74.	(A)	(B)	(C)		114.	(A)	(B)	(C)
75.	(A)	(B)	(C)		115.	(A)	(B)	(C)
76.	(A)	(B)	(C)		116.	(A)	(B)	(C)
77.	(A)	(B)	(C)		117.	(A)	(B)	(C)
78.	(A)	(B)	(C)		118.	(A)	(B)	(C)
79.	(A)	(B)	(C)		119.	(A)	(B)	(C)
80.	(A)	(B)	(C)		120.	(A)	(B)	(C)
81.	(A)	(B)	(C)					
82.	(A)	(B)	(C)					
83.	(A)	(B)	(C)					
84.	(A)	(B)	(C)					
85.	(A)	(B)	(C)					
86.	(A)	(B)	(C)					
87.	(A)	(B)	(C)					
88.	(A)	(B)	(C)					
89.	(A)	(B)	(C)					
90.	(A)	(B)	(C)					
91.	(A)	(B)	(C)					
92.	(A)	(B)	(C)					
93.	(A)	(B)	(C)					
94.	(A)	(B)	(C)					
95.	(A)	(B)	(C)					
96.	(A)	(B)	(C)					
97.	(A)	(B)	(C)					
98.	(A)	(B)	(C)					
99.	(A)	(B)	(C)					
100.	(A)	(B)	(C)					

Exam 3
Afternoon Session

Questions 61–66 relate to Mike Zonding.

Mike Zonding, CFA, is conducting a background check on CFA candidate Annie Cooken, a freshly minted MBA who applied for a stock-analysis job at his firm, Khasko Financial. Zonding does not like to hire anyone who does not adhere to the Code and Standards' professional conduct requirements.

The background check reveals the following:

(i)   While doing a full-time, unpaid internship at Kale Investments, Cooken was reprimanded for working a 30-hour-a-week night job as a waitress.

(ii) As an intern at Lammar Corp., Cooken was fired after revealing to the FBI that one of the principals was embezzling from the firm's clients.

(iii) Cooken performed 40 hours of community service in relation to a conviction on a misdemeanor drug possession charge when she was 16 years old.

(iv) On her resume, Cooken writes, "Recently passed Level II of the CFA exam, a test that measures candidates' knowledge of finance and investing."

During the interview, Zonding asks Cooken several questions on ethics-related issues, including questions about the role of a fiduciary and Standard III(E) Preservation of Confidentiality. He asks her about her internship at Kale Investments, specifically about the working hours. Cooken replies that the internship turned out to require more time than she originally planned, up to 65 hours per week.

Zonding subsequently hires Cooken and functions as her supervisor. On her third day at the money management boutique firm, portfolio manager Steven Clarrison hands her a report on Mocline Tobacco and tells her to revise the report to reflect a buy rating. Cooken is uncomfortable about revising the report.

To supplement the meager income from her entry-level stock-analysis job, Cooken looks for part-time work. She is offered a position working three hours each Friday and Saturday night tending bar at a sports bar and grill downtown. Cooken does not tell her employer about the job.

During her first week, Cooken has lunch with former MBA classmates, including Taira Basch, CFA, who works for the compliance officer at a large investment bank in town. Basch arrives late, explaining, "What a day, it's only noon and already I have worked on the following requests:

1. A federal regulator called and wanted information on potentially illegal activities related to one of the firm's key clients.

2. A rival company's employee wanted information regarding employment opportunities at the firm.

3. A potential client contacted an employee and wanted detailed performance records of client accounts so he can decide whether to invest with the firm."

Zonding appeared on a financial news network program to discuss Orlando Stores, a discount clothing chain. Khasko's investment banking department has completed transactions for Orlando in the past 12 months and currently is working with Orlando to conduct a secondary offering; Khasko has a policy in place that separates the activities of investment banking and research.

At the beginning of the interview, Zonding disclosed that Khasko has an investment banking relationship with Orlando Stores and that his wife holds Orlando shares. He also stated that his research is available on Khasko's website, although he forgot to comment on the risk profile and suitability of investing in Orlando shares.

The host asked Zonding to comment on Khasko's outlook for the stock, given Orlando's recently announced expansion plans. Zonding stated that he officially had a 12-month buy rating on the stock, though he is concerned about potential oversaturation in some of Orlando's markets. When asked about his conviction level in his buy rating, Zonding replied that if there is a sharp share price increase next week when earnings are released, viewers should take the opportunity to sell shares since there are always long-term risks inherent in expansion. Zonding also mentioned that he did not want to be negative about Orlando shares since Orlando is a valuable client of Khasko.

61.   In the context of the Code and Standards, which of the items from the background check would *most likely* indicate that Zonding should not have hired Cooken?
       A. Item i.
       B. Item ii.
       C. Item iii.

62.   Which of the following statements provides the *least appropriate* justification for Cooken's caution about revising the report on Mocline Tobacco?
       A. Cooken knows next to nothing about Mocline stock.
       B. Cooken's uncle, George Whates, is the CFO of Mocline.
       C. In college, Cooken worked for Mocline but never declared the income on her taxes.

63.   By not telling Zonding about the bartending position, Cooken has *most likely* violated:
       A. no Standards.
       B. Standard IV(B) Additional Compensation Arrangements.
       C. Standard IV(A) Loyalty (to employer) and Standard IV(B) Additional Compensation Arrangements.

64.   Which of the requests, if fulfilled, is *most likely* to place Basch in violation of Standard III(E) Preservation of Confidentiality?
       A. Request 1.
       B. Request 2.
       C. Request 3.

65.   Was Zonding in compliance with regard to CFA Institute Research Objectivity Standards (ROS) recommendations on public appearances?
       A. No, because Zonding neglected to discuss Orlando's suitability as an investment.
       B. No, because Zonding failed to disclose Orlando's plans to announce a secondary offering in the near future.
       C. Yes, because Zonding disclosed his firm's relationship with Orlando, his wife's ownership of the shares, and the availability of his Orlando report.

66.   Did Zonding follow the recommended procedures of the CFA Institute Research Objectivity Standards (ROS) with regard to Khasko's rating of Orlando Stores?
       A. No.
       B. Yes, because Zonding stated his rating recommendation and his time horizon on his rating.
       C. Yes, because Zonding discussed his concerns about Orlando's expansion plans, so it was appropriate to recommend selling the shares to capitalize on near-term price increases.

Questions 67–72 relate to Andrea Vrbenic.

Andrea Vrbenic, CFA, was recently promoted to supervisory analyst at a boutique investment bank that specializes in managing initial public offerings for firms in the biotech industry. The firm also manages assets for high net worth clients. Vrbenic will report to Tom Sheffield, a senior manager and director in the investment banking department at the firm.

Wilhelmina Scott, CFA, who also reports to Sheffield, will be Vrbenic's supervisory analyst counterpart on the investment management side. Vrbenic will assume responsibility for all research prepared on subject companies that engage in investment banking business with the firm, while Scott will continue to supervise research covering a small group of companies that constitutes the firm's approved list.

Sheffield assigns Vrbenic the task of ensuring compliance with CFA Institute Research Objectivity Standards that cover herself, Scott, and other analysts at the firm. Sheffield recognizes that this policy is comprehensive and must apply not only to analysts on the investment banking side, but also to research analysts on the investment management side.

Vrbenic soon realizes that investment bankers at the firm use her research reports to help attract new investment banking clients. Vrbenic also learns that coverage of subject companies on the investment banking side will move over to the investment management side if these companies decline to continue an investment banking relationship. Sheffield tells Vrbenic that "the companies are golden while they have an investment banking relationship with us, but may lose their luster after they move to the investment management research side."

Vrbenic and Scott each receive a salary and two bonuses—one based on the investment banking division performance and one based on investment management division performance during a quarter. Sheffield attests annually that the firm has followed CFA Institute Research Objectivity Standards (ROS).

Sheffield attends a meeting with Vrbenic and her analysts. During the meeting, Jamie Verhallen, a research analyst reporting to Vrbenic, presents an overview of a biotech firm that will soon issue additional equity through their investment bank. While Verhallen recommends a favorable rating for the stock, Vrbenic recommends a higher rating due to the investment banking relationship with the firm. Verhallen refuses to sign the report with the changes that Vrbenic recommended during the meeting. Vrbenic transfers responsibility for research on the company to herself and issues the report with a higher rating.

Later that week, Verhallen tells Vrbenic of her father's impending kidney transplant. Verhallen's father has limited income, and Verhallen has agreed to assist with the medical expenses. Verhallen has decided to sell her holdings of the biotech company to raise cash for the operation.

Vrbenic appears on a financial news TV channel that same week describing the positive attributes of the biotech company. To protect her privacy, Vrbenic does not disclose her position in the securities. Vrbenic suggests that members of the audience must become clients prior to receiving any research from her firm.

67.   Under the Research Objectivity Standards, Vrbenic's firm:
        A. may permit Sheffield to supervise investment management research.
        B. must segregate analysts reporting to Scott from the investment banking department.
        C. must prevent research analysts from covering companies that have an investment banking relationship with the firm.

68.   According to the Research Objectivity Standards, Verhallen may sell her stock in the biotech company only if she:
        A. disagrees with a recommendation.
        B. has encountered a financial hardship.
        C. has encountered a financial hardship and disagrees with the recommendation.

69.   Vrbenic's recommendation to raise the biotech company's rating solely based on investment banking relationship violates the Research Objectivity Standards:
        A. only because the analyst reports to her.
        B. because the standards require a reasonable basis for research recommendations.
        C. because the standards require that firms refuse to provide research recommendations when there is any conflict of interest.

70.   Under the Research Objectivity Standards, an acceptable compensation system for research analysts is *most likely* to:
        A. have an incentive component.
        B. align analyst compensation with the accuracy of research at the end of every quarter.
        C. be based on measurable criteria for quality of research.

71. Vrbenic has violated the Research Objectivity Standards through her public appearance by failing to:
    A. disclose her position in the securities but not by failing to provide a copy of the research that she discussed.
    B. provide a copy of the research that she discussed but not by failing to disclose her position in the securities.
    C. disclose her position in the securities as well as by failing to provide a copy of the research that she discussed.

72. To be consistent with the Research Objectivity Standards, Vrbenic's firm is required to issue research reports:
    A. at least annually.
    B. at least quarterly.
    C. on a regular and timely basis.

Questions 73–78 relate to Robert Williams.

Robert Williams is a junior analyst at Anderson Brothers, a large Wall Street brokerage firm. He reports to Will McDonald, the chief economist for Anderson Brothers. McDonald provides economic research, forecasts, and interpretation of economic data to all of Anderson's investment departments, as well as to the firm's clients. McDonald has asked Williams to analyze economic trends in the country of Bundovia. Bundovia has strict capital controls limiting the flow of capital into and out of the country. The currency of Bundovia is the bunco (BUN).

One of Bundovia's major exports is high quality carpets. However, human rights activists have recently begun to complain about child labor practices among Bundovian carpet manufacturers, and this has resulted in negative publicity for the industry. Concerned about the impact on Bundovian exports, the Bundovian government banned child labor and provided oversight authority to the Bundovian carpet manufacturer's association. The Bundovian carpet manufacturer's association is an independent, membership-based organization. Most large carpet manufacturers in Bundovia are members.

McDonald believes that the Bundovian economy is experiencing a hyper-inflationary environment and that the Bundovian government is poised to follow a restrictive monetary and fiscal policy to combat high inflation.

In analyzing Bundovian economic performance, Williams notices that Bundovia has been able to grow rapidly in the past few years and has reached a steady state of growth. Compared to its trading partners, Bundovia has low capital-to-labor ratios; this situation is expected to continue.

Williams is also permitted to trade in the forex markets when he sees an opportunity to make a profit. Williams' bank quotes the following exchange rates to him:

- USD/GBP = 2.0010 – 20
- USD/SFr = 0.8550 – 60

Williams asks the bank for a GBP/SFr cross rate.

Williams receives the following forward rate quotes from the same bank:

- 30-day forward rate: USD/GBP = 2.0045 – 55
- 60-day forward rate: USD/GBP = 2.0075 – 85

Williams decides to go long 1 million GBP (and short USD) in the 60-day forward contract.

30 days after the initiation of the USD/GBP forward contract, the exchange rate and interest rates are as follows:

Quotes	USD/GBP
Spot	2.0086/2.0089
30-day forward	+7.6/+8
60-day forward	+8.7/+9.1
90-day forward	+9.2/+9.8

Interest Rates	USD	GBP
30 day	4.00%	3.00%
60 day	4.25%	3.00%
90 day	4.29%	3.00%

Williams spots another potential arbitrage opportunity in the foreign exchange markets. The current spot rate is $2.00 per BUN. The Bundovian risk-free interest rate is 3%, the one-year forward rate is $2.10 per BUN, and the U.S. risk-free rate is 5%.

73. To carry out the objectives of the Bundovian child labor regulations, the *most important* requirement is that the Bundovian carpet manufacturer's association should:
    A. have the ability to effectively supervise the industry practices.
    B. be properly supervised by the government.
    C. be able to impose sanctions.

74. Based on McDonald's beliefs about Bundovian government monetary and fiscal policies, under the Mundell-Fleming model the Bunco is *most likely* expected to:
    A. depreciate.
    B. appreciate.
    C. remain unchanged in value.

75. Under neoclassical growth theory, the Bundovian growth rate is *most likely* to increase due to:
    A. capital deepening.
    B. technological growth.
    C. either capital deepening or technological growth.

76. Based on the bank's USD/GBP and USD/SFr quotes, Williams's bank is *most likely* to quote a cross rate of:
    A. GBP/SFr = 0.4271 – 78.
    B. GBP/SFr = 2.3375 – 14.
    C. GBP/SFr = 0.4273 – 76.

77.   30 days after initiation of the USD/GBP forward contract, the mark-to-market value of the contract is *closest* to:
        A. USD 860.
        B. USD 1,195.
        C. USD 2,190.

78.   The maximum profit available from covered interest arbitrage in the USD/BUN market by borrowing $1,000 or the BUN equivalent is *closest* to:
        A. $19.05.
        B. $31.50.
        C. $72.50.

Questions 79–84 relate to High Plains Tubular.

High Plains Tubular Company is a leading manufacturer and distributor of quality steel products used in energy, industrial, and automotive applications worldwide.

The U.S. steel industry has been challenged in recent years by competition from foreign producers located primarily in Asia. U.S. producers are experiencing declining margins as labor costs continue to increase. In addition, most U.S. steel mills are technologically inferior to those of foreign competitors and U.S. producers have significant unresolved issues related to complying with environmental protection laws.

High Plains is not immune from the problems of the industry and is currently in technical default under its bond covenants. The default is a result of the firm's failure to meet certain coverage and turnover ratios. High Plains has argued that this is largely due to the favorable credit terms it has given to its customers (major customers are given 90 days to settle) in order to gain market share.

Earlier this year, High Plains and its bondholders entered into an agreement that will give High Plains time to come into compliance with the covenants. If High Plains is not in compliance by year-end, the bondholders can immediately accelerate the maturity date of the bonds. In that case, High Plains would have no choice but to file for bankruptcy.

High Plains follows U.S. GAAP. For the year ended 2014, High Plains received an unqualified opinion from its independent auditor. However, the auditor's opinion included an explanatory paragraph about High Plains' inability to continue as a going concern in the event its bonds remain in technical default.

At the end of 2014, High Plains' Chief Executive Officer (CEO) and Chief Financial Officer (CFO) filed the certifications required by the Securities and Exchange Commission (SEC).

Jon Farnsworth, CFA, is reviewing High Plains' financial accounts to gain a better understanding of credit risk of the company. The first element that causes Farnsworth some concern is the cash flow statement. This is shown in Exhibit 1.

Exhibit 1: Cash Flow Statement

High Plains Tubular Cash Flow Statement		
	Year ended December 31,	
in thousands	**2014**	**2013**
Net income	$158,177	$121,164
Depreciation expense	$34,078	$31,295
Deferred taxes	$7,697	$11,407
Receivables	($144,087)	($24,852)
Inventory	($79,710)	($72,777)
Payables	$36,107	$22,455
Cash flow from operations (CFO)	$12,262	$88,692
Cash flow from investing (CFI)	($39,884)	($63,953)
Cash flow from financing	$82,676	$6,056
Change in cash	$55,054	$30,795
Cash flow from financing	$82,676	$6,056
Change in cash	$55,054	$30,795

Exhibit 2: Selected Financial Footnotes

1. During 2014, High Plains' sales increased 27% over 2013. Its sales growth continues to significantly exceed the industry average. Sales are recognized when a firm order is received from the customer, the sales price is fixed and determinable, and collectability is reasonably assured. In limited cases, some product is sold on a bill-and-hold basis provided that the goods are completed, packaged and ready for shipment; such goods are segregated and the risks of ownership and legal title have passed to the customer. Total revenue from such sales amounted to $907.95 million in 2014. (2013: zero.)

2. The cost of inventories is determined using the last-in, first-out (LIFO) method. Had the first-in, first-out (FIFO) method been used, inventories would have been $152 million and $143 million higher as of December 31, 2014 and 2013, respectively.

3. Effective January 1, 2014, High Plains changed its depreciation method from the double-declining balance method to the straight-line method in order to be more comparable with the accounting practices of other firms within its industry. The change was not retroactively applied and only affects assets that were acquired on or after January 1, 2014.

4. High Plains made the following discretionary expenditures for maintenance and repair of plant and equipment, and for advertising and marketing:

in millions	2014	2013	2012
Maintenance and repairs	$180	$184	$218
Advertising and marketing	$94	$108	$150

5. During the fiscal year ended December 31, 2014, High Plains sold $50 million of its accounts receivable to a third party.

6. High Plains conducts some of its operations in facilities leased under noncancelable finance (capital) leases. Certain leases include renewal options with provisions for increased lease payments during the renewal term.

7. High Plains reclassified $2.9 million of inventory as other assets in 2014. This material had been reported within inventory as work-in-progress in 2013.

After reviewing the cash flow statement and footnotes, Farnsworth analyzes the impact of the bill and hold sales outlined in Exhibit 1 using the assumptions shown in Exhibit 3.

Exhibit 3: Bill-and-Hold Analysis

High Plains EBT margin	5.1%
Average tax rate	28%

79. Which of the following statements regarding High Plains' cash flow quality is *least* accurate?
    A. The transaction described in footnote 5 of Exhibit 2 would have increased cash flow from operations (CFO) in 2014 but decreased the quality of cash flow in 2014.
    B. The decrease in accounts payable in 2013 increased the quality of cash flow as High Plains is paying off suppliers more rapidly.
    C. The divergence between net income and cash flow from operations (CFO) may be an indication of earnings manipulation.

80. What is the *most likely* effect of High Plains' revenue recognition policy on net income and inventory turnover?
    A. Both net income and inventory turnover are overstated.
    B. Only net income is overstated.
    C. Only inventory turnover is overstated.

81. Applying the assumptions in Exhibit 3 to the relevant disclosures given in Exhibits 1 and 2, Farnsworth is *most likely* to conclude that bill-and-hold sales contributed:
    A. more than 20% of net income in 2014.
    B. approximately 10% of net income in 2014.
    C. less than 10% of net income in 2014.

82. Using only the information found in Exhibit 1 and Exhibit 2, which of the following is *most* indicative of lower earnings quality?
    A. High Plains' discretionary expenses.
    B. The change in High Plains' depreciation method.
    C. High Plains' inventory cost flow assumption.

83. Which of the accounting treatments described in footnotes 6 and 7 of Exhibit 2 is *likely* to lower High Plains' financial reporting quality?
    A. Both treatments lower financial reporting quality.
    B. Only the treatment in footnote 6 lowers financial reporting quality.
    C. Only the treatment in footnote 7 lowers financial reporting quality.

84. Which of the following statements about High Plains' financial reporting quality is *least* accurate?
    A. High Plains may have manipulated earnings due to the risk of default.
    B. High Plains' extreme revenue growth will likely revert back to normal levels over time.
    C. Due to High Plains' lengthy credit terms for customers, analysts should place a higher weighting on the accruals-based element of earnings rather than the cash-based element.

Questions 85–90 relate to Stanley Bostwick.

Stanley Bostwick, CFA, is a business services industry analyst with Mortonworld Financial. Currently, his attention is focused on the 20X8 financial statements of Global Oilfield Supply, particularly the footnote disclosures related to the company's employee benefit plans. Bostwick would like to analyze the effect on the reported results of changes in assumptions the company used to estimate the projected benefit obligation (PBO) and net pension cost. But first, Bostwick must familiarize himself with the differences in the accounting for defined contribution and defined benefit pension plans.

Global Oilfield's financial statements are prepared in accordance with International Financial Reporting Standards (IFRS). Excerpts from the company's annual report are shown in the following exhibits.

Exhibit 1: Reconciliation of Projected Benefit Obligation

(in thousands)	20X8	20X7	20X6
Change in projected benefit obligation:			
Benefit obligation at beginning of year	€64,230	€50,534	€39,132
Service cost	8,091	8,038	6,607
Interest cost	4,335	3,158	2,641
Actuarial loss (gain)	(1,932)	5,034	4,590
Benefits paid	(3,824)	(2,534)	(2,436)
Projected benefit obligation at end of year	€70,900	€64,230	€50,534

Exhibit 2: Reconciliation of Fair Value of Plan Assets

(in thousands)	20X8	20X7	20X6
Change in plan assets:			
Fair value of plan assets at beginning of year	€65,164	€44,296	€35,796
Actual return on plan assets	7,084	9,916	(1,868)
Employer contributions	5,000	13,486	12,804
Benefits paid	(3,824)	(2,534)	(2,436)
Fair value of plan assets at end of year	€73,424	€65,164	€44,296

Exhibit 3: Reported Pension Expense

(in thousands)	20X8	20X7	20X6
Service cost	€8,091	€8,038	€6,607
Net interest cost (income)	(63)	390	225
Pension expense	€8,028	€8,428	€6,832

Exhibit 4: Weighted Average Pension Assumptions

	20X8	20X7	20X6
Discount rate	6.75%	6.25%	6.75%
Rate of compensation growth	5.00%	5.00%	5.00%

85. If Global Oilfield's retirement plan is a defined contribution arrangement, which of the following statements would be the *most* correct?
    A. Pension expense and the cash funding amount would be the same.
    B. The potential gains or losses from the assets contributed to the plan are borne by the firm.
    C. The firm would report the difference in the benefit obligation and the plan assets on the balance sheet.

86. If Global Oilfield were to adopt U.S. pension accounting standards, what adjustment, if any, is necessary to its balance sheet at the end of 20X8 assuming no taxes?
    A. Decrease assets by €7,222, decrease liabilities €2,524, and decrease equity by $4,698.
    B Decrease assets by €4,698 and decrease equity by €4,698.
    C. No adjustment is necessary.

87. What was the *most likely* cause of the actuarial gain reported in the reconciliation of the projected benefit obligation for the year ended 20X8?
    A. Increase in the average life expectancy of the participating employees.
    B. Decrease in the expected rate of return.
    C. Increase in the discount rate.

88. Which of the following *best* describes the effects of a decrease in the rate of compensation growth during 20X9 all else equal? Global Oilfield's:
    A. service cost is lower and the projected benefit obligation is higher.
    B. pension expense is lower and the plan assets are higher.
    C. net income is higher and the funded status is higher.

89. As compared to Global Oilfield's reported pension expense, total periodic pension cost expense for the year ended 20X8 is:
    A. higher.
    B. lower.
    C. the same.

90. Assume for this question only that Global reports under U.S. GAAP and that the total periodic pension cost for the year ended 20X8 was €4,250. Ignoring income taxes, which of the following statements *best* describes the adjustment necessary for analyzing Global Oilfield's cash flow statement?
    A. Increase operating cash flow €750 and decrease financing cash flow €750.
    B. Decrease operating cash flow €2,084 and increase investing cash flow €2,084.
    C. Increase operating cash flow €5,000 and decrease financing cash flow €5,000.

Questions 91–96 relate to Valley Airlines.

Jason Bennett is an analyst for Valley Airlines (Valley), a U.S. firm. Valley owns a stake in Southwest Air Cargo (Southwest), also a U.S. firm. The two firms have had a long-standing relationship. The relationship has become even closer because several of Valley's top executives hold seats on Southwest's Board of Directors.

Valley acquired a 45% ownership stake in Southwest on December 31, 2017. Acquisition of the ownership stake cost $9 million and was paid in cash. Valley's stake in Southwest is such that management can account for the investment using either the equity method or the acquisition method. While Valley's management desires to fairly represent the firm's operating results, they have assigned Bennett to assess the impact of each method on reported financial statements.

Immediately prior to the acquisition, Valley's current asset balance and total equity were $96 million and $80 million, respectively. Southwest's current assets and total equity were $32 million and $16 million, respectively.

While analyzing the use of the equity method versus the acquisition method, Bennett calculates the return on assets (ROA) ratio. He arrives at two conclusions:

Conclusion 1:   Compared to the acquisition method, the equity method results in a higher ROA because of the higher net income under the equity method.

Conclusion 2:   Compared to the acquisition method, the equity method results in a higher ROA because of the smaller level of total assets under the equity method.

He also makes the following statements regarding the acquisition method and equity method:

Statement 1:   The framework for determining the method (i.e., equity method or acquisition method) that should be used to account for intercorporate investments is virtually identical under U.S. GAAP and IFRS.

Statement 2:   Both methods report the same net income on the parent's consolidated income statement.

Statement 3:   Both methods report the same equity on the parent's consolidated balance sheet.

In addition, Valley has always wanted to pursue its goal of vertical integration by expanding its scope of operations to include the manufacturing of airline parts for its own airplanes. Therefore, it established a subsidiary, Mountain Air Parts (Mountain), in Switzerland on January 1, 2018. Switzerland was chosen as the location for economic and geographical diversification reasons. Mountain will operate as a self-contained, independent subsidiary. Local management in Switzerland will make the majority of operating, financing, and investing decisions.

The Swiss franc (CHF) is the official currency in Switzerland. On January 1, 2018, the USD/CHF exchange rate was 0.77. At December 31, 2018, the exchange rate had changed to 0.85 USD/CHF. The average exchange rate in 2018 was 0.80 USD/CHF. In its first year of operations, Mountain paid no dividends and no taxes. Mountain uses the FIFO assumption for its flow of inventory.

Mountain Air Parts
Balance Sheet

(in CHF thousands)	12/31/2018	1/1/2018
Assets		
Cash and accounts receivable	600	400
Inventory	500	500
Property, plant, and equipment	600	700
Total assets	1,700	1,600
Liabilities and equity		
Accounts payable	200	100
Long-term debt	100	200
Common stock	1,300	1,300
Retained earnings	100	0
Total liabilities and owner's equity	1,700	1,600

Mountain Air Parts
Income Statement for 2018
(in CHF thousands)

Sales	7,000
COGS	(6,800)
Depreciation	(100)
Net income	100

91. The balance of Valley's current assets as of December 31, 2017, using the acquisition method, is *closest* to:
    A. $87 million.
    B. $119 million.
    C. $128 million.

92. Are Bennett's Conclusions 1 and 2 regarding ROA correct?

Conclusion 1	Conclusion 2
A. Yes	Yes
B. Yes	No
C. No	Yes

93. How many of statements 1–3 made by Bennet are correct?
    A. None.
    B. One.
    C. Two.

94. Using the appropriate method of translation, the amount of total assets reported on Mountain's balance sheet at the end of 2018 is *closest* to:
    A. $1,325.
    B. $1,375.
    C. $1,445.

95. Using the appropriate method of translation, the translation gain (loss) for the year ended 2018 is *closest* to:
    A. $99.
    B. $104.
    C. $109.

96. For this question only, assume that Mountain is operating in a highly inflationary environment. Which of the following statements is *least* correct? Mountain's:
    A. nonmonetary assets and nonmonetary liabilities are adjusted for inflation in accordance with U.S. GAAP.
    B. functional currency is the U.S. dollar.
    C. financial statements are adjusted for inflation, and the net purchasing power gain or loss is recognized in the income statement in accordance with IFRS.

Questions 97–102 relate to Alertron.

Alertron is a pharmaceutical company with approximately $3.5 billion in annual sales that specializes in the development, manufacturing, and marketing of neurology and oncology drug therapies. The firm is seeking to achieve more rapid growth, and Alertron's executive management team feels that the company can grow faster by making acquisitions than it can by trying to grow organically. As a result, management asks the firm's Director of Strategic Planning, Kanna Ozer, CFA, to analyze potential alternatives. At Alertron's next executive management team meeting, Ozer presents the report shown in Exhibit 1 concerning four potential acquisition targets:

Exhibit 1: Report 1—Description of Potential Acquisition Targets

Potential Target	Potential Acquisition Description
BriscoePharm	Firm develops, manufactures, and markets prescription drugs for humans and animals. BriscoePharm has annual sales of $1.2 million, but only certain BriscoePharm drugs are attractive cash flow generators.
Carideo	Firm develops and manufactures oncology and neurology drugs in the United States and abroad. Carideo has annual sales of $1.2 million, and all assets and liabilities would likely be absorbed by Alertron in a potential merger.
Dillon Biotech	Firm designs and manufactures analytical instruments used in drug development. Dillon has $3.5 billion in annual sales. A successful acquisition by Alertron would involve combining operations and forming a new company.
Escarigen	Firm is a pharmaceutical company specializing in cardiology medications. Escarigen is well known among heart surgeons and has a blockbuster cholesterol drug called Karlynivus that is well known in the medical community. In an acquisition, Alertron would want to maintain the successful Escarigen brand and operational structure.

Alertron's executive team agrees that the report is helpful for initiating discussion but decides they need more information concerning the form of each potential acquisition and the most appropriate method of payment. Alertron's management is also concerned whether each potential target would view a takeover attempt as friendly or hostile. Paul Mussara, Alertron's CEO, asks Ozer to prepare a second report that specifically describes the transaction characteristics corresponding to each deal. Ozer's second report is shown in Exhibit 2.

Exhibit 2: Report 2—Merger Transaction Characteristics

Potential Target	Optimal Form of Acquisition	Method of Payment	Likely Attitude of Target Management
BriscoePharm	Asset purchase involving 30% of BriscoePharm's assets	Cash offering	View offer as friendly
Carideo	Stock purchase	Securities offering	View offer as friendly
Dillon Biotech	Stock purchase	Mixed cash and securities offering	View offer as hostile
Escarigen	Stock purchase	Cash offering	View offer as friendly

As Alertron was conducting its analysis, Bhavik Kumar, CEO of Dillon Biotech, hears rumors that Alertron may attempt a hostile takeover of his firm. Kumar calls an emergency meeting with Dillon's four executive vice presidents and expresses his concern that Alertron may attempt a bear hug by submitting a merger proposal directly to the board without informing Dillon's management. Kumar concludes the emergency meeting by asking each executive vice president to brainstorm defense mechanisms that Dillon could employ before a takeover attempt is made and also defenses that could be employed after a hostile takeover offer.

After intense discussions, Alertron decides that a takeover offer for Carideo would be most beneficial due to the net present value of cost reduction synergies of $600 million that Ozer estimates would result from the merger. Mussara asks Ozer to evaluate the deal based on a stock offer in which Alertron would exchange 0.75 shares of Alertron stock for each outstanding share of Carideo stock. Ozer compiles the information shown in Exhibit 3 for her analysis.

Exhibit 3: Merger Evaluation Inputs

	Alertron	Carideo
Pre-merger stock price	$60	$39
Number of shares outstanding (millions)	150	80
Pre-merger market value (millions)	$9,000	$3,120
Estimated NPV of Cost Reduction Synergies	$600 million	

Ozer, and the rest of the executive management team at Alertron, is extremely confident in the $600 million dollar estimate of cost reduction synergies that are likely to result from the merger and feel that the estimate may actually be conservative. However, when analysts at Carideo review the figures, they have a much different opinion and are less certain that $600 million worth of synergies could be realized. While Carideo believes the net present value of synergies from the deal would still be positive, its estimates are much lower than Alertron's.

Carideo's management is also concerned that a merger between Alertron and Carideo could face scrutiny from regulators. Although neither firm is the largest in the pharmaceutical industry, their combined market power could raise antitrust concerns. Phillip Wu, an analyst with Carideo, compiles the following table showing the market share of each of the 12 firms in the pharmaceutical industry to determine whether the concerns were valid. Both Alertron's and Carideo's management teams decide that if regulators are unlikely to challenge the deal, they will proceed with the necessary steps to complete the merger.

Exhibit 4: Market Share of Firms in the Pharmaceutical Industry

Firm Name	Market Share in Pharmaceutical Industry
Munnzer Pharmaceuticals	20%
Spencer Corp.	18%
Alertron	15%
Escarigen	12%
Carideo	10%
Faltysgen	7%
Six other firms	Each have 3% market share

97. Based on Ozer's description of potential acquisition targets, which form of integration and type of merger would *best* describe the transaction if Alertron tried to acquire Escarigen?

	Form of integration	Type of merger
A.	Statutory	Horizontal
B.	Subsidiary	Horizontal
C.	Subsidiary	Vertical

98. Based on the information in Exhibit 2, which of the following statements concerning the transaction characteristics of the potential mergers with Alertron is *most accurate*?
    A. Purchasing Escarigen is likely to reduce Alertron's financial leverage.
    B. Carideo would likely avoid paying corporate taxes in the potential deal with Alertron.
    C. BriscoePharm's shareholders would likely be required to approve the deal with Alertron before any proposed deal is completed.

99. Which of the following *best* satisfies Kumar's request to identify a pair of defense mechanisms that consist of a pre-offer and a post-offer defense?

Pre-offer defense mechanism	Post-offer defense mechanism
A. Poison put	Fair price amendment
B. Greenmail	Restricted voting rights
C. Supermajority voting provision	Leveraged recapitalization

100. Using Ozer's estimates of the cost reduction synergies, the gain that would accrue to Carideo's shareholders as a result of the merger with Alertron is *closest* to:
    A. $108.5 million.
    B. $455.6 million.
    C. $514.2 million.

101. Based on each firm's forecasts of the estimated NPV of synergies from a merger between Alertron and Carideo, what payment method is each firm *likely* to prefer in the deal?
    A. Both firms prefer a cash deal.
    B. Only Alertron prefers a cash deal.
    C. Only Carideo prefers a cash deal.

102. What would be the increase in the Herfindahl-Hirschman Index (HHI) as a result of a merger between Alertron and Carideo, and the *most likely* reaction by regulators to the merger?

Increase in the HHI	Probable response by regulators
A. 75	No antitrust challenge
B. 300	No antitrust challenge
C. 300	Potential antitrust challenge

Questions 103–108 relate to Jacob Marlinton.

Jacob Marlinton, CFA, works for Bantanaya Modros, Inc. (BATNM), a small, independent brewery in the United States. The company was originally privately owned and all profits were distributed to the ownership group at the end of every year. Last year, however, the company wished to expand its operations and used the proceeds of an IPO to fund a bottling plant and expand its distribution network.

At this year's annual general meeting, the board faced several questions about its intended dividend policy in the future. The CEO is currently in favor of a residual policy, which closely matches the policy before the IPO. He believes that a residual dividend policy will have the following two benefits:

1. The policy should boost the company's share price as it will provide a stable long-term dividend.

2. The policy prioritizes investing in positive NPV projects ahead of considering a reduction in dividends.

Marlinton has been asked to calculate the dividend for 2016 if a residual dividend policy is adopted, given capital expenditure levels in the two scenarios in Exhibit 1.

Exhibit 1: Capital Expenditure Levels

Scenario I
The company further expands operations with the opening of a restaurant/brewery. The estimated total required capital expenditure for this plan is $28 million. The project would be financed with a mix of debt and equity in line with the BATNM's target debt and equity weightings. If earnings are not available, the shortfall would be financed with debt, leading to what is expected to be a temporary deviation from the target capital structure.

Scenario II
No significant expansion undertaken. The only capital expenditure would be the replacement of existing equipment. Existing brewing equipment would be sold for $2.2 million and replaced with new equipment costing $3.8 million. The old equipment is three years old and is being depreciated over five years with no salvage value in the financial statements. BATNM received 100% of the cost of the old machine as a tax deduction when it was purchased three years ago because the company is located in a designated tax enterprise zone. The new equipment would similarly qualify for a 100% deduction allowance in the year of purchase. Note that as a result of the replacement of equipment, inventory levels would increase by $200,000.

To help with the calculation, Marlinton has obtained a current summary balance sheet for the firm and a forecasted summary income statement for the year ahead, as shown in Exhibit 2. Marlinton assumes that the current balance sheet levels of debt and equity reflect BATNM's target capital structure. The tax rate for the company is 35%.

Exhibit 2: Summarized Financial Statements (current/forecasted)

Current Balance Sheet
as of 1 January 2016

Assets	($ Thousands)	
Current assets		
Inventory	51,307	
Accounts receivable	36,860	
Cash	76,402	
Other	42,893	
Total		**207,462**
Long-lived assets		
PPE		381,569
Goodwill		3,683
Other		12,447
Total		**605,161**
Liabilities and equity		
Current liabilities		
Accounts payable	22,576	
Short-term debt	120	
Other	74,539	
Total		**97,235**
Long-term liabilities		
Long-term debt		74,953
Other		7,606
Total		**179,794**
Equity		
Common stock		200,458
Additional paid in capital		224,909
Total liabilities and equity		**605,161**

Forecasted Income Statement
Year Ended 31 December 2016

	($ Thousands)
Revenue	248,303
Operating income	40,502
Net income	26,034

Marlinton is concerned that any dividend policy adopted should allow BATNM to stay closely aligned with its target capital structure. He is concerned that any significant increase in debt would lead to a sharp increase in the cost of equity. He has prepared an analysis to test this effect using Modigliani and Miller's theory of capital structure in a world with taxes.

In his analysis, Marlinton assumes that the cost of equity if BATNM was all equity financed would be 15%. He intends to work out the increase in the current cost of equity if $40 million of debt at a cost of 8% was added to the current balance sheet. In his analysis, he intends to also assume that the amount of equity remains constant. Marlinton recognizes that most of the assets of the company (e.g., brewing equipment) are tangible, and, hence, the cost of financial distress will be lower for BATNM relative to companies with mostly intangible assets.

Marlinton believes that maintaining the target capital structure is much more important than dividend policy. He thinks that the company should finance its projects by giving the highest preference to the method with the least potential information content and the lowest preference to the form with the greatest.

103. Regarding the CEO's comments regarding the benefits of a residual dividend policy, Marlinton will *most likely* conclude that:
    A. both are correct.
    B. only benefit 1 is accurate.
    C. only benefit 2 is accurate.

104. The expected 2016 dividend under a residual dividend policy and scenario I is *closest* to:
    A. $3,000,000.
    B. $2,230,000.
    C. zero.

105. The initial outlay to be included in Marlinton's NPV calculation for the project in scenario II is *closest* to:
    A. $3,250,000
    B. $2,900,000
    C. $2,570,000

106. Using Marlinton's assumptions in his capital structure analysis, after the additional debt of $40 million, the cost of equity would *most likely* be:
    A. 16.2%
    B. 17.7%
    C. 18.1%

107. Marlinton's assumptions regarding BATNM's costs of financial distress are *most likely*:
    A. Correct.
    B. incorrect as the costs of financial distress are related to debt levels and not related to assets.
    C. incorrect as the costs of financial distress are higher if the company's balance sheet is made up of mostly tangible assets.

108. Marlinton's suggested method of financing projects is *most likely* to be referred to as:
    A. the pecking order theory.
    B. the static trade-off theory.
    C. Modigliani and Miller proposition II.

Questions 109–114 relate to Trailblazer, Inc.

Louise Valentine, CFA, is analyzing the financial information of Trailblazer, Inc., a company in the retail sector. She is preparing to write a report on her findings. Valentine is considering various valuation approaches and is convinced that a dividend discount model (DDM) would be among the best choices in this case. She notes that Trailblazer does not vary its dividend payments significantly from year to year.

In preparing to estimate a suitable required rate of return on equity for Trailblazer, Valentine notes that the current T-bill rate is 3.5% and that the yield on the company's 10-year bonds is 7.25% while the yield on a 10-year Treasury bond is 4.4%. Additionally, Valentine estimates that the appropriate equity risk premium in excess of the company's cost of debt is 3%. Valentine estimates that average dividend yield for the S&P 500 (the market proxy) is 2.1% and a consensus long-term EPS growth rate of 3.5% is forecast for S&P 500 index.

Valentine also gathers the information shown in Exhibit 1.

Exhibit 1: Trailblazer, Inc. Multifactor Sensitivities (APT)

Factor	Factor Risk Premium	Trailblazer, Inc. Factor Sensitivities
1	1.91%	0.81
2	1.22%	−0.45
3	3.47%	0.24
4	4.15%	0.74

In her report, Valentine makes the following statements about Trailblazer dividends:

Statement 1:   Trailblazer is expected to pay a dividend next year and will continue to do so for the foreseeable future.

Statement 2:   The required rate of return for Trailblazer stock will likely exceed the growth rate of its dividends.

Statement 3:   Trailblazer is in a mature sector of its industry, and accordingly, I expect dividends to decline at a constant rate of 4% indefinitely.

In speaking to a colleague at her firm, Valentine makes the following additional statements after her report is released:

Statement 4:   Trailblazer has a 10-year history of paying regular quarterly dividends.

Statement 5:   Over a recent 10-year period, Trailblazer has experienced one 3-year period of consecutive losses and another period of two annual losses in a row but has been extremely profitable in the remaining five years.

Valentine is concerned with some of the inputs for estimating the cost of equity for other companies that she follows. Based on her research, she makes the following statements:

Statement 6:   We have used historical equity risk premium as input into the CAPM. However, we should adjust the said equity risk premium because it includes some unfavorable surprises in productivity declines and higher inflation due to oil price shocks.

Statement 7:   When estimating beta of a private company using a public company peer, the private company beta should be adjusted for the difference in leverage between the public company and the private company, as well as the difference in their respective sizes.

Valentine is also analyzing the stock of Farwell, Inc. Farwell shares are currently trading at $48 based on current earnings of $4 and a current dividend of $2.60. Dividends are expected to grow at 5% per year indefinitely. The risk-free rate is 3.5%, the market risk premium is 4.5%, and Farwell's beta is estimated to be 1.2.

109.   Based on the APT model and the bond yield plus risk-premium (BYPRP) method, the discount rate Valentine should use in valuing the equity of Trailblazer is *closest* to:

Rate based on APT	Rate based on BYPRP
A. 8.40%	10.25%
B. 4.90%	10.25%
C. 4.90%	7.25%

110.   The forward-looking estimate of average equity risk premium (based on the S&P 500 index as market proxy) is *closest* to:
A. 1.2%.
B. 2.1%.
C. 5.6%.

111. How many of the first three statements Valentine made concerning Trailblazer's dividends are consistent with assumptions of the Gordon growth model (GGM)?
   A. None.
   B. Two.
   C. Three.

112. Do statements 4 and 5 support the decision by Valentine to use a dividend discount model?
   A. Both statements support the use of DDM.
   B. Only Statement 4 supports the use of DDM.
   C. Only Statement 5 supports the use of DDM.

113. Are statements 6 and 7 correct?
   A. Both statements are incorrect.
   B. Only Statement 6 is incorrect.
   C. Only Statement 7 is incorrect.

114. The justified leading and justified trailing P/E ratios of Farwell are *closest* to:

	Justified leading P/E	Justified trailing P/E
A.	16.67	9.42
B.	8.97	17.50
C.	16.67	17.50

Questions 115–120 relate to Tom Vadney.

Tom Vadney, CFA, is president and CEO of Vadney Research and Advisors (VRA), a large equity research firm that specializes in providing international investment and advisory services to global portfolio managers. He has a staff of five junior analysts and three senior analysts covering industries and firms across the Americas, Europe, and Asia-Pacific regions.

In a recent meeting with an institutional portfolio manager, Vadney is asked to review the differences between U.S. GAAP and International Financial Reporting Standards (IFRS) as well as provide a comprehensive industry analysis for the telecommunications sector in Europe and the Asia-Pacific region. Vadney asks Maria Mnoyan, a senior analyst covering the sector, to research the requested information for the client meeting.

Prior to the meeting, Vadney and Mnoyan meet to prepare for the client presentation. They first discuss differences between U.S. GAAP and IFRS. Mnoyan states that although there will be increasing convergence between the two accounting standards, one major difference currently is that IFRS permits either the "partial goodwill" or "full goodwill" method to value goodwill and a noncontrolling interest under the acquisition method, U.S. GAAP requires the full goodwill method. Vadney adds that U.S. GAAP requires equity method accounting for joint ventures, while under IFRS proportionate consolidation is preferred, but the equity method is permitted.

Mnoyan presents the forecast prepared by three junior analysts for Prime Telco. Adams, the first analyst, expects volume growth of 4%, a sales price increase of 2%, and an input price increase of 3%. Analyst Baste's corresponding forecasts are 2%, 5%, and 4%. Finally, analyst Cairns's forecasts are 1% for volume growth, 4% for sales price growth, and 5% for input price growth. Prime's current revenues and COGS are $121 million and $89 million, respectively.

Mnoyan firmly believes that investing in companies located in developing countries provides strong return prospects as the growth rate in labor productivity increases through technological change and increases in capital.

For example, Mnoyan considers Dien Thoai Corporation, a rapidly growing telecommunication firm in an emerging market country. Dien Thoai is likely to be an acquisition target given the global ambitions of larger firms in developed markets. Mnoyan is interested in calculating the present value of growth opportunities (PVGO) for Dien Thoai. She proposes dividing the last dividend paid by Dien Thoai by the required rate of return to find the value of Dien Thoai's assets in place, and then subtracting this from fundamental value to find PVGO.

Dien Thoai's dividend yield based on the most recent dividend paid is 5%. Dividends and earnings are expected to grow 12% next year, but that rate is expected to decrease linearly over the next six years to a long-term rate of 3% per year.

115. Are Mnoyan and Vadney correct about differences between U.S. GAAP and IFRS?
    A. Both are correct.
    B. Only Mnoyan is correct.
    C. Only Vadney is correct.

116. Which analyst is *most likely* to forecast an improvement in gross margin for Prime Telco?
    A. Adams
    B. Baste
    C. Cairns

117. Mnoyan's description of the growth potential of developing countries is *best* described as the:
    A. classical growth theory.
    B. neoclassical growth theory.
    C. endogenous growth theory.

118. What adjustment to her calculation method does Mnoyan need to make to correctly calculate PVGO? The value of assets in place is given by:
    A. the previous dividend multiplied by one plus the sustainable growth rate, divided by the required rate of return.
    B. earnings divided by the required rate of return.
    C. earnings, divided by the required rate of return minus the sustainable growth rate.

119. The required rate of return on Dien Thoai stock implied in its current market price is *closest* to:
    A. 9.5%.
    B. 10.8%.
    C. 11.3%.

120. Which of the following is NOT a strength of multistage Dividend Discount Models?
    A. Models can be used either in forward or reverse to identify values given assumptions of growth and required return or to derive required returns and projected growth rates implied by market prices.
    B. Models are straightforward in the relationship between assumptions and resulting estimates of value, allowing the analyst to review all the assumptions built into the models and to consider the impact of different assumptions.
    C. Models are sensitive to assumptions of growth, allowing variability in potential values.

End of Afternoon Session

Exam 1
Morning Session Answers

To get valuable feedback on how your score compares to those of other Level II candidates, use your Username and Password to gain Online Access at schweser.com and click on the icon that says, *"Practice Exams Volume 1 (Enter answers from book)."*

1. A	21. A	41. C
2. A	22. C	42. A
3. C	23. B	43. B
4. B	24. C	44. B
5. A	25. C	45. C
6. C	26. C	46. C
7. B	27. A	47. A
8. C	28. B	48. C
9. A	29. B	49. A
10. C	30. B	50. C
11. B	31. B	51. C
12. B	32. B	52. C
13. B	33. A	53. A
14. C	34. C	54. C
15. C	35. B	55. B
16. B	36. A	56. C
17. C	37. A	57. B
18. A	38. B	58. C
19. B	39. A	59. B
20. C	40. C	60. B

Exam 1
Morning Session Answers

1. **A** **Standard I(C).** Both Sampson and Lawson have violated Standard I(C) – Professionalism – Misrepresentation. When Sampson prepared biographies with Shadow Mountain Wealth Management Team included in them, she was obviously trying to convey the image that TIM personnel are employees of the bank trust department. This does not portray the correct business relationship between Shadow Mountain and TIM. TIM is an outsourcer to Shadow Mountain and a contract investment management provider, not an employee. Sampson is attempting to create a misleading view of the service level and investment expertise that clients could rightly expect. While Lawson was not a party to preparing such misleading business cards and marketing materials, he participated in the misrepresentation by agreeing to go ahead with the client presentation. (Study Session 1, LOS 2.a)

2. **A** **Standards I(C) and III(D).** Including the BAGF performance is a violation of Standard I(C) – Professionalism – Misrepresentation and Standard III(D) – Duties to Clients – Performance Presentation. When Sampson combines the BAGF performance record with the TIM Composite Equity Composite, this gives potential clients a misleading impression of TIM's long-term equity management performance. The use of this performance data might be acceptable if full disclosure were made as to the source and nature of the data. (Study Session 1, LOS 2.a)

3. **C** **Standard III(A).** Luna has violated the CFA Institute Standards of Professional Conduct – Standard III(A) Duties to Clients – Loyalty, Prudence, and Care. Client brokerage is the property or asset of the client and not TIM. Client brokerage should be used only for research products or services that are directly related to the investment decision-making process and not the management costs of the firm. In this case, Luna should disclose to TIM's clients that their brokerage may be used to purchase research. In addition, Luna should seek to ensure that Turn Byer is providing the best execution for TIM's clients. StockCal is clearly providing equity research products/services that aid TIM in the investment decision-making process and not the general operation or management costs of the firm. StockCal may therefore be properly paid for with client brokerage soft dollars, and this is not a violation of the Standards or Code. However, Add-Invest Software provides TIM's clients with portfolio accounting and performance measurement services and is not related to the investment decision-making process. Therefore, Luna is misusing client resources when she uses client brokerage to purchase Add-Invest Software. Add-Invest is clearly a business expense of TIM and should rightly be paid for by the firm and not the clients. The product or service received must provide proper assistance to the investment manager in following through with his investment decision-making responsibilities. (Study Session 1, LOS 2.a)

4. **B** **Standard III(A).** The increased commission would be a violation, but the cash referral fee would not. Doubling the commission paid to Wurtzel would be a violation of Standard III(A) Duties to Clients – Loyalty, Prudence, and Care. Client brokerage is strictly an asset of the client and must be used for the benefit of clients in research that will assist the investment manager in the investment decision-making process. Client brokerage cannot be used as a reward for bringing clients to TIM and to do so is a misappropriation of client assets. Cash referral fees are acceptable, so long as the referral arrangement is fully disclosed to the clients in advance of opening their accounts. The case mentions that this disclosure will be made. This disclosure allows the client to evaluate any potential conflict(s) of interest in the referral process. (Study Session 1, LOS 2.a)

5. **A** **Standard III(A).** In making a $25,000 contribution to the Hoover Study Center of Unions, Luna has violated Standard III(A) Duties to Clients – Loyalty, Prudence, and Care, which states that Members and Candidates must act for the benefit of their clients and place their clients' interest before their employers' or their own interest. In relationship with clients, Members and Candidates must determine applicable fiduciary duty and must comply with such duty to the persons and interests to whom it is owed. The contribution to the Hoover Study Center of Unions, authorized by the trustees of the union, brings into question this acting for the benefit of the client. Despite providing guidance and governance for the union, trustees are not the client of the union fund; rather, the members of the union and their beneficiaries are the clients of the fund. By making a $25,000 contribution from the client brokerage, Luna and the trustees have used funds that rightly belong to the members of the union and they have done so without direct compensation to the union members. Luna should not have authorized the pension account to make the contribution and having done so violated her duty to loyally guard the assets of her clients as a fiduciary. Luna has an obligation to follow the Code and Standards. Client brokerage is the property of the client, not the trustee or fiduciary representing the client. (Study Session 1, LOS 2.a)

6. **C** **Standard III(A).** In this case, Lutz is the client and, therefore, the direct owner of the client brokerage. If Lutz's desire is to give the soft dollar client brokerage asset to the Roswell Academy, she is free to do so because it is her asset. She is sole owner of her own retirement account. Luna, by following the wishes of the client, is complying with her duty of loyalty. Thus, there is no violation of Standard III(A) Duties to Clients – Loyalty, Prudence, and Care, in the case of the $10,000 contribution to Roswell Academy. (Study Session 1, LOS 2.a)

7. **B** A logarithmic transformation of the dependent variable is the most appropriate transformation to apply when the variable grows at a constant rate over time:

$$\ln(\text{sales}) = a^* + b^*t + e$$

The slope of this equation equals the nominal constant rate. The effective rate equals $e^{b^*} - 1$. (Study Session 3, LOS 11.b)

8. **C** Quarter 1 of 2019 is the 61st quarter (starting with Quarter 1 of 2004): sales = 10 + 16(61) = $986 million. (Study Session 3, LOS 11.a)

9. **A**   The mean reverting value equals the intercept divided by 1 minus slope = 20 / (1 − 0.10) = 20 / 0.90 = $22.22 million. The last change was $50 million as shown in Exhibit 5 (1000 − 950). Therefore, the AR(1) model predicts that the series will fall anytime the current value (the last quarter in 2018) is above the mean reverting value. The change in sales for the last quarter in 2018 was $50 million, which exceeds the mean reverting value. We could also have computed the forecasted change in sales for Quarter 1, 2019 as 20 + (0.1) × 50 = 25 (which is lower than the previous change of 50). (Study Session 3, LOS 11.f)

10. **C**   Seasonality refers to repeating patterns each year. Using quarterly data, tests of seasonality focus on the 4th lag (i.e., "same time last year"). The autocorrelation for the 4th lag is statistically significant. This can be observed by comparing the reported p-value (0.02), which is less than the level of significance (0.05). (Study Session 3, LOS 11.l)

11. **B**   Autoregressive conditional heteroskedasticity refers to an autoregressive equation in which the variance of the errors terms is heteroskedastic (i.e., error variance is not constant). The presence of ARCH is tested with the following regression:

$$e_t^2 = \beta_1 + \beta_2 e_{t-1}^2 + v_t$$

which serves as a proxy for:

$$var(e_t) = \beta_1 + \beta_2 var(e_{t-1}) + v_t$$

Exhibit 4 indicates that the slope estimate in the ARCH equation is not significant (the t-statistic for the slope estimate of the ARCH equation is not significant). Therefore, the squared error does not depend on its lagged value (i.e., if the slope equals zero, then the error variance equals the constant β_1, which indicates no conditional heteroskedasticity in the AR model). ARCH is not present. (Study Session 3, LOS 11.m)

12. **B**   The most recent change in sales reported in Exhibit 5 was $50 million (i.e., an increase from $950 million to $1,000 million). Therefore, the one-step-ahead forecast is 20 + 0.1(50) = $25 million and the two-step-ahead forecast is 20 + 0.1(25) = $22.5 million. (Study Session 3, LOS 11.d)

13. **B**   The snack foods industry, a regulated entity, has found a way to exploit the differences in regulations among the three states and is engaging in regulatory arbitrage. Regulatory competition is a result of actions taken by regulators to attract certain entities. Regulatory capture is the idea that regulatory bodies are influenced or controlled by the regulated industry. (Study Session 4, LOS 15.d)

14. **C**   The carbonated beverages industry is likely to be hurt by the elimination of bigger sizes of drinks. The snack industry can avoid the new manufacturing tax in East by moving manufacture of sweet snacks to the other two states. The demand for corn is expected to remain fairly high so the regulatory changes in East are unlikely to have a major impact on the Tristanyan agricultural industry. (Study Session 4, LOS 15.i)

15. **C**   The increase in driving miles was not the intended effect of the regulation. Unintended effects are not a component of implementation cost. Regulatory burden refers to the cost of regulation for the entity being regulated. If sunset clause provisions were included in the regulation, West's regulators would be required to revisit the cost-benefit analysis and consider the cost of unintended consequences before renewing the regulation. (Study Session 4, LOS 15.h)

16. **B** In order for developed countries to grow, technological development is critical. Proposal 2 most clearly addresses this need. Proposal 1 would be more effective if the focus was on post-secondary education, as developed nations benefit more from innovation and less from applying technology. Proposal 3 is unlikely to have a major impact on labor productivity, as developed nations have high capital-to-labor ratios, and incentives to further increase capital will have relatively little effect on labor productivity. (Study Session 4, LOS 14.h)

17. **C** Neoclassical growth theory concludes that capital accumulation affects the level of output but not the long-run growth rate. (Study Session 4, LOS 14.i)

18. **A** The objectives of regulators in financial markets include prudential supervision, financial stability, market integrity, and economic growth. Low inflation is likely to be an objective of the central bank. (Study Session 4, LOS 15.f)

19. **B** Held-to-maturity securities are reported on the balance sheet at amortized cost. At the end of 2009, the Pinto bonds have a carrying value of $9,260,000 (9,200,000 issue price + 60,000 discount amortization). The amortized discount is equal to the $60,000 difference between the interest expense of $460,000 (9,200,000 × 5%) and the $400,000 coupon payment (10,000,000 × 4%).

Trading securities are reported on the balance sheet at fair value. At the end of 2009, the fair value of the Vega bonds was $7,941,591 (N = 39, I = 2, PMT = 175,000, FV = 7,000,000, Solve for PV).

Thus, at the end of 2009, the investment portfolio is reported at $17.2 million (9,260,000 Pinto bond + 7,941,591 Vega bond). (Study Session 5, LOS 16.a)

20. **C** A $941,591 unrealized gain (7,941,591 FV – 7,000,000 BV) was included in Viper's net income because the Vega bonds were classified as trading securities. Had the Vega bonds been classified as available-for-sale, the unrealized gain would have been reported as a component of stockholders' equity. In that case, net profit margin would have been lower (lower numerator). (Study Session 5, LOS 16.a)

21. **A** Reclassifying a held-to-maturity security to available-for-sale involves stating the investment on the balance sheet at fair value and recognizing the difference in the fair value and the carrying value as other comprehensive income. (Study Session 5, LOS 16.a)

22. **C** <u>Full goodwill method (in millions)</u>
Fair value of Gremlin $1,500 (900 purchase price / 60% ownership interest)
Less: Fair value of Gremlin's
Identifiable net assets <u>1,100</u> (700 CA + 950 NCA – 250 CL – 300 LTD)
Goodwill $400

<u>Partial goodwill method (in millions)</u>
Purchase price $900
Less: Pro-rata share of Gremlin's
Identifiable net assets at FV <u>660</u> (700 CA + 950 NCA – 250 CL – 300 LTD) × 60%
Goodwill $240

Goodwill is not created under the pooling method. (Study Session 5, LOS 16.b)

23. **B**   Viper's post-acquisition LTD is $8,000 million [7,700 million BV of Viper + 300 million fair value (FV) of Gremlin debt]. Viper's post-acquisition equity is equal to $7,300 million (5,800 million Viper pre-acquisition equity + 900 million FV of shares used to acquire Gremlin + 600 million noncontrolling interest). Under U.S. GAAP, the noncontrolling interest is based on the full goodwill method (1,500 million FV of Gremlin × 40% noncontrolling interest). Thus, the long-term debt-to-equity ratio is 1.10 (8,000 million LTD / 7,300 million equity). (Study Session 5, LOS 16.b,c)

24. **C**   According to U.S. GAAP, the goodwill is not impaired because the $1,475 million fair value of Gremlin exceeds the $1,425 million carrying value. Thus, no impairment loss is recognized.

Under IFRS, no impairment loss is recognized because the $1,430 million recoverable amount exceeds the $1,425 million carrying value. (Study Session 5, LOS 16.b)

25. **C**   The institutional guidelines related to developing the specific work product is an input source in the first phase (defining the purpose and context of the analysis). Audited financial statements are an example of an input in the data collection phase. Ratio analysis is an example of the output from the data processing phase. (Study Session 6, LOS 20.a)

26. **C**   If the associate reported the investment in debt securities as held-for-trading instead of designated at fair value, its reported income would be unchanged, because unrealized and realized gains and losses under both methods are reported in the income statement. Additionally, because the investment in associate is reported under equity method by Delicious, it does not report individual assets of the investee. (Study Session 5, LOS 16.b)

27. **A**   Delicious's financial leverage ratio was 1.8 (54,753 average assets / 29,983 average equity) for 2017 and was 1.7 for 2016 (49,354 average assets / 28,738 average equity). Although leverage was higher, the nature of the true leverage was lower. This is because the increasing customer advances (unearned revenue) will not require an outflow of cash in the future and are, thus, less onerous than Delicious's other liabilities. (Study Session 6, LOS 20.b)

28. **B**   As indicated below, the Mexico segment has the lowest EBIT margin, yet it has the highest proportional capital expenditures to proportional assets ratio. Thus, Delicious may be overallocating resources to the Mexico segment.

Segment Analysis for 2017

	EBIT Margin	Total CapEx %	Total Assets %	CapEx % / Assets %
Europe	14.3%	35.0%	72.0%	0.5
Mexico	8.1%	65.0%	28.0%	2.3

(Study Session 6, LOS 20.b)

29. **B** A finance lease is reported on the balance sheet as an asset and as a liability. In the income statement, the leased asset is depreciated and interest expense is recognized on the liability. The lease adjustment involves adding the rental payment back to EBIT and then subtracting the implied depreciation expense. Next, the implied interest expense for the lease is added to reported interest.

Operating Lease Adjustment

in millions	Reported	Adjustments	Pro-Forma	
EBIT	€7,990	69[b] − 50[c]	€8,009	= 17.8
Interest expense	€420[a]	30[d]	€450	

[a] EBIT − EBT: 7,990 − 7,570 = 420
[b] Rent expense (payment)
[c] Depreciation expense: 300 / 6 years = 50
[d] Interest expense: 300 × 10% = 30

(Study Session 6, LOS 20.c)

30. **B** Delicious's implied value without its U.S. associate is €90,736 [€97,525 Delicious market cap − €6,789 share of associate's market cap ($32,330 × 30% × €0.70 current exchange rate)].

Delicious's net income without associate is €6,147 (€6,501 net income − €354 pro-rata share of income from associate).

Implied P/E = 14.8 (€90,736 Delicious implied value without associate / €6,147 Delicious net income without associate). (Study Session 6, LOS 20.e)

31. **B** The justified price-to-book value (P/B) ratio is calculated as:

P/B = (ROE − g) / (r − g)

where:
growth rate: g = ROE × (1 − payout)
Able: g = 0.25 × (1 − 1.00 / 2.50) = 0.15
Baker: g = 0.15 × (1 − 1.60 / 4.80) = 0.10
Charles: g = 0.08 × (1 − 2.50 / 4.00) = 0.03

Justified price-to-book value (P/B):

Able: P/B = (0.25 − 0.15) / (0.20 − 0.15) = 2, implying price = 2 × 10 = $20
Baker: P/B = (0.15 − 0.10) / (0.12 − 0.10) = 2.5, implying price = 2.5 × 32 = $80
Charles: P/B = (0.08 − 0.03) / (0.10 − 0.03) = 0.71, implying price = 0.71 × 50 = $35.5

Able sells for $60, triple its value; Baker sells for $70, 12% below its value; and Charles sells for $35.5, right at its value. (Study Session 11, LOS 32.h,j)

32. **B** The justified price-to-sales (P/S) ratio is calculated as:

P/S = [profit margin × payout ratio × (1 + g)] / (r − g)

Baker: P/S = [(4.80 / 52.80) × (1.60 / 4.80) × (1 + 0.10)] / (0.12 − 0.10) = 1.67

(Study Session 11, LOS 32.h)

33. **A** Able Corporation should sell for [(2.50 / 115) × (1.00 / 2.50) × (1 + 0.15)] / (0.20 − 0.15) = 0.20 × sales, or $23/share. The current market price of $60 is 161% overvalued. Baker trades for $70 versus a value of 1.67 × 52.8 = $88, a discount of 20%. Charles trades for $35.50 versus a value of 1.43 × 25.75 = 37, a negligible discount of 4%. (Study Session 11, LOS 32.i)

34. **C** A high ROE does not make a company a good investment, nor does a high book value. However, Able Corporation does have the highest potential growth rate. Because the justified values for Charles Company are near the market price, there does not appear to be any problem with the valuation inputs (e.g., required return). The similarity between the justified P/B value and the market price of Charles indicates that it is fairly priced and not an especially attractive investment. (Study Session 11, LOS 32.i)

35. **B** Based on the model presented, the predicted P/E ratios can be calculated as:

    Able: 2.74 + 8.21(1.00 / 2.50) + 14.21(0.15) + 2.81(0.25) = 8.85

    Baker: 2.74 + 8.21(1.60 / 4.80) + 14.21(0.10) + 2.81(0.15) = 7.32

    Charles: 2.74 + 8.21(2.50 / 4.00) + 14.21(0.03) + 2.81(0.08) = 8.52

    (Study Session 11, LOS 32.e)

36. **A** Swift has correctly stated that if multicollinearity is present in a model, the interpretation of the individual regression coefficients becomes problematic. The existence of multicollinearity is generally signaled by a high R-squared value and low t-statistics on the regression coefficients. The t-stat for the coefficients for payout ratio, g, and ROE can be calculated as (8.21 / 6.52) = 1.26, (14.21 / 9.24) = 1.54, and (2.81 / 2.10) = 1.34, respectively. Note that all of these t-stats are well below the approximate critical value of 2, indicating they are statistically insignificant. With the high R-squared of 81% and insignificant t-stats, it appears that multicollinearity is indeed present in this model. Swift's comment regarding predictive power is incorrect. Cross-sectional regressions have unknown predictive power outside the specific sample and time period used to generate the regression. (Study Session 11, LOS 32.i)

37. **A** To obtain $F_{(2,5)}$, first calculate the 2-year discount factor P_2 and the 7-year discount factor P_7.

    $P_2 = 1/(1+0.0036)^2$ $= 0.9928$

    $P_7 = 1/(1+0.0227)^7$ $= 0.8546$

    $F_{(2,5)} = 0.8546/0.9928$ $= 0.8608$

    (Study Session 12, LOS 35.b)

38. **B** Spot rates should evolve in line with the current forward rates. (Study Session 12, LOS 35.c)

39. **A** Retail banks typically have little exposure to swaps and, consequently, they typically use the government yield curve. The swap curve is more commonly used by wholesale banks. (Study Session 12, LOS 35.e)

40. **C** The swap spread is the spread paid by the fixed-rate payer of an interest rate swap over the rate on an on-the-run government security with the same maturity as the swap. (Study Session 12, LOS 35.f)

41. **C** The swap spread gives more information about supply and demand, whereas the TED spread more accurately reflects the level of risk in the banking system. (Study Session 12, LOS 35.g,h)

42. **A** The segmented markets theory and the preferred habitat theory both state that rates are influenced by lenders and borrowers, but it is the segmented markets theory that proposes that the maturity sectors are independent. The "b" term in the Cox-Ingersoll-Ross model is the mean reverting level for the short-term interest rate. (Study Session 12, LOS 35.i,j)

43. **B** The CFO is looking to reduce the duration of the fixed-rate bond. The risk here is that market interest rates drop below 6.25%, but we're stuck still paying 6.25%. We can reduce this specific risk by effectively changing that fixed payment into a floating payment. A pay floating and receive fixed swap is most likely to achieve this objective. (Study Session 14, LOS 42.a)

44. **B** TorkSpark has borrowed USD and thus should engage in a USD for GBP swap. At initiation, TorkSpark would exchange USD principal for GBP principal. During the life of the swap, Torkspark would pay GBP interest and the swap dealer would pay USD interest. In order to hedge these flows, the dealer could enter into a GBP for USD swap. Alternately, the dealer could lend USD and borrow GBP. (Study Session 14, LOS 42.a)

45. **C** $/€ spot rate at expiry = 1 / 0.84487 = 1.18361 $/€

    $/€ forward rate at initiation = 1 / 0.89239 = 1.12059 $/€

    $ loss per € = 1.12059 − 1.18361 = $ 0.06302

    Loss on forward contract (given) = $ 189,083

    Total € hedged = 189,083 / 0.06302 = € 3,000,365.

    Given 60% hedged, Total € receivable =3,000,365 / 0.6 = € 5,000,608

    (Study Session 14, LOS 42.a)

46. **C** To protect against downside risk, Garton is using a long put. A call option can be sold to offset the cost of the put, forming a collar. (Study Session 14, LOS 42.g)

47. **A** Required break-even price 38.20 × 1.035 = $39.54

    Jun 38, Jun 42
    Breakeven = $X_L + C_{L0} − C_{H0}$ = 38 + 1.19 − 0.08 = 39.11 (meets criteria)
    Max profit = $X_H − X_L − C_{L0} + C_{H0}$ = 42 − 38 − 1.19 + 0.08 = 2.89 (meets criteria)

    Jun 39, Jun 42
    Breakeven = $X_L + C_{L0} − C_{H0}$ = 39 + 0.70 − 0.08 = 39.62 (too high)
    Max profit = $X_H − X_L − C_{L0} + C_{H0}$ = 42 − 39 − 0.70 + 0.08 = 2.38 (meets criteria)

    Jun 39, Jun 41
    Breakeven = $X_L + C_{L0} − C_{H0}$ = 39 + 0.70 − 0.18 = 39.52 (meets criteria)
    Max profit = $X_H − X_L − C_{L0} + C_{H0}$ = 41 − 39 − 0.70 + 0.18 = 1.48 (too low)

    (Study Session 14, LOS 42.j)

48. **C**   All bull spreads involve buying the low strike price option and writing the higher strike price option. When using puts, this will lead to an initial cash inflow equal to the difference in the two premiums. The difference in premiums would also be the maximum gain—not the maximum loss. (Study Session 14, LOS 42.h)

49. **A**   For industrial properties, the most important factor affecting economic value is retail sales growth, which is expected to be low in West Lundia. The most important factor affecting economic value for apartment REITs are job creation and population growth, which are both expected to be high. For office properties, the most important factor is job creation, which is expected to be high. (Study Session 15, LOS 44.c)

50. **C**   There are two components to this valuation. The first component is the cash flows for the first seven years. The second component is the terminal value.

     PV of CFs in years 1–7:
     PMT = 7.0; I/Y = 10; N = 7. The PV = WL\$34.08 million.

     PV of terminal value:
     An appropriate terminal cap rate can be calculated using the following equation:

     cap rate = discount rate − growth rate = 10% − 3.25% = 6.75%.

     The terminal value is calculated using the following inputs: WL\$8.5 million divided by the terminal cap rate of 6.75%. The value in Year 7 is WL\$125.93 million, discounting this value to the present:
     FV = WL\$125.93 million; N = 7, I/Y = 10 results in a present value of WL\$64.62 million.

     WL\$34.08 + WL\$64.62 = WL\$98.7 million.

     (Study Session 15, LOS 43.g)

51. **C**   NAVPS based on forecasted NOI:

Option #2 (REIT)	(in WL\$ millions)
Recent NOI	140.0
Subtract: Non-cash rents	− 5.0
Add: Full-year adjustment for acquisition	+ 5.0
Pro forma cash NOI	140.0
Projected NOI @ 2.5% growth	143.5
Estimated value of operating real estate @ cap rate of 7.0%	2050.0
Add: Other assets	+ 50.0
Estimated gross value	2100.0
Subtract: Total liabilities	− 300.0
NAV	1800.0

     NAVPS = 1800 / 15 = 120, which is lower than the current market price of WL\$125.00. This REIT is selling at a premium to NAVPS. (Study Session 15, LOS 44.e)

52. **C**   Option 1 represents private investment in real estate, while Options 2 and 3 entail investing through public securities. Tax advantages can be enjoyed by direct investments in real estate, as well as through public securities. Similarly, use of leverage can be pursued by all three options. Option 1 does not have the problem of structural conflicts of interest that may be present in REITs (Option 2). (Study Session 15, LOS 43.c)

53. **A**   The terminal value estimate is 12.0 × WL$13.5 MM for end of year 7 or WL$162.0 MM. The discount rate is the cap rate of 7.0% plus the growth rate of 2.5%, or 9.5%. Discounting this terminal value to find the present value: FV = WL$162.0 MM; I/Y = 9.5; N = 7; PV = WL$85.83 MM. Add the present value of all dividends of WL$39.7 MM for a total of WL$125.53 MM. Divide WL$125.53 MM by 1 million shares outstanding for a value per share of WL$125.53. (Study Session 15, LOS 44.h)

54. **C**   Investment in both public REOCs and public REITs enjoy high liquidity, as shares of both trade on a stock exchange. Tax advantages favor REITs as REOCs are not tax-advantaged. REOCs are more reliant on capital appreciation due to their ability to reinvest cash flows, while REITs tend to have higher current income (i.e., yield). (Study Session 15, LOS 44.a)

55. **B**   VaR has been calculated using the parameters (mean and standard deviation) of the portfolio and assuming a distribution for portfolio risk factors. A historical simulation would instead identify actual returns from the portfolio and identify the 5th percentile. (Study Session 16, LOS 49.b)

56. **C**   To calculate the daily VaR from an annual VaR, the mean and standard deviation must be adjusted using the 250 trading days described.

The mean has been correctly calculated as 9.4% / 250 = 0.0376%

The standard deviation, however, should be divided by $\sqrt{250}$: 14.2% / $\sqrt{250}$ = 0.898%

This would result in a 5% daily VaR = [(0.0376% − (1.65 × 0.898%)] = −1.44%.

(Study Session 16, LOS 49.c)

57. **B**   Liquidating a position when losses exceed a certain amount is an example of a stop loss limit. (Study Session 16, LOS 49.k)

58. **C**   Maximum drawdown is most commonly defined as the worst peak-to-trough decline in a portfolio's returns, or the worst-returning month or quarter for a portfolio. Maximum drawdown is an important risk measure for hedge funds. Redemption risk is a measure for open-end funds of the percentage of a portfolio could be redeemed at peak times. (Study Session 16, LOS 49.h)

59. **B**   The practice of driving the price in one direction with a series of small orders before executing a large order in the other direction is known as painting the tape. (Study Session 17, LOS 52.f)

60. **B**   Wash trading is a kind of market manipulation where the investor buys and sells the same financial instrument simultaneously, in order to simulate demand in the instrument by boosting trading volume. Placing a legitimate trade on one side of the market and several bogus orders on the other side of the market is known as layering. Entering large quantities of fictitious orders into the market and instantaneously canceling them is known as quote stuffing. (Study Session 17, LOS 52.f)

Exam 1
Afternoon Session Answers

To get valuable feedback on how your score compares to those of other Level II candidates, use your Username and Password to gain Online Access at schweser.com and click on the icon that says, *"Practice Exams Volume 1 (Enter answers from book)."*

61. B	81. C	101. A
62. B	82. C	102. A
63. A	83. C	103. C
64. C	84. A	104. C
65. C	85. A	105. C
66. C	86. B	106. A
67. A	87. C	107. B
68. B	88. C	108. B
69. C	89. A	109. A
70. C	90. C	110. C
71. A	91. B	111. B
72. A	92. B	112. B
73. A	93. C	113. A
74. B	94. B	114. A
75. A	95. A	115. A
76. B	96. B	116. C
77. C	97. B	117. B
78. A	98. C	118. B
79. C	99. A	119. A
80. C	100. C	120. C

EXAM 1
AFTERNOON SESSION ANSWERS

61. **B** **Standard VI(A).** The compensation plan is acceptable under Standard VI(A) Conflicts of Interest – Disclosure of Conflicts, but Chester must disclose the plan to clients. The firm's equity strategy is described as "large cap core." The S&P 500 Index is an appropriate benchmark for such a strategy, but the incentive for portfolio managers is to invest outside the index in order to achieve excess returns. Managers may be motivated to invest in securities that would not be consistent with client objectives or risk profiles. (Study Session 1, LOS 2.a)

62. **B** **Standard VI(A).** Rogers must discuss the offer with supervisory personnel at Chester before accepting the offer. His employer then has the opportunity to evaluate the effect of the offer on Rogers's ability to continue to perform his duties for Chester. The foundation is very large, and the position appears likely to consume much of Rogers's time and effort. If compensation is involved, Rogers would have to decline the offer unless Chester consented to the arrangement. (Study Session 1, LOS 2.a)

63. **A** **Standard III(D).** Chester has violated Standard III(D) Duties to Clients – Performance Presentation. The claim in itself is acceptable. Rogers's superior performance has lasted only a short time, and the advertising does not suggest otherwise. However, the superior performance has been achieved by investing in small cap securities, which is inconsistent with the stated style of Chester's equity management. Unless Chester discloses this change in style, the performance claims do not accurately reflect the firm's performance. Chester has not violated the Standards regarding use of and reference to the CFA designation. Rogers's use of the CFA designation is acceptable, and the quote stating that a CFA charterholder is committed to high ethical standards is acceptable as well. (Study Session 1, LOS 2.a)

64. **C** **Standard IV(A).** Pierce should not have taken any employer records, and the computer model was Chester's property, regardless of her co-worker's role in developing the model. Pierce has violated Standard IV(A) Duties to Employers – Loyalty by taking the model without Chester's consent. (Study Session 1, LOS 2.a)

65. **C** **Standard IV(A).** Pierce took no client records with her from Chester. It is reasonable to assume that she is using publicly available information to contact her former clients. So long as Pierce did not have a non-compete agreement, the standards do not preclude her from contacting former clients or encouraging them to move their accounts. The violation in this case was disclosing the new compensation plan. This plan should be disclosed to Chester's clients by Chester. Pierce does not have whistleblower status in this case because she stands to receive a personal gain by bringing her former clients to Cheeri. By disclosing the plan, Pierce has violated Standard IV(A) Duties to Employers – Loyalty by attempting to injure her former employer. Note that the compensation plan is not illegal; it is only a policy that should be disclosed. Had there been an illegal activity, Pierce might have had more justification as a whistleblower. (Study Session 1, LOS 2.a)

66. **C** **Standard III (D).** The problem is that Pierce's performance over the past three quarters arose from large cap securities, not small cap securities. Excluding these results misrepresents her ability as a large cap manager. The Standards do not require compliance with GIPS, nor do they require that previous employer results be excluded. Stating results of a specific style, such as large cap, is acceptable if it is accurate. (Study Session 1, LOS 2.a)

67. **A** 2009 sales forecast = 20.1 + 0.001 × 8,000 + 1,000.6 × 0.05 + 0.1 × 97 − 3.2 × 60,000 − 40.3 × 0.055 = −$191,914 (Study Session 3, LOS 10.e)

68. **B** Using a two-tail test at the 10% significance level, the critical value of the t-statistic equals 1.67 (degrees of freedom equal N − k − 1 = 76 − 5 − 1 = 70). The t-statistic (1.75) exceeds its critical value using a 10% significance level. (Study Session 3, LOS 10.c)

69. **C** As a general rule, any independent variable must have a t-statistic of 2 or more to be statistically significant. There is no indication that sales cannot be modeled. The main weakness in this model is the lack of significance of the PC variable. (Study Session 3, LOS 10.a)

70. **C** The F-value is calculated as (mean regression sum of squares) / (mean squared error) = (412,522/5) / (17,188/70) = 336. (Study Session 3, LOS 10.g)

71. **A** Clark finds that the correlation between the regression errors across time was very close to 1, indicating the presence of significant positive serial correlation. Positive serial correlation causes the standard errors to be too small, which then causes the t-statistics to be too large (biased upward). (Study Session 3, LOS 10.k)

72. **A** A regression exhibits conditional heteroskedasticity if the variance of the regression errors are not constant and are related to the regression independent variables. Clark's Finding 2 indicates that his regression exhibits conditional heteroskedasticity. (Study Session 3, LOS 10.k)

73. **A** The accounting for an ownership interest of between 20% and 50% in an associate is handled using the equity method. Under the equity method, the initial investment is recorded at cost and reported on the balance sheet as a noncurrent asset. Because the acquisition in this case is fully funded by cash, there will be no change to total assets for Hope. (Study Session 5, LOS 16.a)

74. **B** Hope is acquiring a 20% stake in Levitt for $185 million. The pro-rata book value of Levitt's net assets is $119.20 million (= 0.2 × [$824 million − $220 million − $8 million]). The amount of excess purchase price that should be allocated to PP&E is $28.4 million (= 0.2 × [$250 million − $108 million]). Goodwill is then computed as:

Purchase price:	$185.0 million
Less: pro-rata book value of net assets:	$119.2 million
Excess of purchase price:	$ 65.8 million
Less: excess allocated to PP&E:	$ 28.4 million
Goodwill:	$ 37.4 million

(Study Session 5, LOS 16.a)

75. **A** Hope's proportionate share of Levitt's net income is $21.6 million (= 0.2 × $108 million). Levitt's contribution to Hope's EBT is then computed as:

Hope's proportionate share of Levitt's net income:	$21.6 million
Less: additional depreciation expenses:	$ 5.0 million
Equity income:	$16.6 million

(Study Session 5, LOS 16.a)

76. **B** No calculations are required to solve this problem. The increase/decrease to Hope's investment balance is equal to the investment balance at the beginning of year plus equity income less dividends paid. The equity income is positive because Levitt had positive net income, and there is no additional depreciation expense to subtract. Additionally, Levitt is not expected to make any dividend payments for 2011. Based on this, Hope's investment balance will increase. (Study Session 5, LOS 16.a)

77. **C** Both the acquisition method and equity method will report the same net income. The acquisition method (under either partial or full goodwill) will report higher assets than the equity method and hence ROA would be lower under the acquisition method compared to under the equity method. (Study Session 5, LOS 16.c)

78. **A** When the investment constitutes 20% to 50% of the associate, and the investor has significant influence on the associate, IFRS prescribes the equity method for accounting for the investment. (Study Session 5, LOS 16.b)

79. **C** Management incentives are a key factor in light of Mr. Silver's desire to retire in three years and his interest in Flavoring management's capabilities to help guide the combined firm. Diversification is another key motivation because Flavoring's products are consumer based but serve a different market than Fashion's focus on consumer accessories. Because the companies have different product lines, synergies in the form of cost savings or revenue enhancement are unlikely to occur. In addition, the companies are in very different industries, making increased market power in either industry unlikely to occur as a result of the merger. (Study Session 8, LOS 26.b,d)

80. **C** Opportunities to expand its products into different segments of the market for spices are not indicated in the vignette. Flavoring's management appears more interested in geographic expansion of its existing product line. (Study Session 8, LOS 26.b)

81. **C** The bootstrap effect will only occur when Fashion's P/E ratio is higher than Flavoring's and Fashion's P/E post merger does not decline. At the current market price of $30.50, Fashion's P/E is 19.1, based on earnings per share of $1.60 ($80 million earnings/ 50 million shares). At its current market price of $20 and earnings per share of $1.10 ($22 million earnings/20 million shares), Flavoring's stock's P/E is 18.2x. Therefore, the combined earnings per share after the merger would be higher if Fashion issued stock at the current price and bought Flavoring at $20 or less per share. (Study Session 8, LOS 26.c)

82. **C** The following statistics show calculations of estimated takeover value using equal weighting.

Estimated Takeover Value	Flavoring	Mean Multiple	Price/Share	Equal Weight	Est. Value
Sales per share	$5.25	4.13	$21.68	0.25	$5.42
Book value per share	$3.60	5.95	$21.42	0.25	$5.36
Earnings per share	$1.10	19.78	$21.76	0.25	$5.44
Cash flow per share	$2.10	11.58	$24.32	0.25	$6.08
Total estimated value					**$22.30**

(Study Session 8, LOS 26.j)

83. **C** The takeover premium can be based on various statistics (mean, median, mode) of takeover premiums observed for comparable companies. In this case, the takeover premium is based on equally weighting the takeover premium for the four recently acquired companies.

	Jones Foods	Dale Inc.	Hill Brands	Lane Co.	Mean
Preacquisition price (A)	$20	$26	$35	$40	—
Acquisition price (B)	$24	$32	$40	$46	—
Takeover premium = (B – A) / A	20.0%	23.1%	14.3%	15.0%	**18.1%**

(Study Session 8, LOS 26.j)

84. **A** This is a key reason to use the comparable value method, particularly when contrasted with the use of discounted cash flow valuations. Acquisition prices are not necessarily approximations of intrinsic values. A price developed based on comparable transactions does not always indicate the potential value of the acquisition to the purchaser. (Study Session 8, LOS 26.h)

85. **A** Begin by calculating the capital structure of each plan and then multiply the percentage of debt and equity by their component costs and add the results to find the weighted average cost of capital (WACC). The plan with the lowest WACC maximizes the firm's stock price and thus reflects the optimal capital structure. In this case, Plan C meets all the criteria for optimizing X-Sport's capital structure. Plan C's debt-to-equity ratio is 1.22. Thus, there are 1.22 units of debt for every one unit of equity for a total of 2.22 units of capital. Therefore, the percentage of debt is 1.22 / 2.22 = 55%, leaving 45% equity. Thus, the WACC for Plan C is: $(0.55 \times 4.4\%) + (0.45 \times 11.2\%) = 7.46\%$.

Repeating these calculations for Plans A, B, and D, we find that the WACCs are 10.75%, 8.76%, and 7.75%, respectively. (Study Session 7, LOS 22.b)

86. **B** Kelley's report is incorrect regarding the static trade-off theory of capital structure, which states that a company should lever up to the point at which the additional increase in the costs of financial distress exceeds the additional increase in the tax shield from interest rate payments. Once this point is reached, adding more leverage to the company will decrease its value. Kelley's report is correct regarding the net agency costs of equity. Agency costs include equity holders' cost to monitor the firm's executives, management's bonding costs to assure owners that their best interests are guiding the company's actions, and residual losses that result even when sufficient monitoring and bonding exists. Adding additional debt reduces the agency costs to equity holders because less of their capital is at risk. The leverage effectively shifts some agency costs to bondholders. Additionally, managers have less cash to squander when higher leverage is employed because higher interest costs will restrict discretionary free cash flow. (Study Session 7, LOS 22.a)

87. **C** The most likely difference in the cost of debt financing between the current level of 5.0% and the 8.5% for Plan A is that there is a greater probability of bankruptcy. Using the debt-to-equity ratio, we observe that Plan A calls for 2.33 / (2.33 + 1) = 70% debt financing, which is a very large proportion of the capital structure. The chances of bankruptcy are much greater with this heavy reliance on debt financing. (Study Session 7, LOS 22.a)

88. **C** Miller and Modigliani Proposition II states that the cost of equity is a linear function of a company's debt/equity ratio. Pecking-order theory prefers internally generated equity (retained earnings) over new debt and new debt over new equity. Static trade-off theory states that the optimal level of debt is achieved when the extra cost of financial distress equals the tax benefit of debt. (Study Session 7, LOS 22.a)

89. **A** Spin-off transactions involve creating a new entity out of a company's business line or one of its subsidiaries and then granting shares in the new entity to the existing shareholders of the parent company. The shareholders are then free to sell their shares in the spin-off company in the marketplace. Spin-offs are generally viewed as a favorable sign in the market because they often result in greater efficiency for the spin-off company and the parent company. In a carve-out transaction, a new entity is created in a similar manner to the spin-off transaction. The main difference is that a minority of shares is sold to the public while the majority portion of the new shares are held by the parent company (they are not distributed to existing shareholders). (Study Session 8, LOS 26.n)

90. **C** X-Sport's board of directors suffers from a lack of independence from management. The most pressing issue is that the CEO of the company, Richard Haywood, is also the chairman of the board. Judging by his ability to convince the board of his plan to spin off GearTech, Haywood exerts an excessive degree of influence over the board. This lack of independence could negatively impact the value of X-Sport common stock because investors will demand a higher risk premium for holding the stock because there is significant risk that management will not act in the shareholders' best interest. Specifically, there is a great risk (as evidenced by their quick decision to spin off GearTech) that management will enter into future transactions (such as mergers, acquisitions, and divestitures) and assume business risks that are in management's interest but not in the shareholders' best interest. This is known as strategic policy risk, not liability risk. Note that there are two former executives of GearTech on the board who may benefit from spinning off the company. It is possible that the poor corporate governance at X-Sport may call into question the reliability of the financial disclosures of GearTech, but this risk is known as accounting risk, not asset risk. (Study Session 8, LOS 25.f,h)

91. **B**   Firm A should be valued using the one-period dividend discount model. The firm has a history of dividend payments, the dividend policy is clear and related to the earnings of the firm, and (as stated in the presentation) the perspective is that of a minority shareholder. A free cash flow model is more appropriate when examining the perspective of a controlling shareholder.

Firm B should be valued using a residual income model. The residual income approach is most appropriate for firms that do not have dividend histories, have transparent financial reporting, and have negative free cash flow for the foreseeable future (usually due to capital demands). (Study Session 10, LOS 30.a)

92. **B**   Firm C should be valued using an H dividend discount model. A firm that has little competition now, but has competition that is expected to increase, is a candidate for the H-model. Growth can be expected to decline as competitors enter the market. Growth then stabilizes as the industry matures.

Firm D should be valued using a two-stage dividend discount model. A firm that is expected to have a high rate of growth until patents expire, for example, should be modeled by the two-stage model, with one rate of growth before the patent expires and another rate thereafter. (Study Session 10, LOS 30.i)

93. **C**   The firm should be valued using an H dividend discount model given that an initially high rate of growth declines linearly over a specified period. The formula is:

$$V_0 = \frac{[D_0 \times (1+g_L)] + [D_0 \times H(g_S - g_L)]}{r - g_L}$$

where:

$$H = \left(\frac{t}{2}\right) = \text{half-life (in years) of high-growth period}$$

where:
t   = length of high-growth period
g_S = short-term growth rate
g_L = long-term growth rate
r   = required return

Using the figures for Maple:

$$V_0 = \frac{[\$3.00 \times (1+0.07)] + \left[\$3.00 \times \left(\frac{8}{2}\right) \times (0.25 - 0.07)\right]}{0.15 - 0.07} = \$67.13$$

(Study Session 10, LOS 30.l)

94. **B** If you grow the $5.00 dividend out for four years at 18%, the first four dividends are:

D_1	D_2	D_3	D_4
$ 5.90	$ 6.96	$ 8.22	$ 9.69

D5 is then D4 × 1.04 = $10.0816. Discounting the first four dividends at 15%, you obtain:

$PV(D_1)$	$PV(D_2)$	$PV(D_3)$	$PV(D_4)$
$ 5.13	$ 5.26	$ 5.40	$ 5.54

Discounting the dividends from the end of Year 4 to perpetuity using the dividend discount model, you obtain:

10.0816/(0.15 − 0.04) = $91.65. Discounting this figure back to the present, you have 91.65/(1.15⁴) = $52.40.

Summing up the present values of all the above (5.13 + 5.26 + 5.40 + 5.54 + 52.40), you have a total price of $73.73.

Note that your answer may differ slightly from the answer above due to rounding. (Study Session 10, LOS 30.l)

95. **A** The stock price represents the present value of the future dividends (on a no-growth basis) and the present value of the growth opportunities (PVGO):

$$\text{value} = \frac{E_1}{r} + \text{PVGO}$$

Thus the value of a firm's equity has two components: the value of its assets in place (E_1/r) and the present value of its future investment opportunities (PVGO).

$$90 = \frac{6}{0.15} + \text{PVGO}$$

$$\text{PVGO} = 50$$

The P/E for the firm is 90/6 = 15.00.
The P/E of the PVGO is 50/6 = 8.33.

The percentage of Wood Athletic Supplies leading P/E related to PVGO is then 8.33 / 15.00 = 56%. (Study Session 10, LOS 30.e)

96. **B** Statement 1 is incorrect. All of Pacious's description of the initial growth phase is correct except that, in this stage, the free cash flows to equity are actually negative. This is due to the heavy capital investment. Statement 2 is correct. The terminal value in the three-stage dividend growth model can be estimated using either approach. (Study Session 10, LOS 30.j,k)

97. **B** R&D should be capitalized and amortized rather than expensing when incurred. The other adjustments are appropriate. (Study Session 11, LOS 33.a)

98. **C** EVA = NOPAT − $WACC

NOPAT = EBIT × (1 − t) = 28.1 × (1 − 0.45) = 15.455

$WACC = WACC × total capital = 12.5% × 109.2 = $13.65m

For EVA computation, we need beginning 20X6 total capital (i.e., 20X5 ending).

EVA = 15.455 − 13.65 = $1.805m

(Study Session 11, LOS 33.a)

99. **A** Residual income = accounting profit (after tax and interest) minus a charge for equity capital employed.

Net income for 20X6	12.5
Beg. stockholders' equity 85.2[1]	
(−)Cost of equity @ 15%	(12.78)
(=) Residual income	(0.28)

[1]Beginning stockholders' equity = 20X5 ending stockholders' equity = common stock + additional paid-in capital + retained income = 20 + 10 + 55.2 = 85.2.

(Study Session 11, LOS 33.a)

100. **C** Market Value Added = market value of (total) capital − book value of capital

= (145 + 16) − (94.5 + 16)

= $50.5m

(Study Session 11, LOS 33.a)

101. **A** WCInv = 32.4 − 27.2 = 5.2

FCInv = (ending FA − beginning FA + depreciation) = 78.1 − 82.0 + 12 = 8.1

Net borrowing = 16-24 = −8

FCFE = NI + depreciation − WCInv − FCInv + net borrowing

= 12.5 + 12 − 5.2 − 8.1 − 8 = 3.2

(Study Session 11, LOS 31.d)

102. **A** Value of equity = book value of equity + PV of residual income

Value as of 31 December 20X6:

= 94.5 + [5 ÷ (0.15 − 0.05)]

= $144.5m

(Study Session 11, LOS 33.a)

103. **C** The completed binomial tree is as follows:

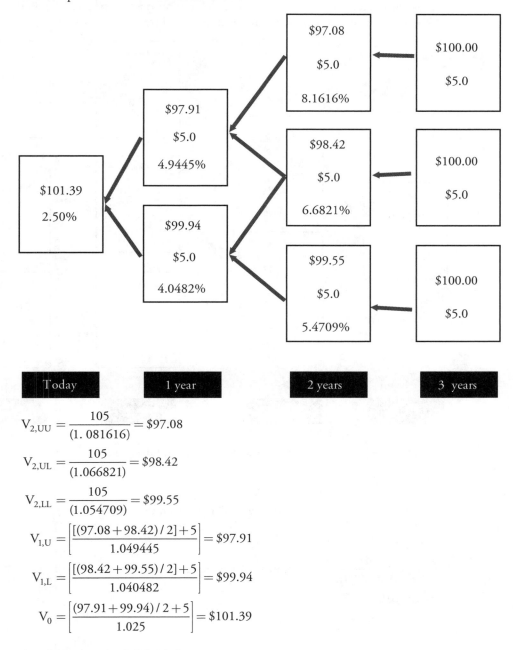

| Today | 1 year | 2 years | 3 years |

$$V_{2,UU} = \frac{105}{(1.081616)} = \$97.08$$

$$V_{2,UL} = \frac{105}{(1.066821)} = \$98.42$$

$$V_{2,LL} = \frac{105}{(1.054709)} = \$99.55$$

$$V_{1,U} = \left[\frac{[(97.08 + 98.42)/2] + 5}{1.049445}\right] = \$97.91$$

$$V_{1,L} = \left[\frac{[(98.42 + 99.55)/2] + 5}{1.040482}\right] = \$99.94$$

$$V_0 = \left[\frac{(97.91 + 99.94)/2 + 5}{1.025}\right] = \$101.39$$

(Study Session 12, LOS 36.d)

104. **C** The value of bond A under interest rate scenario of path X is determined as:

$$\text{Value} = \frac{5}{(1.025)} + \frac{5}{(1.025)(1.049445)} + \frac{105}{(1.025)(1.049445)(1.066821)} = \$101.02$$

(Study Session 12, LOS 36.g)

105. **C** An extendible bond is valued identically to a putable bond. Bond B would be identical to a 3-year putable bond where the underlying option is a European put option exercisable in 2 years at par. The completed binomial tree is given below.

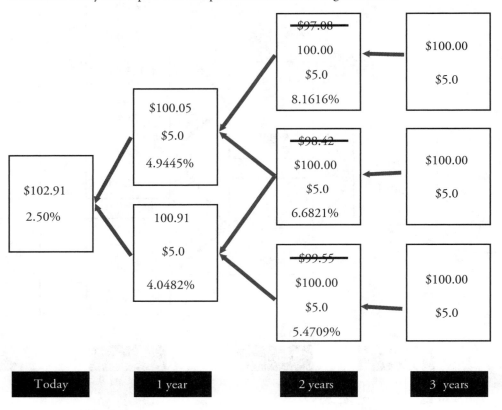

$$V_{2,UU} = \frac{105}{(1.081616)} = \$97.08. \text{ Investor will not extend the bond.}$$

Value = $100

$$V_{2,UL} = \frac{105}{(1.066821)} = \$98.42. \text{ Investor will not extend the bond.}$$

Value = $100

$$V_{2,LL} = \frac{105}{(1.054709)} = \$99.55. \text{ Investor will not extend the bond.}$$

Value = $100

$$V_{1,U} = \left[\frac{[(100.00 + 100.00)/2] + 5}{1.049445} \right] = \$100.05$$

$$V_{1,L} = \left[\frac{[(100.00 + 100.00)/2] + 5}{1.040482} \right] = \$100.91$$

$$V_0 = \left[\frac{(100.05 + 100.91)/2 + 5}{1.025} \right] = \$102.91$$

(Study Session 13, LOS 37.f)

106. **A** Bond B is identical to a 3-year putable bond with the put option exercisable in year 2. If the volatility estimate used to generate the interest rate tree is lower than the actual volatility, the value of the put option and, thus, the value of the putable bond would be underestimated. A lower volatility estimate would underestimate the OAS computed for the putable bond. When the assumed level of interest rate volatility is underestimated, the computed value of the bond using backward induction methodology will be too low; therefore, the OAS needed to force the model price to be equal to the market price will be lower as well. (Study Session 13, LOS 37.d,h)

107. **B** Bond B and Geneva Inc. bonds are of the same credit quality, but Geneva Inc.'s bond offers a lower OAS and, hence, offers lower compensation for taking the same credit risk. Hence, the Geneva Inc. bond is overpriced. The difference in option feature is not relevant, as OAS is computed after adjusting for option risk. (Study Session 13, LOS 37.g)

108. **B** Both callable and putable bonds have an effective duration that is less than or equal to the effective duration of an option-free bond. When the underlying call option is deep out of money, the effective duration of a callable bond and that of an option-free bond will be same. As a result, the statement about effective duration is incorrect. Thomas's statement about one-sided down duration is correct. Due to the limited upside for a callable bond, the change in price of a callable bond for a decrease in interest rates is lower than the change in price for an option-free bond. (Study Session 13, LOS 37.j,k)

109. **A** The futures price can be calculated by growing the spot price at the difference between the continuously compounded risk-free rate and the dividend yield as a continuously compounded rate. The continuously compounded risk-free rate is ln(1.040811) = 4%, so the futures price for a 240-day future is:

$$FP = S_0 e^{(r-d)t} = 1,050 e^{(0.04-0.02)(240/365)} = 1,064$$

(Study Session 14, LOS 40.a)

110. **C** The futures price for a given contract maturity must converge to the spot price as the contract moves toward expiration. Otherwise, arbitrage opportunities would exist. (Study Session 14, LOS 40.a)

111. **B** First, calculate the continuously compounded risk-free rate as ln(1.040811) = 4% and then calculate the theoretically correct futures price as follows:

$$FP = S_0 e^{(r-d)t} = 1,015 e^{(4.0-2.0)(180/365)} = 1,025$$

Then, compare the theoretical price to the observed market price: 1,035 − 1,025 = 10. The futures contract is overpriced. To take advantage of the arbitrage opportunity, the investor should sell the (overpriced) futures contract and buy the underlying asset (the equity index) using borrowed funds. Norris has suggested the opposite. (Study Session 14, LOS 40.a)

112. **B** An increase in the growth rate in dividends for stocks would increase the spot price of the equity index. As the spot price increases, the futures price for a given maturity also increases (holding interest rates constant). Higher dividends during the short period of time until maturity of the futures contract would have only a minimal negative impact on the futures price. (Study Session 14, LOS 40.a)

113. **A** Given the decrease in the index level, the value of the short party's position in a forward contract should be positive. Because the futures contracts are marked to market, the value to the short (or long) party only reflects the change in futures price since the last mark to market. Hence, the value of the futures contract should be lower than the value of the forward contract. (Study Session 14, LOS 40.a)

114. **A** Based on the exchange rate at initiation, the notional principals were €1,000,000 and SF 1,120,000. Sixty days after initiation, the remaining settlement days are 30, 120, 210, and 300 days into the future. The value of the Swiss franc position (per 1 SF notional) is calculated as: (0.0096 / 4) × (0.9996 + 0.9978 + 0.9961 + 0.9932) + 1 × 0.9932 = SF 1.0028. For the notional principal of SF 1,120,000, the value is SF 1,123,136. Based on the current exchange rate, this translates into (1,123,136 / 1.10) euros or €1,021,033.

     The euro position value is given as €1.0014 per €1 notional. For €1 million notional, this translates into a value of €1,001,400. Because Witkowski's client paid the euro notional at initiation, they will receive the euros and have a value of €1,001,400 − €1,021,033 = −€19,633. (Study Session 14, LOS 40.d)

115. **A** $E(R_A) = \Sigma w_{P,j} E(R_{P,j}) - \Sigma w_{B,j} E(R_{B,j}) = 11.07\% - 10.44\% = 0.63\%$

     (Study Session 17, LOS 51.a)

116. **C** Both statements are correct. Information ratio, unlike the Sharpe ratio, is affected by an allocation to cash or by the use of leverage. For an unconstrained optimization, a change in aggressiveness in active weights changes both the active return and active risk proportionally, leaving the information ratio unchanged. (Study Session 17, LOS 51.b)

117. **B** IR(Dena) = IR(Orient)
     $(0.2) \times (0.99) \times \sqrt{12} = (0.25) \times (0.80) \times \sqrt{X}$
     $\sqrt{X} = 3.429; X = 11.76$

     (Study Session 17, LOS 51.c)

118. **B** IC = 2(% correct) − 1
     $IC_A = 2(0.52) - 1 = 0.04$
     $IC_B = 2(0.58) - 1 = 0.16$
     $IC_C = 2(0.59) - 1 = 0.18$

     $IR = IC\sqrt{BR}$
     $IR_A = 0.04\sqrt{12 \times 2} = 0.20$
     $IR_B = 0.16\sqrt{4 \times 3} = 0.55$
     $IR_C = 0.18\sqrt{2 \times 2} = 0.36$

     Any investor should always choose the fund with the highest information ratio. The amount of active risk can then be adjusted by changing the allocation of portfolio to the benchmark versus the active fund. (Study Session 17, LOS 51.c,d,e)

119. **A** Both statements are incorrect. The portfolio with the highest information ratio will have the highest Sharpe ratio. Recall that the Sharpe ratio of the portfolio is computed as $SR_P^2 = SR_B^2 + IR_P^2$. Given that benchmark Sharpe ratio (SR_B) is the same for all similar active portfolios, the active portfolio with the highest information ratio will also be the portfolio with the highest Sharpe ratio. The optimal active risk for a constrained portfolio = TC × optimal active risk for an unconstrained portfolio. Given that TC < 1 for constrained portfolio, the optimal active risk for a constrained portfolio will be lower than the optimal active risk for an unconstrained portfolio. (Study Session 17, LOS 51.c,d)

120. **C** Active risk is comprised of the uncertainty from benchmark tracking risk and uncertainty about the true information coefficient (σ_{IC}). Hence, an increase in uncertainty about the information coefficient will increase active risk.

The basic fundamental law relates expected active return to the information coefficient as follows:

$$E(R_A) = \frac{IC}{\sigma_{IC}} \sqrt{BR}\ \sigma_A$$

Hence, an increase in the uncertainty of the information coefficient leads to a decrease in the expected active return and a decrease in the information ratio. (Study Session 17, LOS 51.f)

Exam 2
Morning Session Answers

To get valuable feedback on how your score compares to those of other Level II candidates, use your Username and Password to gain Online Access at schweser.com and click on the icon that says, *"Practice Exams Volume 1 (Enter answers from book)."*

1. C	21. A	41. C
2. A	22. B	42. B
3. C	23. C	43. C
4. C	24. A	44. A
5. B	25. C	45. A
6. A	26. C	46. B
7. B	27. B	47. A
8. C	28. B	48. C
9. C	29. C	49. A
10. A	30. C	50. B
11. A	31. B	51. C
12. B	32. C	52. B
13. A	33. A	53. C
14. A	34. A	54. C
15. C	35. A	55. A
16. B	36. C	56. A
17. C	37. C	57. C
18. B	38. A	58. A
19. C	39. C	59. C
20. A	40. A	60. C

Exam 2
Morning Session Answers

1. **C** There is no violation of the Standards in Transaction A. Connor is basically hedging any potential loss from a decline in the price of Stock A prior to the completion of his sale transaction. There is no apparent attempt to manipulate the market in this transaction. (Study Session 1, LOS 2.a,b)

2. **A** A critical factor in assessing any violation of Standard II(B) Integrity of Capital Markets – Market Manipulation is the intent of the parties involved. In this case, Connor is hoping that his options transaction drives up the price of Stock B, which would improve the reported performance of the Biogene Fund. This type of manipulation would be a violation of the Standard. (Study Session 1, LOS 2.a,b)

3. **C** Transactions meant to minimize tax liabilities are not prohibited by the Standards. If the Biogene Fund benefits, the investors in the fund will presumably benefit also. (Study Session 1, LOS 2.a,b)

4. **C** Connor was not pressured to take the IPO, and he believed it was a good investment. Connor received no confidential information. The IPO had been made available to all Apple clients prior to Biogene. There is no evidence of a violation of either of these Standards. (Study Session 1, LOS 2.a,b)

5. **B** By suggesting that Biogene might need to acquire more shares to support the price in the future, Arnold is suggesting that Apple would be willing to manipulate the market by creating false trading volume. This is transaction-based manipulation in violation of Standard II(B) Integrity of Capital Markets – Market Manipulation. (Study Session 1, LOS 2.a,b)

6. **A** By changing his previous decision and accepting the 2% based on Arnold's e-mail, Connor has violated the Standards related to material nonpublic information. He has acted based upon the receipt of inside information. Arnold has violated the Standards related to both material nonpublic information and preservation of confidentiality. Arnold violated Standard III(E) – Duties to Clients – Preservation of Confidentiality by revealing information he received based upon a special relationship with Stock D. By passing that information to another area of Apple, Arnold has violated Standard II(A) Integrity of Capital Markets – Material Nonpublic Information as well. (Study Session 1, LOS 2.a,b)

7. **B** Krosse is a developing nation with the highest α (share of capital in GDP) among all the countries. A high value of α indicates that the next unit of capital added will increase output almost as much as the previous unit of capital. Developing nations with a high α are more likely to benefit from capital deepening, which should result in an increase in productivity (at least in the short term). (Study Session 4, LOS 14.d)

8. **C** Krosse's labor growth rate is greater than that of Procken's. Labor growth can be accomplished by an increase in the labor force participation rate, an increase in average hours worked, additional supply of labor by immigration, or a higher population growth rate. We are told that the population growth rate is equal for the two countries. The only choice that allows for higher labor growth rate is then higher average hours worked. (Study Session 4, LOS 14.g)

9. **C** Growth rate in potential GDP = long-term growth rate of technology + α × (long-term growth rate of capital) + $(1 - \alpha)$ × (long-term growth rate of labor).

    The growth rate in potential GDP using a calculator: PV = –$4,800; FV = +$5,778; N = 5; solve for I/Y. I/Y = 3.78%.

    Rearrange the equation to solve for long-term growth rate of technology.
    3.78% = LTGRT + (0.225) × 3.8% + (0.775) × 0.8%
    LTGRT = 3.78% – 0.86% – 0.62%
    LTGRT = 2.30%
    (Study Session 4, LOS 14.e)

10. **A** If the neoclassical theory holds then the sustainable growth rate of output of G* is the same as the long-term rate of capital.

    The growth rate in potential GDP using a calculator:
    Procken (Past = 4.0%): PV = –$250; FV = +$306; N = 5; solve for I/Y = 4.12%.
    Krosse (Past = 4.7%): PV = –$250; FV = +$315; N = 5; solve for I/Y = 4.73%.
    Weira (Past = 4.5%): PV = –$4,500; FV = +$5,262; N = 5; solve for I/Y = 3.18%.
    Toban (Past = 3.8%): PV = –$4,800; FV = +$5,778; N = 5; solve for I/Y = 3.78%.

    Weira's stock market appreciation rate of 4.5% exceeds the potential growth rate of GDP of 3.2% significantly. The difference between potential GDP growth rate and past stock market appreciation for the other three countries differences is relatively smaller. (Study Session 4, LOS 14.b,i)

11. **A** It is stated in the vignette that Weira has reached steady-state. In steady state (i.e., in equilibrium), the marginal product of capital (MPK = $\alpha Y/K$) and marginal cost of capital (i.e., the *rental price of capital*, r) are equal; hence: $\alpha Y/K = r$.

    r = (0.25)(4,500) / (18,750) = 0.06 or 6%

    (Study Session 4, LOS 14.d)

12. **B** Based on the data in the vignette, Krosse and Procken are developing countries. The GDP per capita for Krosse is $250 billion divided by 20.0 million people, which is equal to $12,500. The GDP per capita for Procken is $250 billion divided by 20.4 million people, which is equal to $12,255. Krosse is more likely to achieve convergence because Krosse is showing more willingness towards opening up the economy to trade and financial flows than is Procken; Krosse's international trade as a proportion of GDP is higher than Proken's, and comments by Krosse's representative indicate that inflow of foreign capital would be welcome. Finally, comments by Procken's representative indicate an inward-oriented policy, which could hinder convergence. (Study Session 4, LOS 14.j)

13. **A** Inventory turnover is cost of sales divided by inventory. A decrease in inventory is likely to cause the ratio to increase as the amount of inventory relative to the cost of goods sold decreases. (Study Session 6, LOS 20.d)

14. **A** Ending inventory and other current assets are both included within total assets, so the reclassification will not alter total assets or revenue. (Study Session 6, LOS 19.d)

15. **C** Biased accounting choices are reflected not only in the numbers presented but also in the manner of disclosure of information. The lack of transparency of GAAP-compliant net income relative to the headline net income suggests that the financial statements are not very decision-useful. (Study Session 6, LOS 19.b)

16. **B**

	2014	2013	2012
Headline Net Income	**1,262.7**	**1,104.4**	**1,086.0**
Network costs (from note A)	885.5	325.0	202.0
Settlements (from note A)	24.8	22.1	20.0
Net Income	**352.4**	**757.3**	**864.0**

Net Income CAGR $[(352.4/864)^{1/2}] - 1 = -0.36 = -36\%$

Average stockholders' equity = (8,380 + 7,980)/2 = 8,180

Return on stockholders' equity for 2014 = 352.4/8,180 = 4.31%

Earnings quality refers not only to compliance with GAAP but also to the persistence and level of earnings. The GAAP-compliant net income does not satisfy the minimum return requirement; hence, earnings are low (and therefore of low quality). (Study Session 6, LOS 19.h)

17. **C** An investment in associates is accounted for using the equity method, while investment in a subsidiary is accounted for using the acquisition method. Using either method, net income will be the same. However, fixed assets and total revenue will be lower under the equity method. (Study Session 6, LOS 19.k)

18. **B**

	2014	**2013**	**2012**	**2011**
	(£000)	(£000)	(£000)	(£000)
Revenue	998.5	918.6	817.6	
Net Income	44.4	31.2	26.7	
Income from Associates	17.8	11.2	8.4	
NI Excluding Associates	26.6	20.0	18.3	
Total Assets	1,260.8	1,166.6	1,043.2	1,012.1
Investment in Assoc.	101.6	83.8	72.6	64.2
Total Assets (Ex assoc.)	1,159.2	1,082.8	970.6	947.9
Equity	638.4	569.8	542.5	524.2
Average Equity	604.1	556.2	533.4	510.2
Average Assets	1,213.7	1,104.9	1,027.7	500.8
Average Assets (Ex assoc.)	1,121.0	1,026.7	959.3	
Net Margin (Ex assoc.)	2.66% (26.6 / 998.5)	2.18% (20.0 / 918.6)	2.24% (18.3 / 817.6)	
Net Margin	4.45% (44.4 / 998.5)	3.40% (31.2 / 918.6)	3.27% (26.7 / 817.6)	
Asset TO (Ex assoc.)	0.891 (998.5 / 1121.0)	0.895 (918.6 / 1026.7)	0.852 (817.6 / 959.3)	
Asset Turnover	0.823 (998.5 / 1213.7)	0.831 (918.6 / 1104.9)	0.796 (817.6 / 1027.7)	
Leverage	2.01 (1213.7 / 604.1)	1.99 (1104.9 / 556.2)	1.93 (1027.7 / 533.4)	
ROE Total	7.35% (44.4 / 604.1)	5.61% (31.2 / 556.2)	5.01% (26.7 / 533.4)	
ROE (Ex assoc.)	4.77% (0.0266 × 0.891 × 2.01)	3.87% (0.0218 × 0.895 × 1.99)	3.68% (0.0224 × 0.852 × 1.93)	

(Study Session 6, LOS 20.a)

19. **C** Assuming International Oilfield is an integrated sales division and Continental Supply makes virtually all of the decisions, the functional currency is likely the presentation currency. Thus, the temporal method is used. Under the temporal method, remeasurement gains and losses are reported in the income statement.
(Study Session 5, LOS 18.d)

20. **A** International Oilfield is carrying 867 (i.e., 975 − 108) LCU original cost of equipment purchased in 2014 on their books. The 2015 losses due to fire and related insurance settlement do not affect depreciation in 2016 (other than depreciating fewer assets). The new equipment purchased during the year would be depreciated for a half year in 2016. Depreciation will be translated at the historical exchange rate under the temporal method.

Equipment	Calculation	LCU Depreciation	Historical Exchange Rate	USD Depreciation
Originally purchased in 2014	867 / 10	86.7	1	$ 86.70
Purchased in 2016 (1/2 year)	1/2 × (225 /10)	11.25	1.25	$ 9.00
Total				$ 95.70

(Study Session 5, LOS 18.d)

21. **A** Under the current rate method, gains and losses that occur as a result of the translation process do not show up on the income statement but are instead accumulated in a balance sheet account called the cumulative translation adjustment account (CTA). The translation gain or loss in each year is calculated and added to the account, acting like a running total of translation gains and losses. The CTA is simply an equity account on the balance sheet.

    To compute the CTA for Continental's balance sheet, force the accounting equation (A = L + E) to balance with the CTA; [(120 million cash and receivables + 631.3 million inventory + 820.7 million equipment − 600 million liabilities) / 1.50] − $350 million capital stock − $525 retained earnings = −$227 million. The LCU 350 capital stock was issued at the end of 2013 at an exchange rate of LCU 1 = $1. The $525 retained earnings figure was given in the text. (Study Session 5, LOS 18.d)

22. **B** Compared to the temporal method, the current rate method will result in a higher gross profit margin percentage (higher numerator) when the local currency is depreciating as is the case in this scenario (the exchange rate has risen from LCU 1 per $1 to LCU 1.25 per $1; thus, it costs more LCUs to buy $1 which is the result of a depreciating LCU). Under the temporal method, COGS is remeasured at the historic rate; thus, COGS is not impacted by the depreciating currency. Under the current rate method, COGS is translated at the average rate; thus, COGS is lower because of the depreciating currency. Lower COGS results in a higher gross profit margin percentage.
(Study Session 5, LOS 18.e)

23. **C** Both the numerator (cash + receivables) and denominator (current liabilities) of the quick ratio are remeasured at the current exchange rate under the temporal method. Inventories are ignored in the quick ratio. Since the same rate is used to remeasure both the numerator and denominator, the ratio does not change when stated in the presentation currency. (Study Session 5, LOS 18.e)

24. **A** The temporal method is required if the foreign subsidiary is operating in a highly inflationary environment, defined as cumulative inflation of more than 100% in a 3-year period. Compounded inflation of 30% annually for three years is approximately 120% ($1.30^3 - 1$). Under the temporal method, remeasurement gains and losses are recognized in the income statement. In this case, International Oilfield has a net monetary liability position (monetary liabilities of 600 million > monetary assets of 120 million). Holding net monetary liabilities denominated in a currency that is depreciating will result in a gain. (Study Session 5, LOS 18.g)

25. **C** CEO compensation is consistent with market estimates, so no adjustment is necessary. Long-term leases on facilities are legally binding; hence, no adjustment is necessary until the lease comes up for renewal. Elimination of excessive perks is a valid adjustment. (Study Session 11, LOS 34.e)

26. **C**

Normalized EBITDA	32
(–) Depreciation	11
(=) EBIT	21
Taxes @ 25%	5.25
Operating income after tax	15.75
(+) Depreciation	11
(–) Capex	6
(–) WCInv	5
(=) FCFF	15.75

(Study Session 11, LOS 34.e)

27. **B** Sampson intends to make a purchase offer for controlling equity interests in the target companies. Cash flow models are more appropriate because a controlling interest allows Sampson to set the target company's financing, investment, and distribution policies. (Study Session 9, LOS 27.h)

28. **B** NavTech recently has decided to capitalize much of its research and development expense, thereby deferring much of its R&D expense (rather than immediately recognizing R&D as expense on the income statement). This is an example of aggressive accounting, especially if revenues cannot be matched directly with R&D expense. By reducing the investment return assumption on its pension investments, Sampson is moving to a more conservative approach. By capitalizing its leases (treating as finance leases rather than operating leases), Aerospace Communications more clearly reports its liabilities and assets. (Study Session 9, LOS 27.e)

29. **C** If the company's business model is not sustainable, the liquidation value is more appropriate than its value as a going concern (which could be negative). Balance sheet value is an accounting concept, not a valuation concept. (Study Session 9, LOS 27.b)

30. **C** Defining P_0 as the current stock price, D_1 as the expected year-end dividend, r as the required cost of equity, and g as the dividend growth rate, the present value formula for constant growth dividends is:

$$P_0 = \$21.40 = \frac{D_1}{r-g} = \frac{\$1.07}{0.12-g}$$

$$0.12-g = \frac{\$1.07}{\$21.40}$$

$$g = 0.12 - \frac{\$1.07}{\$21.40} = 0.07 = 7\%$$

(Study Session 9, LOS 27.d; and Study Session 10, LOS 30.d)

31. **B** An analyst must review the cash flows from a company's operating, investing, and financing activities to generate a useful free cash flow, while dividends are simply set by the board of directors. Analysts use free cash flow whenever an investor takes a control perspective, such as in the event of an acquisition. The P/E model is considered weak because accounting issues can impact earnings. Companies that do not generate free cash flow in the long run are in financial trouble. (Study Session 11, LOS 31.a)

32. **C** Free cash flow to the firm (FCFF) can be calculated in many ways but in this question, you are given enough information to calculate the measure in the following way:

FCFF = net income + non-cash charges + interest (1 − t) − fixed capital investment − working capital investment

$FCFF_0$ = 20,000,000 + 1,250,000 + 0 − 8,450,000 − (9,985,000 − 7,460,000) = 10,275,000

The next step is to forecast the future FCFFs and the terminal value:

$FCFF_1$ = 10,275,000(1.25) = 12,843,750

$FCFF_2$ = 12,843,750(1.25) = 16,054,688

terminal value = 16,054,688(1.12) / (0.15 − 0.12) = 599,375,000

Next, calculate the present value of the FCFFs and the terminal value:

$$PV_{FCFs} = \frac{12,843,750}{1.15} + \frac{(16,054,688 + 599,375,000)}{(1.15)^2} = 476,521,739$$

If a firm has non-operating assets (e.g., land held for investment) on its balance sheet, the value of these assets must be added to the value of the operating assets (determined using the present value of the FCFFs and terminal value) to find the total firm value.

total firm value = value of operating assets + value of non-operating assets

total firm value = 476,521,739 + 875,000 = 477,396,739

(Study Session 11, LOS 31.j)

33. **A** If BioTLab established a dividend there would no impact on either FCFF or FCFE. Changing the company capital structure by increasing debt will not impact FCFF, although it will initially increase FCFE by the amount of debt issued and then reduce FCFE thereafter by the after-tax interest expense. (Study Session 11, LOS 31.g)

34. **A** The FCFF model is better than the FCFE model in valuing debt laden, cyclical companies, and companies with a changing capital structure. Since Groh Group does not pay a dividend, the DDM model would be the least appropriate model to value the company. (Study Session 11, LOS 31.a,g)

35. **A** WACC = (0.35 / 1.35)(0.06)(1 − 0.40) + (1 / 1.35)(0.13) = 10.56%

    FCFF = FCFE + Int(1 − T) − net borrowing
    $\qquad$ = 20,000,000 + 4,000,000(1 − 0.40) − 1,600,000
    $\qquad$ = 20,800,000

    $$\text{firm value} = \frac{FCFF_0\,(1+g)}{WACC - g}$$

    $$483,508,770 = \frac{20,800,000\,(1+g)}{0.1056 - g}$$

    $$g = 0.06$$

    (Study Session 11, LOS 31.j)

36. **C** FCFF can be inflated by decreasing capital expenditures relative to depreciation. All other statements are true. (Study Session 11, LOS 31.e,g)

37. **C** *Interest rate tree*: Discount maturity value back one year at different 1-year forward rates, then take the equally weighted average of those values discounted back to today at today's 1-year rate:

    V = 0.5 × [(108 / 1.08530) + 8] / 1.0725 + 0.5 × [(108 / 1.06983) + 8] / 1.0725

    V = 0.5 × (99.512 + 8) / 1.0725 + 0.5 × (100.951 + 8) / 1.0725

    V = 50.122 + 50.793 = 100.915

Today	Year 1	Year 2
		108
	107.512	
100.915		108
	108.951	
		108

    (Study Session 12, LOS 36.d)

38. **A** Use the same method as in the previous problem, but remember that if the value at one node exceeds the call price, then the call price should be used for that node. In this case, the value at the lower node would be 108 / 1.06983 = 100.951. The assumption is that the bond would be called at the call price one year from now, or 100.

V = 0.5 × (99.512 + 8) / 1.0725 + 0.5 × (100 + 8) / 1.0725

V = 50.122 + 50.350 = 100.472

(Study Session 13, LOS 37.f)

39. **C** Statement 1 is correct. The value of the option would be the difference between the value calculated with no call feature (the Bratton bonds) and the value calculated assuming the bond is callable (the Hardin bonds). Recall that the vignette stated the Bratton and Hardin bonds were identical except for the call feature in the Hardin bonds. The option value would therefore be: 100.915 – 100.472 = 0.443. Statement 2 is also correct. Increased volatility would increase the value of the option, thus lowering the value of the callable bond. (Study Session 13, LOS 37.b,h)

40. **A** The OAS accounts for compensation for credit and liquidity risk after the optionality has been removed (i.e., after cash flows have been adjusted). Since in this case the credit risk of the bonds is similar, the OAS could prove helpful in evaluating the relative liquidity risk. OAS will be affected by different assumptions regarding the volatility of interest rates. (Study Session 13, LOS 37.g)

41. **C** Option-free Bratton bonds will have higher one-sided down duration compared to the callable Hardin bonds when the underlying option is at- or near-the-money. Due to the underlying call option, the appreciation of Hardin bonds in a declining interest rate scenario will be limited. (Study Session 13, LOS 37.k)

42. **B** The duration formula given will calculate the percentage change in price for a 100 basis point change in yield, regardless of the actual change in rates used to derive BV_- and BV_+. The standard backward induction process would ensure that the derived values of BV_- and BV_+ reflect any potential change in cash flows due to embedded options. (Study Session 13, LOS 37.i)

43. **C** An option that is deep in-the-money will have the largest delta. Call options that are deep in-the-money will have a delta close to one, while put options that are deep in-the-money will have a delta close to –1. Options that are out-of-the-money will have deltas close to zero. Put F is the option that is deepest in-the-money, and therefore has the largest delta (even though it is negative, the change in the price of Put F given a change in the price of BIC stock will be larger than any of the other options). Call C is the deepest out-of-the-money option, and thus has the smallest delta. (Study Session 14, LOS 41.k)

44. **A** An option's gamma measures the change in the delta for a change in the price of the underlying asset. The gamma of an option is highest when an option is at-the-money since the probability of moving in or out of the money is high. Put E is close to being at-the-money and because it has a gamma of greater than zero, the sensitivity of Put E's price to changes in BIC's stock price (i.e., the delta) is likely to change. The higher the gamma, the greater the change in delta given a change in stock price. (Study Session 14, LOS 41.l)

45. **A** As the option moves further into the money and as the expiration date approaches, the delta of a put option moves closer to –1. (Study Session 14, LOS 41.k)

46. **B** The premium on Put D has risen from $2.31 to $3.18 and there is still time left until expiration. Therefore, the increase in value must have come from either a decrease in stock price, an increase in volatility, or both of these events. Choice A would be correct if the option was at expiration and the $3.18 represented only intrinsic value. Since we are not yet at the expiration date, the stock price must be above $26.82. A negative earnings surprise would most likely cause a drop in the market price of the stock. Since there is no indication of the exact amount of the drop in price, the premium observed is a possibility. A decrease in BIC volatility would reduce the put premium, not increase it. (Study Session 14, LOS 41.k)

47. **A** To protect a portfolio against an expected decrease in the value of a long equity position, put options can be purchased (i.e., a protective put strategy). The number of puts to purchase depends on the hedge ratio, which depends on the option's delta. Because the delta of the put options is negative, as the option delta moves closer to −1, the number of options necessary to maintain the hedge falls. (Study Session 14, LOS 41.l)

48. **C** Grimell is incorrect in both of his statements. Using put-call parity, Mabry could create a position in which he would earn the risk-free rate of return but he would need to sell calls and buy puts with the same strike price, not the same premium. As the vega (volatility relative to price) of an option increases, it would become more sensitive to changes in the volatility of the underlying asset. Therefore, the price would likely rise, not fall. (Study Session 14, LOS 41.k, LOS 42.b)

49. **A** A monthly VaR cannot be annualized by simply multiplying by 12. The monthly return and standard deviation would need to be annualized and VaR recalculated. An assumption of a normal distribution is invalid if options were in the portfolio. (Study Session 16, LOS 49.b)

50. **B** The estimated loss under the condition that VaR has been exceeded is known as conditional VaR. (Study Session 16, LOS 49.e)

51. **C** The $225,000 is a minimum loss that will be exceeded 5% of the time. The maximum possible loss is the value of the portfolio. (Study Session 16, LOS 49.a)

52. **B** The description is of reverse stress testing, which is a form of scenario analysis, not sensitivity analysis. A Monte Carlo simulation would run many repeated scenarios. (Study Session 16, LOS 49.h)

53. **C** Execution algorithms are not designed to profit from arbitrage opportunities, rather they are used to minimize the impact of large trades by slicing them up into smaller trades and releasing to the market in stages. (Study Session 17, LOS 52.c)

54. **C** Market fragmentation occurs when the number of venues trading the same instrument increases. As a response, algorithms are used to aggregate liquidity and route orders to the venues that have the best price and market depth. (Study Session 17, LOS 52.d)

55. **A** The models in equations 1 through 4 employ factors derived from macroeconomic variables. (Study Session 16, LOS 48.d)

56. **A**   The intercept in a macroeconomic factor model equals the expected return for the portfolio examined in the model (assuming no surprises in the macroeconomic variables). The factors in the multifactor equations, F_{IS} and F_{BC}, are factor "surprises," which by definition are expected to equal zero (i.e., by definition, zero "surprise" is "expected"). So, by assumption, F_{IS} and F_{BC} are expected to equal zero. Therefore, the expected return for Portfolio A equals its intercept (17.5%). (Study Session 16, LOS 48.d)

57. **C**   The multifactor equation for Portfolio A is used to answer this question. Simply insert the factor surprises for F_{IS} and F_{BC}. From Exhibit 1, $F_{IS} = 0.01 - 0.02 = -0.01$ and $F_{BC} = 0.02 - 0.03 = -0.01$. Therefore, both factor surprises equal -1%. Substituting into the multifactor equation for Portfolio A and including the firm-specific surprise return: $0.1750 + 2(-0.01) + 1.5(-0.01) + 0.012 = 15.2\%$. (Study Session 16, LOS 48.d)

58. **A**   A portfolio that has a sensitivity of 1.0 to one of the macroeconomic factors, and zero sensitivity to the remaining macroeconomic factors is called a factor portfolio. Portfolios D and E are factor portfolios. A portfolio that has factor sensitivities that equal the sensitivities of the benchmark is called a tracking portfolio. Portfolio Z has factor sensitivities that exactly match those of the S&P 500. (Study Session 16, LOS 48.f)

59. **C**   According to the Arbitrage Pricing Model, the expected return equals risk-free rate + $b_1 RP_1 + b_2 RP_2$, where RP_i is the risk premium for factor i. Portfolio D is designed to have sensitivity equal to one to the investor sentiment risk factor and sensitivity equal to zero to the business cycle risk factor. Similarly, Portfolio E is a portfolio designed to have sensitivity equal to zero to the investor sentiment risk factor and sensitivity equal to one to the business cycle risk factor. Portfolios that have a sensitivity equal to 1.0 to one factor and zero sensitivity to the remaining factors are called *factor portfolios*. Therefore, Portfolio D is the investor sentiment factor portfolio, and Portfolio E is the business cycle factor portfolio. According to the multifactor equations, the expected return for the investor sentiment factor portfolio (D) equals 9% and for the business cycle factor portfolio (E) equals 8%. Risk premiums are defined as the difference between the expected return on the appropriate factor portfolio and the risk-free rate. The risk-free rate is 5% (the long-term government bond yield). Therefore, the investor sentiment risk premium equals $0.09 - 0.05 = 0.04$. Similarly, the business cycle risk premium equals $0.08 - 0.05 = 0.03$. Therefore, the expected return for Portfolio P equals $0.05 + 1.25(0.04) + 1.1(0.03) = 13.3\%$. (Study Session 16, LOS 48.d)

60. **C**   Active factor risk is caused by deviations of a portfolio's factor sensitivities from the benchmark factor sensitivities. Deviations are quite large for both Portfolios D and E, but Portfolio Z's factor sensitivities match those of the S&P 500 benchmark (1.5 and 1.25). (Study Session 16, LOS 48.f)

Exam 2
Afternoon Session Answers

To get valuable feedback on how your score compares to those of other Level II candidates, use your Username and Password to gain Online Access at schweser.com and click on the icon that says, *"Practice Exams Volume 1 (Enter answers from book)."*

61. A	81. C	101. B
62. C	82. A	102. B
63. C	83. B	103. B
64. A	84. C	104. B
65. C	85. B	105. C
66. A	86. C	106. C
67. A	87. A	107. C
68. A	88. B	108. A
69. C	89. C	109. C
70. C	90. B	110. B
71. C	91. A	111. A
72. C	92. C	112. B
73. C	93. B	113. B
74. B	94. C	114. C
75. C	95. B	115. B
76. A	96. B	116. A
77. C	97. B	117. B
78. A	98. C	118. C
79. C	99. C	119. C
80. C	100. A	120. A

Exam 2
Afternoon Session Answers

61. **A** CFA Institute Research Objectivity Standards recommend that rating systems include the following three elements: (1) the recommendation or rating category, (2) time horizon categories, and (3) risk categories. Holly's report on BlueNote provides all three elements (strong buy, 6- to 12-month time horizon, average level of risk) and also includes the recommended disclosure on how investors can obtain a complete description of the firm's rating system. (Study Session 1, LOS 3.a,b)

62. **C** Standard II(A). Holly has utilized public information to conduct an intensive analysis of BlueNote and has also utilized information obtained from a supplier that, while nonpublic, is not by itself material. When combined with his knowledge of BlueNote's material public information, however, the information from the supplier allows Holly to make a significant and material conclusion that would not be known to the public in general. This situation falls under the Mosaic Theory. Holly is free to make recommendations based on her material nonpublic conclusion on BlueNote since the conclusion was formed using material public information combined with *nonmaterial* nonpublic information. Thus, the BlueNote report did not violate Standard II(A) Integrity of Capital Markets – Material Nonpublic Information, and since there appears to be a reasonable and adequate basis, does not appear to violate any other Standards either. Holly's report on BigTime, however, is based in part on a conversation that he overheard between executives at BigTime. The information he overheard related to the sale of one of BigTime's business units was both material and nonpublic. The fact that several other analysts overheard the conversation as well does not make the information public. Because Holly is in possession of material nonpublic information, he is prohibited by Standard II(A) from acting or causing others to act on the information. Therefore, his report on BigTime violates the Standard. (Study Session 1, LOS 2.a,b)

63. **C** CFA Institute Research Objectivity Standards (ROS) require disclosures of conflicts of interest such as beneficial ownership of securities of a covered firm. The ROS recommend that such disclosure be made either in the supporting documents or on the firm's Web site. It is further recommended that the disclosure, or a page reference to the disclosure, be made in the report itself. Holly owns shares of BigTime that may potentially benefit from his recommendation. His best course of action would be to disclose the conflict on both the firm's Web site and in the report. (Study Session 1, LOS 3.a,b)

64. **A** Standard II(B) – Market Manipulation. Holly has issued a buy recommendation on BigTime stock. The analysis is based on a very optimistic analysis of the company's fundamentals. Yet, three days after issuing the report, Holly decides to sell all of his clients' holdings as well as his own holdings of BigTime stock after observing a rise in the price of the stock. Holly's report, which caused an increase in the price of BigTime stock, was intended to deceive market participants into believing the company was a good investment when, as indicated by his subsequent sale of the shares, Holly believed otherwise. The combination of actions indicates that Holly is likely attempting to manipulate the price of the stock for his clients', and his own, benefit. Thus, he has likely violated Standard II(B) – Integrity of Capital Markets – Market Manipulation. (Study Session 1, LOS 2.a,b)

65. **C**   Standard I(B) – Professionalism: Independence and Objectivity. Members and candidates are prohibited from accepting any gift that could reasonably be expected to interfere with their independence and objectivity. The desk pen is a token item with little material value and can be accepted without violating the Standard. However, the concert tickets are likely to have a very substantial amount of material value since the concert is sold out and involves a popular musical act. Best practice dictates that Holly should not accept the concert tickets since they could reasonably be expected to compromise Holly's independence and objectivity. (Study Session 1, LOS 2.a,b)

66. **A**   Standard V(B) – Communication With Clients and Prospective Clients. Standard V(B) requires members and candidates to promptly disclose any changes that materially affect investment processes. Holly has provided a detailed description of the new valuation model that will be used to generate investment recommendations and has disclosed the new limitations on the investment universe (i.e., no alcohol or tobacco stocks). Therefore, it does not appear that he has violated Standard V(B). Holly also has not violated any other standards. It is acceptable for him to e-mail those clients with e-mail addresses and send his letter by regular mail to those who do not. Standard III(B) – Fair Dealing does not require that all clients receive investment recommendations or other communications at exactly the same time, only that the system treats clients fairly. (Study Session 1, LOS 2.a,b)

67. **A**   The standard error can be determined by knowing the formula for the t-statistic:

t-statistic = (slope estimate – hypothesized value) / standard error

Therefore, the standard error equals:

standard error = (slope estimate – hypothesized value) / t-statistic

The null hypothesis associated with each of the t-statistics reported for the slope estimates in Table 1 is: H_o: slope = zero. So, the standard error equals the slope estimate divided by its t-statistic: 0.2000 / 2.85 = 0.07.

The confidence interval equals: slope estimate ± (t_{crit} × standard error), where t_{crit} is the critical t-statistic associated with the desired confidence interval (as stated in the question, the desired confidence interval equals 99%). Exhibit 3 provides critical values for a portion of the Student t-distribution. The appropriate critical value is found by using the correct significance level and degrees of freedom. The significance level equals 1 minus the confidence level = 1 – 0.99 = 0.01. The degrees of freedom equal N – k – 1, where k is the number of independent variables: 30 – 3 – 1 = 26 degrees of freedom. Note that the table provides critical values for one-tail tests of hypothesis (area in upper tail). Therefore, the appropriate critical value for the 99% confidence interval is found under the column labeled "0.005," indicating that the upper tail comprises 0.5% of the t-distribution, and the lower tail comprises an equivalent 0.5% of the distribution. Therefore, the two tails, combined, take up 1% of the distribution. The correct critical t-statistic for the 0.01 significance level equals 2.779. Therefore, the 99% confidence interval for the FORECAST slope coefficient is:

0.2000 ± 2.779(0.07) = (0.0055, 0.3945)

The lower bound equals 0.0055 and the upper bound equals 0.3945. (Study Session 3, LOS 9.f and 10.e)

68. **A**   The *F*-statistic is used to test the overall significance of the regression, which is formulated with the null hypothesis that all three slopes simultaneously equal zero. Note that this null hypothesis is identical to a test that the *R*-square equals zero. (Study Session 3, LOS 10.g)

69. **C**   Pilchard should test the following null hypothesis: $H_o: b_2 \geq 0$. The alternative hypothesis is: $H_A: b_2 < 0$ (a negative estimate for b_2 supports the small firm effect). The test is a one-tail hypothesis test. The critical value at the 0.01 value for a one-tail test equals –2.479 (area in lower tail equals 0.01; degrees of freedom equal 26). Exhibit 1 indicates that the *t*-statistic for the b_2 estimate equals –2.50, which exceeds the critical value. Therefore, the null hypothesis that small firms do not outperform large firms, after controlling for COVERAGE and FORECAST should be rejected in favor of the alternative hypothesis that small firms outperform large firms (after controlling for COVERAGE and FORECAST). (Study Session 3, LOS 9.g and 10.e)

70. **C**   The slope on the dummy variable (COVERAGE), which is 0.05 or 5%, equals the change in average returns between neglected and non-neglected firms after controlling for SIZE and FORECAST. (Study Session 3, LOS 10.j)

71. **C**   The ANOVA (Analysis of Variance) Table provides data on the sources of variation in the dependent variable (stock returns). The degrees of freedom for the regression sum of squares (a.k.a., the explained sum of squares) equals *k*, the number of independent variables: k = 3 in Pilchard's regression. The total sum of squares equals the numerator of the sample variance formula for the dependent variable. Recall from Level I Quantitative Methods that the denominator of a sample variance equals N – 1. The denominator in the sample variance equals the degrees of freedom for the numerator (the total sum of squares). Therefore, the degrees of freedom for the total sum of squares in Pilchard's regression equals 30 – 1 = 29. (Study Session 3, LOS 9.j and 10.g)

72. **C**   The estimated regression equation equals:

return = 0.06 + 0.05Coverage – 0.003LN(SIZE) + 0.20Forecast

where:
coverage equals zero if number of analysts exceeds 3

Therefore, the predicted return for Eggmann Enterprises equals:

return = 0.06 + 0 – 0.003LN(500) + 0.20(0.50)

return = 14.14%

(Study Session 3, LOS 9.h and 10.e)

73. **C**   Angle uses the uncovered interest rate parity relationship to forecast future spot rates. If the Canadian dollar is expected to depreciate relative to the U.S. dollar and the Mexican peso, then nominal interest rates in Canada must be higher than those in the United States and Mexico. The 13% nominal interest rate in Mexico is higher than the nominal interest rate in the U.S., so the nominal interest rate in Canada must be greater than 13%. (Study Session 4, LOS 13.e)

74. **B**   Hohlman is incorrect regarding the implications of an expansionary monetary policy in the U.S. under the Mundell-Fleming model, which predicts a depreciation of the dollar. The asset market approach focuses on fiscal policy—not monetary policy. (Study Session 4, LOS 13.k)

75. **C** If relative purchasing power parity holds, then inflation differentials drive future exchange rates. If the international Fisher relationship holds, then inflation differentials will be equal to interest rate differentials. Hence, when both relative purchasing power parity and the international Fisher relationship hold, uncovered interest rate parity should also hold. Covered interest rate parity always holds (by arbitrage) and is not a necessary additional condition. Real interest rate parity links the Fisher effect to the international Fisher relationship. (Study Session 4, LOS 13.f)

76. **A** When the expected future spot rate is equal to the forward rate (and covered interest parity holds—by arbitrage), uncovered interest rate parity should hold as well. The international Fisher relationship links relative purchasing power parity to uncovered interest rate parity. Real interest rate parity links the Fisher effect to the international Fisher relationship. (Study Session 4, LOS 13.f)

77. **C** Angle assumes the forward rate is an accurate predictor of the expected future spot rate, so we will use ¥200/£ as the future spot rate.

Angle states that uncovered interest rate parity holds.

Given a quote structure of ¥/£,

S_0 (1 + Yen interest rate) / (1 + GBP interest rate) = $E(S_1)$

S_0(1.064 / 1.097) = 200

S_0 = 206.20

Notice that the exchange rate will move from ¥206/£ to ¥200/£. So it takes fewer yen to buy one pound (i.e., the yen has strengthened), which uncovered interest rate parity predicts because the Japanese interest rate is lower. (Study Session 4, LOS 13.e,f)

78. **A** Statement 3: Hohlman is correct regarding absolute purchasing power parity. It is based on the law of one price, which states that the price of goods should not differ internationally. Absolute purchasing power parity is not used to predict exchange rates.

Statement 4: Hohlman is correct regarding relative purchasing power parity. It does not hold in the short-run and therefore is not useful for predicting short-run currency values. It does tend to hold in the long run, however, and is therefore useful for long-run exchange rate forecasts. (Study Session 4, LOS 13.e)

79. **C** Total assets, liabilities, revenues, and expenses are higher under proportionate consolidation as compared to the equity method. However, net income and stockholders' equity are the same under either method. Accordingly, profit margin and return on assets are typically lower under proportionate consolidation than under the equity method. Return on equity will be same under either method. (Study Session 5, LOS 16.a)

The following financial statements are provided for informational purposes only. The numbers in the acquisition method are derived as EPI + EP/BM LLC, except for the equity items.

In Millions, Year End 2018	EPI	EP/BM LLC	Acquisition Method
Revenue	$3,115	$421	$3,536
Cost of goods sold	$2,580	$295	$2,875
SG&A	$316	$50	$366
EBIT	$219	$76	$295
Interest expense	$47	$8	$55
Equity in earnings of EP/BM	$22		N/A
Pretax income	$194	$68	$240
Income tax	$60	$24	$84
(–) Noncontrolling interest			$22*
Net income	$134	$44	$134

In Millions, December 31, 2018	EPI	EP/BM LLC	Acquisition Method
Assets			
Cash	$118	$13	$131
Accounts receivable	$390	$50	$440
Inventory	$314	$41	$355
Property	$1,007	$131	$1,138
Investment	$38		N/A
Total	$1,867	$235	$2,064
Liabilities and Equity			
Accounts payable	$274	$35	$309
Long-term debt	$719	$125	$844
Equity	$874	$75	$911**
Total	$1,867	$235	$2,064

*50% of EP/BM LLC's net income of $44
**$874 + noncontrolling interest (50% of EP/LLC's equity of $75)

80. **C** current ratio = current assets / current liabilities; (131 + 440 + 355) / 309 = 3.0. (Study Session 5, LOS 16.c)

81. **C** interest coverage = EBIT / interest expense; 295 / 55 = 5.36. (Study Session 5, LOS 16.c)

82. **A**

   Under Equity Method:

   Long-term debt to equity ratio = 719 / 874 = 0.82

   Under Acquisition Method:

   Long-term debt to equity ratio = 844 / 911 = 0.93

   (Study Session 5, LOS 16.a)

83. **B**   Regardless of the upstream/downstream sale, the net income would be identical under equity method and under acquisition method. All assets (including inventory) would be higher under acquisition method, regardless of upstream/downstream sale.
   (Study Session 5, LOS 16.a)

84. **C**   Net income will be the same under the acquisition method (partial or full goodwill) and proportionate consolidation. Stockholders' equity will be higher under the acquisition method due to minority interest; thus, ROE will be higher under proportionate consolidation relative to the acquisition method. (Study Session 5, LOS 16.a)

85. **B**   The final period cash flow will include the project cash flows, the return of net working capital, and the after-tax sale of fixed capital used in the project. Because Tera is a replacement project, the incremental cash flows must be calculated. In other words, we are concerned with the additional sales and costs derived from the new equipment.

   incremental sales = 708,000 − 523,000 = $185,000

   incremental cash expenses = 440,000 − 352,000 = $88,000

   incremental depreciation = 110,667 − 40,000 = $70,667

   incremental project cash flows = (185,000 − 88,000 − 70,667) × (1 − 0.40) + 70,667 = $86,467

   return of incremental net working capital = $110,000

   In the final year, the book value of the old machine (if not replaced) = 120,000 − 3 × 40,000 = 0. Similarly, the book value of the new machine (if replaced) = 332,000 − 3 × 110,667 = 0.

   incremental cash flow from after-tax sale of equipment = (113,000 − 90,000) − 0.40[(113,000 − 90,000) − (0 − 0)] = $13,800

   total cash flow in final period = 86,467 + 110,000 + 13,800 = $210,267

   (Study Session 7, LOS 21.a)

86. **C**   In scenario analysis, the analyst simultaneously changes several key variables to generate several different scenarios. Generally, three scenarios are created: (1) worst case, (2) most likely, and (3) optimistic. For the worst case scenario, for example, the analyst will use the slowest growth in sales, highest growth in expenses, and highest discount rate to derive an NPV under the worst of all possible situations. A similar approach is used to generate the optimistic scenario, but the best possible growth in each of the variables is used. The most likely is simply what the analyst thinks are the most reasonable assumptions for the discounted cash flow forecast under normal conditions. Using the different cases, the analyst can assess the risk of the project. (Study Session 7, LOS 21.d)

87. **A** Once the Tera Project is begun, the project will be necessary for continuing operations. This is likely a result of the replacement nature of the project. If the equipment necessary for GigaTech's operations is replaced with newer equipment, abandoning the project is not really an option. Management does have the option of scaling up the project after initiation, which is known as an expansion option. Management can also wait up to nine months to make a decision on the Tera Project, giving them a timing option (note that this is not one of the answer choices). Finally, the equipment used in the Tera Project can support additional shifts if demand for GigaTech's products temporarily exceeds supply, giving them a flexibility option (specifically a production-flexibility option). (Study Session 7, LOS 21.f)

88. **B** The least common multiple of lives approach requires estimating the least common denominator between two mutually exclusive projects with unequal lives. Since the Zeta and Sigma projects have lives of 3 and 2, the least common multiple is 6. The cash flows must be stated over a 6-year period, repeating the cash flow pattern as often as necessary (two times for Zeta and three times for Sigma). The cash flows are then discounted to find the net present value (NPV). The project with the highest NPV is selected. The cash flows are as follows:

				Year			
	0	**1**	**2**	**3**	**4**	**5**	**6**
Zeta Project	−360,000	250,000	220,000	190,000			
				−360,000	250,000	220,000	190,000
Total	−360,000	250,000	220,000	−170,000	250,000	220,000	190,000
Sigma Project	−470,000	330,000	390,000				
			−470,000	330,000	390,000		
					−470,000	330,000	390,000
Total	−470,000	330,000	-80,000	330,000	−80,000	330,000	390,000

Before calculating the NPV of each project, the cost of capital must be restated in nominal terms since the cash flow projections are stated in nominal terms. The nominal cost of capital is equal to 15.0% = (1 + 0.1058)(1 + 0.04). The NPV of each project is calculated as follows:

$$NPV_{Zeta} = -360,000 + \frac{250,000}{1.15} + \frac{220,000}{1.15^2} + \frac{-170,000}{1.15^3} + \frac{250,000}{1.15^4} + \frac{220,000}{1.15^5} + \frac{190,000}{1.15^6}$$
$$= 246,425$$

$$NPV_{Sigma} = -470,000 + \frac{330,000}{1.15} + \frac{-80,000}{1.15^2} + \frac{330,000}{1.15^3} + \frac{-80,000}{1.15^4} + \frac{330,000}{1.15^5} + \frac{390,000}{1.15^6}$$
$$= 260,381$$

Since its NPV is greater, GigaTech should select the Sigma project.
(Study Session 7, LOS 21.c)

89. **C**   The comments in the memo from GigaTech's board of directors are both incorrect. Earnings per share (EPS) is not a suitable criteria to evaluate capital budgeting projects. Under capital rationing, a firm selects the projects that increase the value of the firm by the greatest amount (i.e., have the highest NPV) subject to the capital constraints of the firm's budget. It is perfectly possible that projects that increase EPS will not get selected. For example, if a project has an NPV of $80 and increases EPS by $0.50 and a second project has an NPV of $200 but will initially reduce EPS by $0.20, the firm should select the second project (if its capital budget will allow it) since it adds more value. The capital budgeting process should not consider sunk costs (i.e., past costs that do not affect the cash flows of the project) such as costs to find investment projects. The cash flow projections should consider the economic impact from increased competition resulting from highly profitable investment projects. (Study Session 7, LOS 21.c)

90. **B**   When evaluating potential capital investment projects, the discount rate should be adjusted for the risk of the project under consideration. This is frequently accomplished by determining a project beta and using this beta in the CAPM security market line equation: $r_i = R_F + \beta_i[E(R_M) - R_F]$. Project betas can be determined in a number of ways including using proxy firms with operations similar to the project under consideration, estimating an accounting beta, or through cross-sectional regression analysis. Whatever method used to determine the discount rate, it should be clear that the weighted average cost of capital (WACC) is only appropriate for projects with risk similar to the overall firm. If a project is more (less) risky than the overall firm, the discount rate used to evaluate the project should be greater (less) than the firm's WACC. (Study Session 7, LOS 21.e)

91. **A**   If assets are purchased rather than shares, payment is made to the target company; the company will pay tax on any capital gains, not the shareholders. Purchasing assets instead of the share capital is a way to avoid assumption of liabilities, and when less than 50% of a target's assets are sold, shareholder approval is not normally required. (Study Session 8, LOS 26.e)

92. **C**

	# Shares (millions)	Share Price ($)	Value ($ million)
Broadstore value	20.00	19.20	384.00
Sagan value	15.75	16.20	255.15
PV synergy (2.3 / 0.08)			28.75
Value new entity			**667.90**
Original # shares	20.00		
Shares issued	13.00		
Total			**33.00**
Share price of merged entity		20.24	
Broadstore holding	20.00	20.24	404.79
Broadstore original value			384.00
Gain			**20.79**
Sagan holding	13	20.24	263.11
Sagan original value			255.15
Gain			**7.96**

(Study Session 8, LOS 26.k)

93. **B**   In Scenario 2, Sagan Termett shareholders receive cash for their shares and are, therefore, not affected by the realization of synergies; in this case, the acquirer bears all the risk. In Scenario 1, the Sagan Termett shareholders hold shares in the new entity; both sets of shareholders are affected by the realization of synergistic gains. (Study Session 8, LOS 26.l)

94. **C**

Exellar (per share)			Avg. Metric	Value $
Earnings	$2.73	×	12.67	34.59
Sales	$21.21	×	1.47	31.18
Book value	$13.92	×	2.57	35.77
Mean				$33.85
Premium				35%
Value	$33.85	×	1.35	$45.69

(Study Session 8, LOS 26.j)

95. **B**   The risk that managers enter into transactions, which may result in personal gains but are not in the best interests of shareholders, is known as strategic policy risk. (Study Session 8, LOS 25.h)

96. **B**   The utilitarian approach focuses on the best possible balance of good consequences over bad. The Kantian approach is based on the idea that people are not instruments and should be treated with respect. The Friedman doctrine argues that the only social responsibility of a business is to increase profits while staying within the rule of the law. (Study Session 8, LOS 24.d)

97. **B** $\beta_u \approx \left[\dfrac{1}{1+\left(D/E\right)}\right]\beta_E = \left[\dfrac{1}{1+\left(40/60\right)}\right]0.90 = 0.54$

The calculation is not required if you understand the steps involved. Since Midwest News has no debt and Freedom's beta must be unlevered, the beta to be used must be less than 0.90 (Freedom's beta). (Study Session 9, LOS 28.d)

98. **C** $\text{required return estimate} = \dfrac{\text{year-ahead dividend}}{\text{market price}} + \text{expected dividend growth rate}$

$\text{required return estimate} = \dfrac{\left(\$3.00 \times 0.40\right)}{\left(\$15,000\ \text{million}/375\ \text{million}\right)} + 0.06 = 0.09$

Since Freedom Corporation has a dividend policy of paying 40% of earnings, dividend growth equals earnings growth.

The assumption is that Freedom's stock is correctly valued.

(Study Session 9, LOS 28.a)

99. **C**   The Gordon growth model calculates the equity risk premium by starting with the dividend yield on the market index, adding the consensus long-term earnings growth rate and subtracting the current long-term government bond yield. The expected growth in the market index's P/E ratio is an input used in the macroeconomic model. (Study Session 9, LOS 28.b)

100. A r_i = risk-free rate + equity risk premium + size premium$_i$ + specific-company premium$_i$

r_i = 3.5% + 4.0% + 3.5% + 2.0% = 13.0%

(Study Session 9, LOS 28.b)

101. B $$V_0 = B_0 + \frac{(ROE - r)(B_0)}{r - g}$$

$$B_0 = \frac{\$79.5 \text{ million}}{1.5 \text{ million}} = \$53 \text{ per share}$$

ROE = $19.5 million / $79.5 million = 0.245

r = 0.15 (given in problem)

g = 0.03 (given in Exhibit 2)

$$V_0 = 53 + \frac{0.245 - 0.15}{0.15 - 0.03}(53) = \$94.96 \text{ per share}$$

(Study Session 11, LOS 33.d)

102. B An issue not described in Exhibit 2 is control premium. Any control premium adjustment is normally added directly to a company's value estimate. Statement 1 is not correct. Since Midwest News does not pay a dividend, the free cash flow model would be better suited to compute the company's equity value rather than the dividend discount model. Statement 2 is correct. (Study Session 9, LOS 28.c; and Study Session 11, LOS 31.f)

103. B Both the probability of default and expected loss will vary with the state of the economy, so a weighted average may be taken. The expected loss is (the probability of default) × (loss given default), not the recovery rate. The present value of expected loss may be higher or lower than the expected loss, as the risk premium may be higher than the discount from the time value of money. (Study Session 13, LOS 38.a)

104. B The option analogy for debt states that a long position in risky debt is equivalent to a long position in a riskless bond plus a short European put on the company's assets. (Study Session 13, LOS 38.d)

105. C European call on assets is the correct analogy for equity under the structural model for credit analysis. (Study Session 13, LOS 38.d)

106. C The expected loss per year can be calculated as the difference between the average yield on risk-free debt and the average yield on the corporate bond. This assumes frictionless markets and hence a yield spread that is entirely due to credit risk.

Average risk-free yield = 0.01257
Average corporate yield = 0.02991
Expected percentage loss per year = 2.991% − 1.257% = 1.73%

(Study Session 13, LOS 38.g)

107. C Reduced form models do allow for the systematic default of companies. A key advantage of reduced form models is that default probability is linked to the state of the economy. While one of the assumptions of reduced form model is that a zero-coupon bond trades, other liabilities can be used in the place of the zero-coupon bond. (Study Session 13, LOS 38.e)

108. **A** An asset-backed security does not default when a portion of the collateral defaults; thus, the probability of default is not relevant. (Study Session 13, LOS 38.i)

109. **C** To calculate the fixed payment in pesos, first use the Mexican term structure to derive the present value factors:

$Z_{360} = 1 / [1 + 0.050(360 / 360)] = 0.9524$

$Z_{720} = 1 / [1 + 0.052(720 / 360)] = 0.9058$

The annual fixed payment per peso of notional principal would then be:

$FS(0,2,360) = (1 - 0.9058) / (0.9524 + 0.9058) = 0.0507$

The annual fixed payment would be: $0.0507 \times \$100M / 0.0893 = 56.8$ million pesos. (Study Session 14, LOS 40.c)

110. **B** A payer swap can be replicated using a long payer swaption and short receiver swaption with the same exercise rates. Torrey's statement 1 about how if the premiums of the two options are equal, the exercise rate must be equal to the market swap fixed rate is correct. (Study Session 14, LOS 41.j)

111. **A** Statement 2 is correct. (Study Session 14, LOS 41.j)

112. **B** Given the exercise rate of 5%, the call option has a positive payoff for nodes C++ and C+−.

The value of the option at node C++ can be calculated as:
$[\text{Max}(0, 0.083 - 0.05)] \times \$2,000,000 = \$66,000$

Similarly, the value at node C+− can be calculated as:
$[\text{Max}(0, 0.0504 - 0.05)] \times \$2,000,000 = \$800$

Value at node C+ = $[(0.5 \times 66,000) + (0.5 \times 800)] / (1.0531) = \$31,716$

Value at node C− = $[(0.5 \times 800) + 0] / (1.0322) = \$388$

And the value at node C = $[(0.5 \times 31,716) + (0.5 \times 388)] / (1.04) = \$15,435$

(Study Session 14, LOS 41.d)

113. **B** The fixed dollar payment under the swap using the original yield curve is computed as:

$Z_{360} = 1 / [1 + 0.040(360 / 360)] = 0.9615$

$Z_{720} = 1 / [1 + 0.045(720 / 360)] = 0.9174$

The annual fixed payment per dollar of notional principal would then be:

$FS(0,2,360) = (1 - 0.9174) / (0.9615 + 0.9174) = 0.044$

The annual fixed payment would be:

$0.044 \times \$100M = \$4.4$ million

Using the new U.S. term structure to derive the present value factors:

$Z_{180}(360) = 1 / [1 + 0.042(180 / 360)] = 0.9794$

$Z_{180}(720) = 1 / [1 + 0.048(540 / 360)] = 0.9328$

The present value of the fixed payments plus the $100M principal is:

$4.4M × (0.9794 + 0.9328) + $100M × 0.9328 = $101.69 million

(Study Session 14, LOS 40.d)

114. **C** Use the new Mexican term structure to derive the present value factors:

$Z_{180}(360) = 1 / [1 + 0.050(180 / 360)] = 0.9756$

$Z_{180}(720) = 1 / [1 + 0.052(540 / 360)] = 0.9276$

The present value of the fixed payments plus the principal is:

0.0507 × (0.9756 + 0.9276) + 0.9276 = 1.0241 per peso

Apply this to notional principal and convert at current exchange rate:

1.0241 × ($100M / 0.0893) × 0.085= $97.48 million

The value of the swap is the difference between this value and the pay dollar fixed present value derived in the previous question:

$97.48 – $101.69M = – $4.21 million (Study Session 14, LOS 40.d)

115. **B** The risk that the private equity portion of the IS University's Endowment Fund would most likely suffer from is illiquidity. It can be difficult to trade the private equity investments because they are usually not listed on secondary securities markets. The private equity investments are diversified in terms of vintage and strategies. The IS endowment fund is exempt from taxation on capital gains or dividends. (Study Session 15, LOS 45.f; and Study Session 16, LOS 47.e)

116. **A** Percentage management fee = management fee / paid-in capital

paid-in capital = Σ called-down

2016 % management fee = 1.95 / (75 + 25 + 30) = 0.015

(Study Session 15, LOS 43.h,i)

117. **B** $195 million Alpha Fund (all data in millions)

Year	Called-down	Mgmt. Fees	Operating Results	NAV before Distributions	Carried Interest	Distributions	NAV after Distributions
2014	30	0.45	−10	19.55		0	
2015	25	0.83	55	98.72		0	
2016	75	1.95	75	246.77	10.35	0	236.42

2014 NAV before distributions = 30 − 0.45 + (−10) = 19.55

2015 NAV before distributions = 19.55 + 25 − 0.83 + 55 = 98.72

2016 NAV before distributions = 98.72 + 75 − 1.95 + 75 = 246.77

When NAV before distribution exceeds committed capital, the 20% carried interest is applied. (246.77 − 195) × 0.2 = 51.77 × 0.2 = 10.35

In years 2017 and beyond, the 20% carried interest is applied to the change in NAV before distributions. For example, if the 2017 NAV before distributions was 296.77, then the carried interest would equal (296.77 − 246.77) × 0.2 = 50 × 0.2 = 10.

The NAV after distributions subtracts carried interest and distributions from NAV before distributions.

(Study Session 15, LOS 45.i)

118. **C** Venture capital investments require considerable capital to develop and grow. Companies that require venture capital usually have significant cash burn as they develop new products. Venture capital investments are primarily funded through equity and utilize little or no debt. Risk measurement of venture capital investments is difficult because of their short operating history, and the required development of new markets and technologies. (Study Session 15, LOS 45.c)

119. **C** post-money valuation = $V / (1 + r)^t$

V = $300 million; r = 40%; t = 5 years

post-money valuation = 300 million / $(1 + 0.4)^5$ = 55.78 million

Note that the adjusted discount rate incorporating the probability of failure is directly given in the question as 40%. (Study Session 15, LOS 45.j)

120. **A** The ownership proportion of the venture capital (VC) investor is f = INV / POST = $9,000,000 / 90,000,000 = 0.10 or 10%.

$shares_{VC} = shares_{Founders}(f / 1 − f)$ = 2,500,000 × (0.10 / 0.90) = 277,778

price = INV / $shares_{VC}$ = $9,000,000 / 277,778 = $32.40 per share

(Study Session 15, LOS 45.j)

Exam 3
Morning Session Answers

To get valuable feedback on how your score compares to those of other Level II candidates, use your Username and Password to gain Online Access at schweser.com and choose the menu item *"Practice Exams Volume 1 (Enter answers from book)."*

1. A	21. A	41. B
2. A	22. B	42. B
3. B	23. A	43. C
4. C	24. C	44. C
5. C	25. B	45. C
6. B	26. C	46. B
7. B	27. A	47. B
8. C	28. C	48. C
9. A	29. A	49. C
10. A	30. C	50. C
11. C	31. A	51. C
12. B	32. B	52. B
13. B	33. A	53. A
14. B	34. C	54. C
15. A	35. C	55. A
16. A	36. B	56. A
17. A	37. C	57. A
18. A	38. C	58. A
19. A	39. A	59. B
20. A	40. B	60. B

©2017 Kaplan, Inc.

Exam 3
Morning Session Answers

1. **A** Cost of finished jewelry = 11.06 + 2.897 × (cost of gold)
   $2,000 = 11.06 + 2.897× (cost of gold)
   Price of gold = ($2,000 − 11.06) / 2.897 = $686.55

   (Study Session 3, LOS 9.h)

2. **A** Singh is correct that a change in the relationship between gold prices and jewelry costs would be an example of parameter instability.

   Hara is correct to fail to reject the null hypothesis that the value of the slope coefficient is equal to 4.0 at the 5% level of significance.

   The critical t-value for the slope coefficient with 31 − 2 = 29 df at the 5% level for a two-tailed test is 2.045. The test statistic is (2.897 − 4.000)/0.615 = −1.79. The absolute value (1.79) is less than 2.045, and the correct decision is to fail to reject the null hypothesis that the slope coefficient is equal to 4.0. (Study Session 3, LOS 9.g, LOS 11.h)

3. **B** Biscayne is incorrect in the specification of the formula because the appropriate R^2 to use in calculating a Breusch-Pagan chi-square statistic is not the R^2 of the regression of jewelry prices on gold prices but rather the R^2 of the regression of squared residuals from the original regression on the independent variable(s). (Study Session 3, LOS 10.k)

4. **C** Singh is incorrect because a potential result of misspecifying a regression equation is nonstationarity (not stationarity, which is desirable).

   Biscayne is incorrect because the effect of omitting an important variable in a regression is that the regression coefficients are often biased (not unbiased) and/or inconsistent. (Study Session 3, LOS 10.m)

5. **C** While Hara is correct about the remedy for multicollinearity (i.e., remove one or more of the highly correlated independent variables), he is incorrect about the effect of reducing the number of independent variables on the coefficient of determination R^2. R^2 never increases when independent variables are dropped. (Study Session 3, LOS 10.h, l)

6. **B** Biscayne is incorrect because a serial correlation problem can be corrected by using the Hansen method to adjust the coefficient standard errors, not the R^2. (Study Session 3, LOS 10.k)

7. **B**

	2012	*2013*	*2014*	*2014 Restated*
Revenue	14,000	13,720	15,915	15,915
Accounts Receivable	1,789	1,907	2,610	3,010
Receivables Turnover (Revenue/AR)	7.83	7.20		5.29
DSO (365 × AR/Revenue)	47	51		69
Percentage increase			(69/47) − 1 = 47%	

(Study Session 6, LOS 19.c)

8. **C** Bill and hold transactions record revenue for inventory that is still held by the firm. While this practice will increase reported revenues and accounts receivable, it does not alter the timing of billing and collections and will not boost cash flows. (Study Session 6, LOS 19.d)

9. **A** The cash component of earnings is more persistent than the accruals component of earnings. The formula given shows β as the coefficient of earnings persistence; β captures the relationship between current period earnings and earnings in the prior period. A higher β indicates a higher persistence in earnings. (Study Session 6, LOS 19.f)

10. **A**

As Reported	*2015*	*2016*	*Excluding Associates*	*2015*	*2016*
Revenue	12,071	12,795	Net Income	770	585
Net Income	770	585	Less Associates	(63)	(94)
				707	491
Net Margin	**6.38%**	**4.57%**	**Net Margin**	**5.86%**	**3.84%**
Average Total Assets	15,302	15,893	Average Total Assets	15,302	15,893
			Less Associate	1,812	1,952
				13,490	13,941
Asset Turnover	**0.79**	**0.81**	**Asset Turnover**	**0.89**	**0.92**
Average Equity	4,513	4,938			
Leverage	**3.39**	**3.22**	Leverage	**3.39**	**3.22**
ROE	17.06%	11.84%		17.68%	11.38%

We have no information on how the associates are funded, so no adjustment is made to leverage.

Contribution in 2015: 17.06% − 17.68% = −0.62%

Contribution in 2016: 11.84 − 11.38 = +0.46%

(Study Session 6, LOS 20.c)

11. **C**

Lease Obligations	
	$ million
2016	148
2017	148
2018	148
2019	148
2020	98
2021–25	98/yr
PV @ 4%	**$976**
Debt As Reported	2,367
Lease Obligation	976
Total	**3,343**
Equity	**4,936**
Debt to Equity	**67.73%**

(Study Session 6, LOS 20.d)

12. **B** Operating leases treat the entire least payment as rent, an operating expense, which reduces operating profit. Capital lease accounting instead expenses depreciation and interest. Of these two expenses, only depreciation is charged against operating profit and, hence, operating profit will be typically higher under a capital lease. Capital lease accounting results in a higher reported interest expense and lower coverage ratio. (Study Session 6, LOS 20.d)

13. **B** The beta of 1.04 is estimated from the slope coefficient on the independent variable (the return on the market) from the regression.

From the CAPM: required return on equity = 0.03 + [1.04 (0.07 − 0.03)] = 0.072 = 7.2%. (Study Session 9, LOS 28.c)

14. **B** The value of the stock in early 2019 is the present value of the future dividends. After 2021, dividends are expected to grow at the rate of 4%. The dividend that begins the constantly growing perpetuity is $2.63 × 1.04 = $2.74. You are given the cost of equity of 10%. Note that for the third cash flow, we add the third dividend ($2.63) to the present value of the constantly growing perpetuity that begins in the fourth year = $2.74 / (0.10 − 0.04) = $45.67. This is valid since they both occur at the same point in time (i.e., at the end of the third year). Using a financial calculator we can estimate the value of one share of O'Connor stock as follows:

CFO = 0; C01 = $2.13; C02 = $2.36; C03 = $2.63 + $45.67 = $48.30; I = 10; CPT → NPV = $40.18

(Study Session 10, LOS 30.b)

15. **A** De Jong's estimate of value of $75.00 (based on a high-growth period of three years) is greater than the market's consensus of $70.00, which means the market's consensus high-growth duration must be less than three years, all else equal.
(Study Session 10, LOS 30.b)

16. **A** In order for the dividend discount model to produce a reasonable estimate of share price, the investor should have a non-control perspective. For the FCFE model to be appropriate, there should be a link between FCFE and profitability. (Study Session 10, LOS 30.a)

17. **A** $H = 6 / 2 = 3$, $D_0 = 1.92$, $r = 0.095$, $g_s = 0.11$, $g_L = 0.04$

$$P_0 = \frac{D_0(1+g_L)}{(r-g_L)} + \frac{D_0 \times H \times (g_s - g_L)}{(r - g_L)}$$

$$= \frac{1.92(1.04)}{(0.095 - 0.04)} + \frac{1.92 \times 3 \times 0.07}{(0.095 - 0.04)} = \$43.64$$

(Study Session 10, LOS 30.l)

18. **A**

$$r = \left[\left(\frac{D_0}{P_0}\right) \times \left[(1+g_L) + [H \times (g_S - g_L)]\right]\right] + g_L$$

$$= \left[\left(\frac{1.92}{48}\right) \times \left[(1.04) + (2.5 \times 0.07)\right]\right] + 0.04 = 0.0886$$

(Study Session 10, LOS 30.m)

19. **A** Increasing invested capital to take advantage of positive NPV projects will increase NOPAT and the dollar cost of capital ($WACC). Because NPV is positive, the increase in NOPAT will be larger than the increase in $WACC, so EVA will increase. (Study Session 7, LOS 23.e and Study Session 11, LOS 33.a)

20. **A** All of the justifications noted by De Jong are appropriate reasons to use the residual income model. (Study Session 11, LOS 33.j)

21. **A** When residual income is expected to persist at its current level forever, the persistence factor is highest. When ROE declines over time to the cost of equity, residual income declines over time to zero, and the persistence factor will have a value between 0 and 1. When residual income falls to zero immediately, the persistence factor has a value of zero. (Study Session 11, LOS 33.h)

22. **B** Residual income = net income – equity charge
Equity charge = equity capital × cost of equity capital
Equity charge = $73,000,000 × 0.08 = $5,840,000
Residual income = $10,035,000 – $5,840,000 = $4,195,000

EVA = NOPAT – (C% × TC)

EVA = $28,517,640 – (0.054 × $324,000,000) = $11,021,640
(Study Session 11, LOS 33.a)

23. **A** We need to solve for g in the relationship:

$$V_0 = B_0 + \left(\frac{ROE - r}{r - g}\right) B_0$$

$$\$70.00 = \$4.29 + \left(\frac{0.1184 - 0.08}{0.08 - g}\right) \$4.29$$

Solving for g, we get $g = 7.75\%$. (Study Session 11, LOS 33.g)

24. **C** Only Statement 2 is correct. Residual income valuation is related to P/B. When the present value of expected future residual income is negative, the justified P/B based on fundamentals is less than 1. Statement 1 is not correct: residual income models recognize value *earlier* than other valuation models. (Study Session 11, LOS 33.e,i)

25. **B** The bond will be called in the lower node if the interest rate (including OAS) is 5.0% because the present value of the remaining cash flows ($100.95) is greater than the call price ($99.50). The bond will not be called if rates increase to 7.5% in the upper node because the value of the bond ($98.60) is less than the call price ($99.50). The value of the callable bond according to the model is 101.01:

$$V_0 = \frac{1}{2} \times \left[\frac{98.60 + 6.00}{1.04} + \frac{99.50 + 6.00}{1.04}\right] = 101.01$$

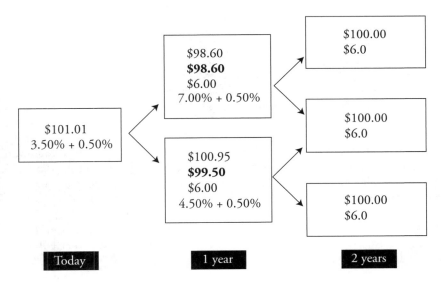

(Study Session 13, LOS 37.f)

26. **C** The value of a putable bond is equal to the value of an otherwise equivalent option-free bond plus the value of the embedded put option. The value of the embedded put option will decrease if yield volatility decreases. The value of the option-free bond will not be affected by changes in yield volatility, so the value of the putable bond will also decrease. Evermore is incorrect in her analysis of both effects. (Study Session 13, LOS 37.d)

27. **A** The computed value of a putable bond decreases with a decrease in the assumed level of volatility and therefore the OAS needed to force the model price to be equal to market price will be lower. (Study Session 13, LOS 37.h)

28. **C** The benchmark securities used to create the tree are Treasury securities, so the OAS for each callable corporate bond reflects additional credit risk and liquidity risk relative to the benchmark. The bonds are overvalued if their OAS are smaller than the required OAS and undervalued if their OAS are larger than the required OAS. The required OAS for both bonds is the *Z*-spread over Treasuries on comparably-rated securities with no embedded options. That required spread is not provided in the vignette.

    The BB-rated issue is overvalued because its OAS is less than zero, which means it must be less than the required OAS. Therefore, Evermore is correct in her analysis of the BB-rated issue.

    The AA-rated issue has a positive OAS relative to the Treasury benchmark, but we don't know the required OAS on similar bonds, so we can't determine whether or not the AA-rated issue is over or undervalued based on the information given. Therefore, Evermore is incorrect to conclude that the issue is undervalued. (Study Session 13, LOS 37.g)

29. **A** Davenport has correctly outlined the appropriate methodology for using a binomial model to estimate effective duration and effective convexity. Evermore fails to adjust for the OAS and, instead, simply adds 100 basis points to every rate on the tree rather than shifting the yield curve upward and then recreating the entire tree using the same rate volatility assumption from the first step. Even if both use the same rate volatility assumption and the OAS is equal to zero, the two methodologies will generate significantly different duration and convexity estimates. (Study Session 13, LOS 37.i)

30. **C** The value of a callable convertible bond is equal to the value of an option-free bond plus the value of the conversion option on the stock minus the value of the call option on the bond.

    A decrease in the volatility of Highfour's common stock returns will decrease the value of the conversion option on the stock. Consequently the value of the convertible bond will also decrease. Evermore was correct in her analysis, and Davenport was incorrect to disagree with her.

    A decrease in the yield volatility will decrease the value of the embedded call option. The investor has written the call option, so a decrease in the value of the call option will increase the value of the convertible bond. Evermore is incorrect in her analysis, and Davenport was correct to disagree with her. (Study Session 13, LOS 37.o)

31. **A** Each of the portfolios has an effective duration of five, so a parallel shift in the yield curve will have the same effect on each portfolio, and each will experience the same price performance. (Study Session 12, LOS 35.k)

32. **B** The exposure of each portfolio to changes in the 5- and 10-year rates are equal to the sum of the 5- and 10-year key rate durations:

portfolio 1 exposure = 0.20 + 0.15 = 0.35
portfolio 2 exposure = 0.40 + 4.00 = 4.40

Portfolio 2 has the largest exposure, and portfolio 1 has the smallest exposure. If the 5- and 10-year key rates increase, portfolio 1 will fall by the smallest amount and will experience the best price performance (i.e., the smallest decrease in value).

You can confirm this by doing the calculations for a 20 basis point increase:

% change in portfolio 1 = (−0.20 × 0.002 × 100) + (−0.15 × 0.002 × 100)
= (−0.35 × 0.002 × 100) = −0.07%

% change in portfolio 2 = (−0.40 × 0.002 × 100) + (−4.00 × 0.002 × 100)
= (−4.40 × 0.002 × 100) = −0.88%

(Study Session 12, LOS 35.k)

33. **A** Statement 1 is correct. Swap markets tend to have more maturities with which to construct a yield curve as compared to government bond markets. Statement 2 is correct. Retail banks tend to have little exposure to swaps and hence are more likely to use the government spot curve as their benchmark. (Study Session 12, LOS 35.e)

34. **C** The value of a 3-year bond extendible by one year is equal to an otherwise identical 4-year bond that is putable in three years. Accordingly, the value of bonds B and C should be the same. (Study Session 13, LOS 37.a)

35. **C** The steps in the process of calculating the effective duration of a callable bond using a binomial tree are as follows:

Step 1: Given assumptions about benchmark interest rates, interest rate volatility, and the call and/or put rule, calculate the OAS for the issue using the binomial model.

Step 2: Impose a small parallel shift in the on-the-run yield curve by an amount equal to $+\Delta y$.

Step 3: Build a new binomial interest rate tree using the new yield curve.

Step 4: Add the OAS to each of the 1-year forward rates in the interest rate tree to get a "modified" tree. (We assume that the OAS does not change when interest rates change.)

Step 5: Compute $BV_{+\Delta y}$ using this modified interest rate tree.

Step 6: Repeat steps 2 through 5 using a parallel rate shift of $-\Delta y$ to estimate a value of $BV_{-\Delta y}$.

There is no restriction on the relationship between the assumed change in the yield (Δy) and the OAS. (Study Session 13, LOS 37.i)

36. **B**   An upward sloping yield curve predicts an increase in short-term rates according to the pure expectations theory but not necessarily the liquidity premium theory.

   The liquidity theory says that forward rates are a biased estimate of the market's expectation of future rates because they include a liquidity premium. Therefore, a positive sloping yield curve may indicate either (1) that the market expects future interest rates to rise or (2) that rates are expected to remain constant (or even fall), but the addition of the liquidity premium results in a positive slope. (Study Session 12, LOS 35.i)

37. **C**   The present value of the next coupon payment (per $100 face value) is

$$\frac{2.50}{1.04^{\left(\frac{182}{365}\right)}} = 2.4516.$$

   The no-arbitrage forward price is $(98.25 - 2.4516) \times 1.04^{\left(\frac{270}{365}\right)} = 98.62$.

   (Study Session 14, LOS 40.b)

38. **C**   PV of the coupon is now $\dfrac{2.50}{1.04^{\left(\frac{122}{365}\right)}} = 2.4674$, and the value of the forward contract to

   the long is $98.11 - 2.4674 - \dfrac{98.62}{1.04^{\left(\frac{210}{365}\right)}} = -0.77693$ per $100, or –$77,693.

   The value to the short is +$77,693. (Study Session 14, LOS 40.a)

39. **A**   Adams used the 90-day rate (0.0352) and the time period (90/360) in the numerator instead of the 150-day rate (0.0392) and the 150-day time period (150/360). The denominator is correct, so two out of the four terms are used correctly. The correct calculation is:

$$\left[\frac{1 + 0.0392\left(\frac{150}{360}\right)}{1 + 0.0332\left(\frac{60}{360}\right)} - 1\right]\left(\frac{360}{90}\right) = \left[\frac{1.01633}{1.00553} - 1\right](4) = 4.30\%$$

   (Study Session 14, LOS 40.b)

40. **B** $(0.0430 - 0.0414) \times \$10 \text{ million} \times \dfrac{90}{360} = \$4,000$ (expected payoff in 120 days)

   PV of payoff is $\dfrac{\$4,000}{1 + 0.0392\left(\frac{120}{360}\right)} = \$3,948$

   (Study Session 14, LOS 40.a)

41. **B** $1.1854\left(\dfrac{1.03}{1.04}\right) = \$1.174$ (Study Session 14, LOS 40.a)

42. **B** The arbitrage-free forward price = 1.0210(1.03)/(1.02) = 1.0310. The forward price in the market is spot price + forward premium = 1.0210 + 0.0301 = 1.0511. Therefore, the quoted forward price is higher than the arbitrage-free forward price. An arbitrage profit can be earned by selling Swiss francs at the forward price of $1.0511 while buying francs in the spot market (using borrowed USD). (The francs purchased in the spot market are invested at the Swiss interest rate for the duration of the futures contract.)

Note: These extensive calculations are not actually required to solve this problem.

At time t=0:

Begin with nothing.

Borrow $100 at 3% (repayment of $103 is required at t=1).

Convert the $100 USD into 100/1.0210 = CHF 97.9432

Invest (lend) CHF 97.9432 at the Swiss 2% rate (to produce CHF 99.902 at t=1)

Sell 99.902 CHF forward at the $1.0511 rate.

At t=1

Convert CHF 99.902 to USD at the previously locked in rate of 1.0511, yielding 99.902 × 1.0511 = $105.01

Repay $103 for USD loan (with interest).

Arbitrage profit = $105.01 − $103 = $2.01

(Study Session 14, LOS 40.a)

43. **C** Current term structure:

LIBOR		Discount Factor
$LIBOR_{180}$	0.029	0.98571
$LIBOR_{360}$	0.030	0.97087
$LIBOR_{540}$	0.032	0.95420
	ΣDF =	2.91078

SFR_{New} = (1 − 0.95420) / (2.91078) ≈ 0.015735 semiannually or 3.1469% annually.

Value (to payer) = ΣDF × (SFR_{New} − SFR_{Old}) × (days / 360) × notional

= 2.91078 × (0.031469 − 0.035) × (180 / 360) × $150 million ≈ −$770,000

(Study Session 14, LOS 40.c)

44. **C** Current term structure:

LIBOR	Discount Factor
$LIBOR_{60}$ 0.027	0.99552
$LIBOR_{150}$ 0.0285	0.98826
$LIBOR_{240}$ 0.0295	0.98071

Fixed-rate payment: $0.037 \times 90 / 360 = 0.00925$
Value to GD (fixed payer) per $ notional principal:
$(1892.23 / 1926.64) - 0.98071 - 0.00925(0.99552 + 0.98826 + 0.98071) = -0.02599$
Value $= -0.02599 \times \$250,000,000 = -\$6,497,910$

(Study Session 14, LOS 40.c)

45. **C** The original contract was a 90-day FRA on 180-day LIBOR. As 50 days have passed, the equivalent contract is now a 40-day FRA on 180-day LIBOR. Hernandez needs the 40-day rate and the 220-day rate to reprice the FRA and discount the gain or loss back to today. (Study Session 14, LOS 40.a)

46. **B** POPRT is part of the index CDS. GD sold protection of $350 million over the 125 equally weighted entities, meaning that it has effective exposure of $350 million / 125 = $2.8 million.

   On the single-name POPRT CDS, GD purchased protection of $2.5 million, leaving a net notional exposure of 2.8 − 2.5 = $0.3 million. (Study Session 13, LOS 39.d)

47. **B** As the credit spread for TRTRS has widened and GD has purchased protection, GD will gain by selling protection at a higher premium. (Study Session 13, LOS 39.c)

48. **C** Typically, an LBO will result in an increase in the probability of default due to the large increase in debt levels. An investor would, therefore, seek to buy protection, as the premium would rise along with the probability of default. Due to the takeover premium that would result from the LBO, Eagen would also benefit by going long TRTRS stock. (Study Session 13, LOS 39.e)

49. **C** Private equity funds add value to their portfolio investments in a variety of ways including utilizing optimal financial leverage, incentivizing portfolio company management, and creating operational improvements. Incentivizing the GP is a mechanism to reduce conflict of interest between LP and GP and not a mechanism to add value. (Study Session 15, LOS 45.a)

50. **C** Relative to demand for natural gas, seasonality in demand for oil is lower. Cold winters increase the demand for gas for heating fuel and hot summers increase the demand for gas as well (for cooling) because gas is a primary source of fuel for electrical power generation. (Study Session 15, LOS 46.a)

51. **C** The supply shortage would result in an increase in convenience yield, which will in turn lower the futures price relative to the spot price. (Study Session 15, LOS 46.f)

52. **B** In a total return swap, the variable payments are based on the change in price of a commodity. In an excess return swap, the variable payments are based on the difference between the price of a commodity and a benchmark value. In a basis swap, the variable payments are based on the difference in prices of two commodities. (Study Session 15, LOS 46.i)

53. **A** The case provides that the pricing in cattle futures market reflects contango; futures prices are higher than spot prices. The hedging pressure hypothesis can explain contango pricing by suggesting that farmers that wish to hedge their commodity price risk may be outnumbered by commodity consumers reducing their risk by taking long positions in the futures market. The insurance perspective suggests that farmers should dominate the hedging market, which results in backwardation and would be least likely to explain a contango pricing behavior. The theory of storage relies on the convenience yield to predict the relationship between spot and futures prices; it links storage costs and storability to the convenience yield. Existence of high inventory levels could reduce the convenience yield and hence push futures prices higher, potentially leading to contango. (Study Session 15, LOS 46.f)

54. **C** Since futures prices are less than spot prices, the roll return will be positive. Convergence will create identical spot and futures prices at maturity; maturing contracts will be replaced with the next shortest futures contract, which will have a lower price. (Study Session 15, LOS 46.h)

55. **A**

Asset Class (i)	Portfolio Return $E(R_{Pi})$	Benchmark Return $E(R_{Bi})$	Active Weight (Δw_i)	$(\Delta w_i)\,(E(R_{Bi}))$
Equities	13%	12%	10%	1.20%
Bonds	7%	5%	−11%	-0.55%
Cash	3%	3%	1%	0.03%
Total				0.68%

Expected active return from asset allocation = $\Sigma \Delta w_j E(R_{B,j})$ = 0.68%

(Study Session 17, LOS 51.a)

56. **A** Both statements are correct. The global optimal risky portfolio is the portfolio with the highest Sharpe ratio. Investors customize their portfolios based on their risk tolerance by combining this optimal risky portfolio and the risk-free asset. A market-neutral long-short equity fund would have beta of zero, and, hence, the appropriate benchmark would be the risk-free asset. The excess return in the numerator is the same for both the information ratio and the Sharpe ratio when the risk-free asset is the benchmark. Additionally, by definition, the active risk will be same as total risk when the benchmark is risk-free (i.e., zero volatility). (Study Session 17, LOS 51.b)

57. **A** Transfer coefficient can be thought of as a cross-sectional correlation between the forecasted active returns and active weights, adjusted for risk. (Study Session 17, LOS 51.c)

58. **A** Prime has the highest information ratio and, hence, is most suitable for the investor regardless of the active risk constraint. In this instance, the investor would invest ⅚ or 83.33% in Prime and the remaining 16.67% in the benchmark portfolio to meet the maximum active risk constraint.

Fund	Prime	Redux	Optimus
Expected active return	2.40%	1.25%	1.28%
Active risk	6%	5%	4%
Information ratio	0.40	0.25	0.32

(Study Session 17, LOS 51.d)

59. **B** Manager B has an information coefficient (IC) of 2(0.55) − 1 or 0.10.

Given unconstrained optimization for Manager B, TC = 1.0

Manager B information ratio = $IC \times \sqrt{BR}$ = $0.10 \times \sqrt{12}$ = 0.35

Manager A information ratio = $TC \times IC \times \sqrt{BR}$ = $0.4 \times 0.20 \times \sqrt{BR}$

Setting Manager A information ratio = 0.35, $\sqrt{BR}$ = 4.375 and BR = 19.14.

(Study Session 17, LOS 51.e)

60. **B** Closet index funds are characterized by low active risk and a Sharpe ratio equal to that of the benchmark. The information ratio for closet index funds tends to be zero (or negative after fees). Low information ratio can also occur for (unsuccessful) active funds. (Study Session 17, LOS 51.b)

Exam 3
Afternoon Session Answers

To get valuable feedback on how your score compares to those of other Level II candidates, use your Username and Password to gain Online Access at schweser.com and choose the menu item *"Practice Exams Volume 1 (Enter answers from book)."*

61. A	81. A	101. A
62. C	82. A	102. C
63. A	83. C	103. C
64. C	84. C	104. B
65. A	85. A	105. C
66. A	86. C	106. A
67. B	87. C	107. A
68. B	88. C	108. A
69. B	89. B	109. A
70. C	90. A	110. A
71. A	91. B	111. C
72. C	92. C	112. B
73. B	93. C	113. C
74. B	94. C	114. C
75. B	95. C	115. B
76. A	96. A	116. B
77. A	97. B	117. C
78. B	98. B	118. B
79. B	99. C	119. A
80. A	100. C	120. C

EXAM 3
AFTERNOON SESSION ANSWERS

61. **A** Item (i) is a likely violation of the Code and Standards. Working as a waitress is not a conflict of interest for an investment analyst, but Cooken's employer can reasonably assume that a 30-hour-a-week side job could be tiring, depriving the company of her skills and ability during her internship, which would violate Standard IV(A) Loyalty (to employer).

    Cooken's description of the CFA exam is accurate, and she takes no liberties with a title. Thus she has not violated Standard VII(B) Reference to CFA Institute, the CFA Designation, and the CFA Program.

    One conviction as a teenager before working as an investment professional is not a violation of Standard I(D) Misconduct. Standard IV(A) Loyalty (to employer) does not hold when illegal activities are involved, and Cooken's willingness to talk to the FBI would most likely not be considered a violation. The Standards do suggest, however, that the member consult with his employer's compliance personnel or outside counsel before disclosing any confidential client information. (Study Session 1, LOS 2.a)

62. **C** While Cooken's tax avoidance may represent a professional-conduct issue, it has no bearing on her ability to write a report on Mocline. While Clarrison may be an expert on Mocline Tobacco, Cooken does not know enough about the stock to write about it without taking the risk of being in violation of Standard V(A) Diligence and Reasonable Basis. Because of Cooken's relationship to the CFO of Mocline and ownership of Mocline stock, her objectivity might be questioned. (Study Session 1, LOS 2.a)

63. **A** Standard IV(A) Loyalty (to employer) requires that members and candidates act for the benefit of their employer and not deprive the employer of their skills and abilities. In addition, members and candidates must not cause harm to their employers. It's safe to say that a bar does not compete with a stock-analysis company, and a 6-hour-a-week part-time job should not interfere with her ability to perform analysis duties. Standard IV(B) Additional Compensation Arrangements relates to additional compensation related to an employee's services to the employer. The moonlighting is not related to her analysis job and, as such, does not violate the standard. There is nothing inherently unethical about working as a bartender, and moonlighting as a barkeeper does not compromise Cooken's professional reputation, integrity, or competence. Thus, Standard I(D) Misconduct has not been violated. (Study Session 1, LOS 2.a)

64. **C** Request 3 is a likely violation. Potential clients are not entitled to performance data beyond what the company chooses to disclose. Providing data, particularly client-specific data, could be a violation of the clients' confidentiality.

    Members and candidates must answer questions asked by CFA Institute's Professional Conduct Program. Members and candidates may report illegal activities (and in some cases may have a legal obligation to report such activities) on the part of clients without fear of violating Standard III(E) Preservation of Confidentiality, so 1 is not likely a violation. And unless the firm's policy requires silence about job openings, answering questions about them is ethical, if not always wise, so 2 is not likely a violation. (Study Session 1, LOS 2.a)

©2017 Kaplan, Inc.

65. **A** Although Zonding directed the audience to his published report, the ROS also recommends that, during any public appearances, sufficient information be included for investors to assess the appropriateness of the investment for their own personal risk profile. (Study Session 1, LOS 3.b)

66. **A** Zonding recommended that viewers sell shares on share price increases despite his 12-month buy rating. Firms should not allow analysts to suggest trading actions that differ from the current published rating. (Study Session 1, LOS 3.b)

67. **B** The CFA Institute Research Objectivity Standards require that research analysts be separated from the investment banking department. The firm must not allow Vrbenic to report to Sheffield, the head of investment banking, in order to avoid compromising the independence of Vrbenic's analysis. (Study Session 1, LOS 3.b)

68. **B** The requirement is that firms have policies and procedures covering employees' personal investments and trading activities. These policies must prohibit employees and their immediate families from trading contrary to recently published recommendations, except in cases of extreme hardship. Since the analyst needs the money to pay for her father's kidney transplant, Verhallen may sell the securities contrary to the recommendation. (Study Session 1, LOS 3.b)

69. **B** Research analysts must be prohibited from promising a subject company a favorable report or price target or threatening to change reports, recommendations, or price targets. Sheffield's unique insight may or may not lead to a change in recommendation, but changing the recommendation based on whether the subject company does investment banking business violates the ROS. The ROS require that all conflicts of interest be disclosed but they do not prohibit coverage of companies where such a conflict of interest may be present. (Study Session 1, LOS 3.b)

70. **C** Firms must establish and implement salary, bonus, and other compensation programs that are tied to the quality of the research and the accuracy of the recommendations over time (not necessarily every quarter). Firms must avoid directly linking analyst compensation to investment banking or corporate finance activity on which the analyst may be collaborating. (Study Session 1, LOS 3.b)

71. **A** Firms must provide full and fair disclosure of all potential conflicts of interest. Vrbenic's failure to disclose her position in the securities violates the ROS. Vrbenic is not, however, required to provide research to audience members, although the ROS recommends that the firm make the reports available even if they charge for them. The standards recommend—but do not require—that firms disclose availability of subject company research reports and how the audience might acquire such a report, if the firm makes it available to non-clients. This firm does not. (Study Session 1, LOS 3.b)

72. **C** In order to comply with the CFA Institute Research Objectivity Standards *recommendations*, firms should issue research reports at least quarterly, or whenever material facts about the subject company change if sooner. However, there is no specific frequency of report issuance required by the Research Objectivity Standards. The only *requirement* is that firms issue their research on a regular and timely basis. (Study Session 1, LOS 3.b)

73. **B** While ability of the self-regulating organizations (SROs) and their enforcement powers are important, the most important element is being properly supervised by formal government authorities. (Study Session 4, LOS 15.b)

74. **B**   Given low capital mobility, a restrictive monetary and fiscal policy should lead to domestic currency appreciation under the Mundell-Fleming model. (Study Session 4, LOS 13.k)

75. **B**   Under the neoclassical growth theory, capital deepening affects the level of output but not the growth rate in the long run. Once an economy reaches steady-state growth, only further technological progress will increase the growth rate. (Study Session 4, LOS 14.i)

76. **A**   GBP/SFr = GBP/USD × USD/SFr.

We are given USD/GBP, so we convert the provided quotes:

$$\left(\frac{GBP}{USD}\right)_{bid} = \frac{1}{\left(\frac{USD}{GBP}\right)_{offer}} = \frac{1}{2.0020} = 0.4995$$

and

$$\left(\frac{GBP}{USD}\right)_{offer} = \frac{1}{\left(\frac{USD}{GBP}\right)_{bid}} = \frac{1}{2.0010} = 0.4998$$

Now,

$$\left(\frac{GBP}{SFr}\right)_{bid} = \left(\frac{GBP}{USD}\right)_{bid} \times \left(\frac{USD}{SFr}\right)_{bid} = 0.4995 \times 0.8550 = 0.4271$$

and

$$\left(\frac{GBP}{SFr}\right)_{offer} = \left(\frac{GBP}{USD}\right)_{offer} \times \left(\frac{USD}{SFr}\right)_{offer} = 0.4998 \times 0.8560 = 0.4278$$

The GBP/SFr quote should be: GBP/SFr = 0.4271 − 78. (Study Session 4, LOS 13.b)

77. **A**   The original 60-day forward contract calls for long GBP. So the all-in forward price FP = 2.0085. After 30 days, the contract would still have 30 days remaining to expiration. The new 30-day all-in forward price to sell GBP is 2.0086 +(7.6/10,000) = 2.00936. The relevant 30-day USD interest rate is 4%.

$$V_t = \frac{(FP_t - FP)(\text{Contract size})}{\left[1 + R\left(\frac{\text{Days}}{360}\right)\right]} = \frac{(2.00936 - 2.0085)(1,000,000)}{\left[1 + 0.04\left(\frac{30}{360}\right)\right]} = \text{USD } 857.14$$

(Study Session 4, LOS 13.d)

78. **B**   Covered interest rate parity requires that $F = \dfrac{(1+R_\$)}{(1+R_{BU})} \, S_0$

$F = (1.05 \ / \ 1.03) \times 2.00 = \$2.0388/BU$

The BUN should trade at a forward premium of 1.9%. However, the BUN is actually trading at a premium of 5%. Therefore, the appropriate arbitrage strategy is to sell BUN in the forward market as below:

1. Borrow $1,000 at 5%. At the end of one year, Williams will be obligated to repay $1,000(1.05) = $1,050.

2. Convert the $1,000 to BUN at the spot rate, which yields $1,000 / ($2/BUN) = BUN500.

3. Simultaneously enter into a 1-year forward contract to convert BUN to USD at the forward rate of $2.1000/BUN.

4. Invest BUN 500 at 3%. In one year, Williams will receive proceeds of BUN500(1.03) = BUN515.

5. Convert the BUN515 back to USD at the forward rate, which was locked in at the beginning of the year and yields BUN 515($2.1/BUN) = $1,081.50.

6. Arbitrage profits = $1,081.50 – $1,050 = $31.50.

(Study Session 4, LOS 13.e)

79. **B**   In Exhibit 1, the cash flow statement shows that payables contributed positively to cash flow for 2013. This means payables increased during the period, suggesting High Plains was *delaying* payments to suppliers to boost CFO. (Study Session 6, LOS 19.i)

80. **A**   Revenue should be recognized when earned and payment is assured. High Plains is recognizing revenue as orders are received. Because High Plains has not yet fulfilled its obligation to deliver the goods, revenue is not yet earned. By recognizing revenue too soon, net income is overstated and ending inventory is understated. Understated ending inventory would result in an overstated inventory turnover ratio. (Study Session 6, LOS 19.h)

81. **A**

Net income		$158,177,000
Bill-and-hold revenue	$907,950,000	
EBT margin	5.1%	
Bill-and-hold pre-tax income	$46,305,450	
Tax rate	28%	
Bill-and-hold post-tax income		$33,339,924
		21.08%

(Study Session 6, LOS 19.h)

82. **A** Discretionary expenses, such as maintenance and repairs, and advertising and marketing expenses, are declining over time even as sales and capital expenditures are increasing. Investment in capital assets is increasing because cash flow from investing activities (CFI) is greater than depreciation expense for the period. The change to the straight-line depreciation method is certainly less conservative. However, measuring earnings quality based on conservative earnings is an inferior measure as most accruals will correct over time. Note that using LIFO as an inventory cost flow assumption during periods of stable or rising prices would cause net earnings to reflect economic (real) earnings, thereby leading to a higher quality of earnings. (Study Session 6, LOS 19.f)

83. **C** A finance (capital) lease is reported on the balance sheet as an asset and as a liability. In the income statement, the leased asset is depreciated and interest expense is recognized on the liability. Thus, capitalizing a lease *enhances* earnings quality. An *operating* lease classification *lowers* earnings quality. The reclassification of inventory will impact the calculation of inventory turnover and inventory days. Reclassifications make trend analysis more difficult and lower financial reporting quality. (Study Session 6, LOS 19.d)

84. **C** It appears that High Plains manipulated its earnings in 2014 to avoid default under its bond covenants. Extreme earnings (including revenues) tend to revert to normal levels over time (mean reversion). Because of the estimates involved, a *lower* weighting should be assigned to the accrual component of High Plains' earnings. (Study Session 6, LOS 19.g)

85. **A** In a defined contribution plan, pension expense is equal to the amount contributed by the firm. The plan participants bear the shortfall risk. There is no pension obligation in a defined contribution plan. (Study Session 5, LOS 17.a)

86. **C** Under U.S. GAAP and under IFRS, Global Oilfield would report the funded status in its balance sheet. (Study Session 5, LOS 17.b)

87. **C** The assumed discount rate increased from 6.25% in 20X7 to 6.75% in 20X8 (Exhibit 4). There is an inverse relationship between the discount rate and the present value of a future sum. Thus, the increase in the discount rate resulted in an actuarial gain (lower PBO). An increase in life expectancy would result in an actuarial loss. Decrease in expected rate of return would increase reported pension expense but would not affect PBO. (Study Session 5, LOS 17.d)

88. **C** A decrease in the compensation growth rate will reduce service cost. Lower service cost will result in lower pension expense and, thus, higher net income. Lowering the compensation growth rate will also reduce the PBO. A lower PBO will increase the funded status of the plan (make the plan appear more funded). The compensation growth rate assumption has no effect on the plan assets. (Study Session 5, LOS 17.d)

89. **B** For the year-ended 20X8, Global Oilfield's reported pension expense was €8,028 (Exhibit 3), and its total periodic pension cost was €3,410. Total periodic pension cost can be calculated as plan contributions minus the change in funded status [€5,000 − (€2,524 funded status for 20X8 − €934 funded status for 20X7)]. (Study Session 5, LOS 17.f)

90. **A** Total periodic pension cost represents the true cost of the pension. If the firm's contributions exceed its true pension expense, the difference can be viewed as a reduction in the overall pension obligation similar to an excess principal payment on a loan. Pension contributions are reported as operating activities in the cash flow statement while principal payments are reported as financing activities. Thus, the adjustment involves increasing operating cash flow by €750 (€5,000 employer contributions − €4,250 total periodic pension cost) and decreasing financing cash flow by the same amount. (Study Session 5, LOS 17.e)

91. **B** Consolidated current assets are equal to $119 million ($96 Valley current assets − $9 cash for investment in Southwest + $32 Southwest current assets). (Study Session 5, LOS 16.a)

92. **C** ROA is calculated as net income / total assets. Both methods result in the same net income, so conclusion 1 is incorrect. However, the acquisition method leads to higher reported total assets. Hence, the ROA is greater under the equity method and lower under the acquisition method (conclusion 2 is correct). (Study Session 5, LOS 16.b)

93. **C** The applicability of equity method and acquisition method is identical under U.S. GAAP and IFRS (convergence project) and hence statement 1 is correct. While equity method reports the same net income as acquisition (statement 2 is correct), due to the inclusion of minority interest in equity under the acquisition method, the amount of equity reported under the acquisition method is higher than the amount of equity reported under the equity method (statement is 3 incorrect). (Study Session 5, LOS 16.b)

94. **C** See the table in the solution to the next question. (Study Session 5, LOS 18.d,e)

95. **C** (Study Session 5, LOS 18.d,e)

The following financial statements reflect the use of the current rate method (functional currency is the CHF) since Mountain is a self-contained company and is less dependent on Valley.

Income Statement (in $ thousands)

Sales	$5,600	= 0.80 × 7,000
Cost of goods sold	$5,440	= 0.80 × 6,800
Depreciation	80	= 0.80 × 100
Net income	$80	

Balance sheet (in $ thousands)

Cash and accounts receivable	$510	= 0.85 × 600
Inventory	425	= 0.85 × 500
Fixed assets	510	= 0.85 × 600
Total assets	$1,445	
Accounts payable	$170	= 0.85 × 200
Long-term debt	85	= 0.85 × 100
Common stock	1,001	= 0.77 × 1,300
Retained earnings	80	= 0 + 80
FC translation adjustment	109	Calculated as plug figure
Total liabilities and equity	$1,445	

96. **A** Under U.S. GAAP, the nonmonetary assets and liabilities of the foreign subsidiary are not restated for inflation. Under IFRS, the subsidiary's financial statements are adjusted for inflation, and the net purchasing power gain or loss is recognized in the income statement. Then, the subsidiary is translated into U.S. dollars using the current rate method. If Mountain operates in a highly inflationary environment, the appropriate method is the temporal method. Under the temporal method, the functional currency is considered to be the parent's presentation currency. Thus, Mountain's functional currency is the U.S. dollar. (Study Session 5, LOS 18.g)

97. **B** Ozer's memo states that in an acquisition, Alertron would want to maintain the successful Escarigen brand and operational structure. As a result, the most likely form of integration would be a subsidiary merger in which Escarigen would become a subsidiary of Alertron. Most subsidiary mergers occur when the target has a well-known brand that the acquirer wants to maintain, which is the case here. Note that in a statutory merger, the target company would cease to exist as a separate entity. Since both Alertron and Escarigen are involved in the pharmaceutical industry, the type of merger would be best described as horizontal. The merger would not be vertical as Alertron would not be moving up or down the supply chain. (Study Session 8, LOS 26.a)

98. **B** The potential acquisition of Carideo is described as a stock purchase, which means that Carideo's shareholders would be responsible for paying capital gains taxes on the deal and no taxes would be levied against Carideo at the corporate level. The other answers are incorrect. The potential deal with Escarigen is described as a cash offering. In most cash offerings, the acquirer borrows money to raise cash for the deal, which would increase the acquirer's financial leverage. In the potential deal with BriscoePharm, shareholders generally only approve asset purchases when the purchase is substantial (greater than 50% of firm assets). In this case, shareholder approval would not be required. In a proxy battle for Dillon Biotech, Alertron would try to have shareholders approve new members of the board of directors to try to gain control of the company. Trying to purchase shares from shareholders individually is a tender offer. (Study Session 8, LOS 26.e)

99. **C** The only pair combination that correctly identifies a pre-offer and post-offer defense, respectively, is a supermajority voting provision, which is a pre-offer defense requiring shareholder approval in excess of a simple majority; and a leveraged recapitalization, which is a post-offer defense where a target borrows money to repurchase its own shares. Pre-offer defenses suggested include poison puts, fair price amendments, restricted voting rights, poison pills, and staggered board elections. The only other post-offer defense suggested was greenmail, which was incorrectly categorized. (Study Session 8, LOS 26.f)

100. **C** First, calculate the value of the combined firm after the merger:

Post merger value of the combined firm: $V_{AT} = V_A + V_T + S - C$

V_A = \$9,000
V_T = \$3,120
S = \$600
C = \$0 because no cash is changing hands

The value of the combined firm is therefore V_{AT} = \$9,000 + \$3,120 + \$600 − 0 = \$12,720

Next, to account for the dilution and to find the price per share for the combined firm, P_{AT}, divide the post merger value by the post merger number of shares outstanding. Since we are told that Alertron would exchange 0.75 shares of its stock for each share of Carideo, the number of new shares issued is:

80 million shares × 0.75 = 60 million new shares

So, $P_{AT} = \dfrac{\$12{,}720}{150 + 60} = \$60.57$

This means the actual value of each share given to Carideo's shareholders is \$60.57 and the actual price paid for Carideo is:

$P_T = (N \times P_{AT}) = (60 \times \$60.57) = \$3{,}634.20$

Carideo's gain in the merger as the target is:

$Gain_T = TP = P_T - V_T = \$3{,}634.20 - \$3{,}120 = \$514.20$

Note that Carideo's gain simply represents the takeover premium in the transaction. (Study Session 8, LOS 26.k)

101. **A** In a cash offer, the acquirer assumes the risk and receives the potential reward from the merger, while the gain to the target shareholders is limited to the takeover premium. In this case, Alertron is comfortable with the estimate of synergies and thinks the estimate may even be conservative. By making a cash offer, the takeover premium realized by Carideo would remain unchanged, with any excess benefit from synergies going to Alertron. Based on its forecasts, Alertron would prefer a cash deal.

However, if the synergies were less than expected, the takeover premium realized by Carideo would still be unchanged with a cash deal, but Alertron's gain may decrease. Since Carideo management believes the estimate of synergies is too high, they would also prefer a cash deal to lock in the gain they realize from the takeover premium. (Study Session 8, LOS 26.l)

102. **C** Pre-merger HHI = $\begin{aligned}&(0.20\times100)^2+(0.18\times100)^2+(0.15\times100)^2+(0.12\times100)^2+\\&(0.10\times100)^2+(0.07\times100)^2+\left[(0.03\times100)^2\times6\right]=1,296\end{aligned}$

The post merger market share of the combined firms would be 15% + 10% = 25%.

Post-merger HHI = $\begin{aligned}&(0.25\times100)^2+(0.20\times100)^2+(0.18\times100)^2+(0.12\times100)^2+\\&(0.07\times100)^2+\left[(0.03\times100)^2\times6\right]=1,596\end{aligned}$

Change in HHI = 1,596 − 1,296 = 300

A post-merger HHI that is between 1,000 and 1,800 indicates a moderately concentrated industry. With a change in an HHI that is greater than 100, there is certainly the potential for an antitrust challenge by regulators. (Study Session 8, LOS 26.g)

103. **C** Benefit 1 is incorrect. Depending on the level of earnings versus positive NPV projects available, the dividend can swing from very high to low (or zero). Positive NPV projects will be financed using earnings, and there will be no dividend if all earnings are used in this way. (Study Session 7, LOS 23.g)

104. **B**

Debt	Short-term			120
	Long-term			74,953
	Total			**75,073**
Equity	Common stock			200,458
	APIC			224,909
	Total			**425,367**
Capital structure		Debt	**15.00%**	75,073 / (75,073 + 425,367)
		Equity	**85.00%**	425,367 / (75,073 + 425,367)
Capital expenditure				28,000
Financed by debt		4,200		28,000 × 0.15
Financed by earnings		23,800		28,000 × 0.85
Earnings for year				26,034
Required by capex				23,800
Residual Dividend				**2,234**

(Study Session 7, LOS 23.g)

105. **C**

			Outlay
Proceeds from sale	2,200,000		**2,200,000**
Tax base	0	(full allowance in year 1)	
Taxable gain	2,200,000		
Tax rate	35%		
Tax payable	770,000		(770,000)
Cost new machine	3,800,000		(3,800,000)
Investment in working capital	200,000		(200,000)
Net outlay			(2,570,000)

Note that investment in working capital is not tax deductible. Annual tax allowable depreciation on the new machine would be relevant when calculating the tax paid for operating cash flows (at the end of the year).

(Study Session 7, LOS 21.a)

106. **A**

All equity cost   15%
Cost of debt   8%
Current D/E   0.18   Debt 75,073   New D/E 0.27   Debt   115,073
Tax Rate   35%   Equity 425,367   Equity   425,367

$r_e = r_o + [(r_o - r_d) \times (1-t) \times (D/E)]$

$= 15\% + [(15\% - 8\%) \times 0.65 \times 0.27]$

$= 16.2\%$

(Study Session 7, LOS 22.a)

107. **A** The costs of financial distress will indeed be lower if the company has tangible, marketable assets, compared to a company with mostly intangible assets.

(Study Session 7, LOS 22.a)

108. **A** The pecking order theory suggests that managers prefer to finance internally as it has the lowest potential information content, followed by debt and finally new equity.

(Study Session 7, LOS 22.a)

109. **A** Based on the APT, the appropriate discount rate for Trailblazer is:

$$E\left(R_{Trailblazer}\right) = 3.5\% + (0.81 \times 1.91\%) - (0.45 \times 1.22\%) + (0.24 \times 3.47\%) + (0.74 \times 4.15\%) = 8.4\%$$

Based on the BYPRP method, the required return on Trailblazer's equity = 7.25% + 3% = 10.25%. (Study Session 9, LOS 28.c)

110. **A** Equity risk premium = dividend yield + LT EPS growth rate − LT government bond yield

    = 2.1% + 3.5% − 4.4% = 1.2%

    (Study Session 9, LOS 28.b)

111. **C** All three statements are consistent with the assumptions of the Gordon growth model. Regarding Statement 3, there is nothing to prevent the growth rate from being negative. The model can still be applied in this case. (Study Session 10, LOS 30.d)

112. **B** For a DDM to be appropriate for valuation purposes, dividends must be a reasonably good measure of the cash flow of a firm. Dividends are appropriate for measuring cash flow when a company has a history of dividend payments, when the dividend policy is clear and related to the firm's earnings, and when the perspective is that of a minority shareholder. The two statements relate to the history of dividends and the relationship between dividends and earnings. Statement 4 supports the use of dividends since the history of paying dividends is fairly long and consistent. Statement 5 suggests that the relationship between dividends and earnings is not very strong since the company continues to pay regular dividends regardless of whether losses are incurred or profits are earned. (Study Session 10, LOS 30.a)

113. **C** Statement 6 is correct. Adjusted historical equity risk premium removes any biases in the historical data series. Statement 7 is incorrect. While we adjust peer public company beta for leverage differences, differences in size are not accounted for via adjustment to beta. It is better to account for size differences by additional risk premium for size.

    (Study Session 9, LOS 28.b,d)

114. **C** required return = 3.5% + (1.2 × 4.5%) = 8.9%

    retention ratio = b = ($4.00 − $2.60)/ $4.00 = 0.35

    payout ratio = (1 − b) = 1 − 0.35 = 0.65

    justified leading P/E = $\dfrac{1-b}{r-g} = \dfrac{0.65}{0.089-0.05} = 16.67$

    justified trailing P/E = $\dfrac{(1-b)\times(1+g)}{(r-g)} = \dfrac{0.65\times1.05}{0.089-0.05} = 17.50$

    Notice that the current market price is irrelevant for calculating justified P/E ratios. (Study Session 10, LOS 30.f)

115. **B** Mnoyan is correct. IFRS permits either the partial goodwill or full goodwill method to value goodwill and the noncontrolling interest under the acquisition method. U.S. GAAP requires the full goodwill method. Vadney is incorrect. Both IFRS and U.S. GAAP require equity method accounting for joint ventures. (Study Session 5, LOS 16.b)

116. **B** % Revenue growth = (1 + % Δvolume) × (1 + % Δprice) − 1

Forecasted revenue = current revenue × (1 + revenue growth rate) = $121 × (1 + revenue growth rate)

% growth in COGS = (1 + % Δvolume) × (1 + % Δinput price) − 1

Forecasted COGS = (current COGS) × (1 + COGS growth rate) = $89 × (1 + COGS growth rate)

Analyst	Adams	Baste	Cairns
Revenue growth	6.08%	7.10%	5.04%
COGS growth	7.12%	6.08%	6.05%
Forecasted revenues	$128.36	$129.59	$127.10
Forecasted COGS	$95.34	$94.41	$94.38
Forecasted gross margin	25.72%	27.15%	$25.74%

Current gross margin = ($121 − $89) / $121 = 26.45%

Thus, analyst Baste is most likely to forecast an improvement in gross margin.

(Study Session 11, LOS 33.i)

117. **C** The neoclassical growth theory relates technological change to increases in labor productivity; however, increases in capital and labor would not increase growth rate in output per worker permanently under neoclassical growth theory.

The endogenous growth theory holds that technological advances lead to increases in labor productivity. Additionally, capital deepening investments would lead to social benefits and hence lead to further technological advances—increasing growth rate of output per worker.

Classical growth theory maintains that any increase in per capita GDP above subsistence level is mean reverting. (Study Session 4, LOS 14.i)

118 **B** The value of assets in place is E/r. The difference between this value and the fundamental value is PVGO. (Study Session 10, LOS 30.e)

119. **A** $r = \left[\left(\dfrac{D_0}{P_0}\right) \times \{(1 + g_L) + [H \times (g_s - g_L)]\} + g_L\right]$

Given: dividend yield = 5%, g_s = 12%, g_L = 3% and H = 6 / 2 = 3.

r = [(0.05) × {(1.03) + 3(0.12 − 0.03)}] + 0.03 = 0.095 or 9.5%

(Study Session 10, LOS 30.m)

120. **C** Sensitivity to assumptions of growth is a limitation, not a strength. (Study Session 10, LOS 30.h,i)

Notes

Notes

Notes

Notes

Notes

Notes

Notes

Notes

Notes